Inspecting and advising

Along with the rest of the education system, the role of the local adviser or inspector has undergone a sea change in recent years. There is now considerable pressure for local advisory services to take on an inspectorial and evaluative role. At the same time, the need for schools to have access to the disinterested advice of professional colleagues in a time of institutional upheaval has never been greater.

This book offers sound practical guidance to advisers, inspectors and advisory teachers at all levels on how to carry out this difficult but crucial task. It considers the aims of the advisory service in the fields of inspection, support and staff development and it sets out the means by which these aims can be achieved. These include the development of interpersonal skills in dealing with school staff and with other sections of the advisory networks, inter- viewing, organising advisory teams and managing one's own work. In all these areas, Joan Dean gives advice based on 28 years in the advisory services. Her book is an essential handbook not only for advisors themselves but also for staff in schools and in higher education who collaborate with them in the development of schools and teacher.

Joan Dean recently retired after seventeen years as Chief Inspector for Surrey. Her previous experience includes work as a Senior Primary Adviser for Berkshire, two headships of primary schools, a period as a lecturer in higher education, and experience of classroom teaching. She is the author of twenty books for teachers, including *Managing the Secondary School* and *Managing the Primary School*. In 1980 she was awarded an OBE for her services to teaching.

Educational Management Series

Series editor: Cyril Poster

Inspecting and advising

A handbook for inspectors, advisers and advisory teachers

Joan Dean

London and New York

First published 1992
by Routledge
11 New Fetter Lane, London EC4P 4EE

Simultaneously published in the USA and Canada
by Routledge
a division of Routledge, Chapman and Hall, Inc.
29 West 35th Street, New York, NY 10001
Reprinted 2002 by RoutledgeFalmer
RoutledgeFalmer is an imprint of the Taylor & Francis Group

© 1992 Joan Dean

Typeset by LaserScript Limited, Mitcham, Surrey
Transferred to digital printing 2003

British Library Cataloguing in Publication Data

A catalogue record for this book is available from the British library.

0–415–05611–X

Library of Congress Cataloging-in-Publication Data

Has been applied for.

ISBN 0–415–05611–X

To my husband, David Dean
who has supported me
through twenty-eight enjoyable years
in advisory work

Contents

Illustrations

Foreword

Joan Dean's books need little introduction to those interested in education management at every level. This volume now joins in the Education Management series *Managing the Secondary School* (1985) and *Managing the Primary School* (1987), both originally published by Croom Helm but now available under the Routledge imprint, and *Special Needs in the Secondary School* (1989) published by Routledge. Like her other works, this new book demonstrates a lifetime's dedication to improving educational standards coupled with a genuine understanding of the issues that face teachers, advisers and administrators in the present decade.

I know of no other book which offers so much sound and practical advice to those in the advisory service of LEAs. Teachers may feel themselves challenged, even threatened, by change; advisers, inspectors and advisory teachers are no less so. Their role is undergoing a radical reappraisal. As the inspectorial functions demanded of advisers and inspectors by recent legislation come increasingly to the fore, it is vital that schools continue to have access to professional colleagues to whom they can turn for advice. If advisory teams are to be able still to offer this service, then their skills have to be honed and their time deployed to the best advantage. This book makes a valuable contribution towards enabling them, in a climate of increasing constraint, to function even more effectively than before. Since her retirement, Joan Dean has added to her many years of experience as an adviser a wealth of reading and practical research which illuminates this book.

This is not a book solely for advisers, inspectors and advisory teachers. It deserves to be read by those in managerial roles in schools, by LEA administrators who work alongside the advisory service and by those in higher education who have a commitment to in-service training.

Cyril Poster

Preface

This book is designed mainly for local advisers, inspectors and advisory teachers. It contains much that should be of interest to HMI, to administrators and to anyone concerned with inspecting or advising teachers.

The book sets out to offer advisers, inspectors and advisory teachers suggestions about ways of tackling each aspect of their work, taking into account the changes which have recently come about. The book starts with an account of recent researches in advisory work and goes on to look at the roles of advisers, inspectors and advisory teachers. An early chapter looks at the interpersonal skills needed. There is a substantial chapter on inspection which reviews possible ways of undertaking the responsibility for monitoring the work of schools and looks in detail at the process of formal inspection, giving some suggestions for ways of costing this process. Other chapters look at ways of supporting teachers, providing in-service education, relationships with other groups, making appointments of advisers and others, training inspectors, advisers and advisory teachers and personal organisation. A chapter on organising the advisory team looks at the advantages and disadvantages of the various possible forms of organisation, at the roles of the chief and senior advisers/inspectors and at communication and evaluation.

The book could be read as a whole, but is also intended to be useful for looking at particular aspects of the work. It should be of particular interest to advisers and inspectors entering the service, but is also intended to support the work of more experienced advisers and inspectors.

A number of people have helped me in writing this book, mainly by reading and commenting on the various chapters. I should particularly like to thank the following: Roger Bailess, Roger Gill, Joan Greenfield, Freda Handley, Barbara Heritage, John Lambert, Jim Shallcross, Anita Straker. I should also like to thank the following LEAs, Barnsley, Hereford and Worcester, Richmond-upon-Thames and Warwickshire, for permission to include material from their internal papers.

Note

It is now extremely difficult to decide what to call the officers who hold different kinds of advisory posts. While there are now some areas which have both advisers and inspectors, each with a different role, others have inspectors or advisers who have both roles. I therefore refer generally to 'advisers and inspectors' when both roles are encompassed, reverting to 'adviser' or 'inspector' when describing the distinctive aspects of their work.

A similar problem occurs with advisory teachers, who may also be called teacher advisers or support teachers or even some other name. In some LEAs these terms refer to different roles. Nevertheless, there is a greater similarity of function and I refer to all in such posts as 'advisory teachers'.

There are also problems about how to refer to the team of advisers, inspectors and advisory teachers. When the whole group of people in all three roles is referred to I have used the term 'advisory team'. When I refer only to advisers and inspectors I speak of the 'advisory/inspectorate' team.

Similar problems occur in trying to find terms which describe all the educational institutions of an LEA. I have therefore used the term 'establishment' or 'institution' where it seems appropriate.

Chapter 1

The advisory service

All organisations are the product of their history and the advisory service is no exception. It has grown slowly since it was established in a few authorities towards the end of the last century but the pace of change has accelerated and the service has been particularly affected by recent changes. In 1974 the reorganisation of local government gave many LEAs the chance to rethink the role and structure of their advisory services and there was considerable development at that time. Unfortunately the reorganisation was followed fairly quickly by the oil crisis and recession and by falling rolls so that many of the planned posts fail to materialise but other posts were lost to the service, sometimes through redeployment, sometimes through redundancy and sometimes by not filling the posts of people who had left. This left many teams with an unsatisfactory structure. It also led to the allocation of responsibilities to inspectors/advisers addition to their normal work and for which they were, in some cases, not qualified. For example, a study of the responsibilities held by inspectors/advisers in 1979 found some people with responsibility for half a dozen subjects but expert in only one.

In the 1980s we have seen developments coming from central government, many of which have involved the appointment of advisory teachers. The Education Reform Act is making new demands upon the service and there are substantial changes in the structure and organisation of many advisory teams. The most recent changes in the funding of local authorities and in-service work appear to be leading to a reduction in the number of support posts.

Findings of studies of advisory services

There have been two studies of advisory services which give us a picture of the situation as it was before LEAs started to reorganise their advisory services to meet the demands of the 1988 Act. These are described in the NFER study, *The LEA adviser – a changing role* (Stillman and Grant 1989) and in *Assuring quality in education* by the Audit Commission (1989b). These studies make the following points:

General

There was a wide variety of practice in different LEAs The variation among LEAs was greater than it might at first appear. People might have similar titles but undertake different tasks. The structure of a service might look similar to that of another service, but in practice might work in a very different way. Stillman and Grant (1989), in particular, found it difficult to generalise about what was happening because the variety was so great. They found that there was no single task that was common to all inspectors and advisers. The Audit Commission had similar findings.

The work of the service had grown by accretion without proper consideration of what was involved. The brief outline given above will explain some of the reasons why this has happened. The problem was particularly serious in small LEAs, where there are too few posts to allow for a proper coverage of all the areas of curriculum needed. In this situation, LEAs had often allocated subject areas to inspectors or advisers whether or not they had any expertise in the area concerned. Stillman and Grant (1989) noted that a third of all inspectors/advisers were responsible for subjects in which they had had no initial training.

Inspectors and advisers were severely overworked This is too well known to need comment. Every study of the use of time by inspectors/advisers shows them working very long hours. For example, a study in 1988 of a large county area showed that the average working week was fifty-six hours, with one or two people working in excess of seventy hours. Stillman and Grant also make the point that most inspectors and advisers enjoyed their work, which perhaps accounts for the readiness to work such long hours.

Many advisory/inspectorate services reflected yesterday's needs in the way they were structured and staffed. Most advisory/inspectorate services had continued to structure themselves according to the pattern set out in 1974 and this was no longer appropriate. There was also the problem that inspectors and advisers tend to stay a long time in one post, so that someone appointed for a need at one point in time might continue in post long after that need had been met. Not enough effort was made to reorganise to provide for change.

The tasks of inspectors and advisers were not sufficiently clearly defined and the amount of work to be done overall had rarely been considered. One reason why inspectors and advisers were overworked was that new tasks were added continually with very little being taken away. The overall work to be done was generally greater than even the largest teams could manage and most inspectors' and advisers lived with a permanently guilty conscience. This was made worse by the fact that jobs were not clearly defined. Only a limited number of inspectors/advisers had job descriptions and not all of these gave clearly defined tasks.

Too much advisory work was ad hoc The pressures of advisory work meant that a good deal of inspectors' and advisers' time was spent in fire-fighting and not enough time was spent in planned activity. The Audit Commission paper says:

> The major influences on the use of inspector/adviser's time appeared to be *ad hoc* requests both from institutions and from a variety of officers and the personal professional interests of individual advisers.
>
> (Audit Commission 1989b)

There were insufficient primary inspectors/advisers for the number of schools and the service tended to be secondary orientated. Most advisory/inspectorate services were staffed on the basis of needing subject specialists for each major subject in the curriculum. Although very often the specialists recruited had a responsibility for their subjects in primary as well as secondary schools, they were likely to be recruited from secondary schools and might have a great deal to learn about primary education. The number of inspectors and advisers with primary school backgrounds did not reflect the number of teachers in primary and secondary schools or the needs at the different levels.

There was insufficient experience of senior management in schools in a number of services. Head teachers in primary and secondary schools and principals of colleges of further education need advice on many aspects of their work. There were usually only a limited number of people in any advisory/inspectorate service who could offer this advice and these might not have experience of headship. This becomes even more important as schools become more independent, with heads needing advice on more aspects of their work. However, this posed problems because of the relationship between the salaries of inspectors/advisers and headteachers, which did not attract heads and deputy heads in secondary schools or principals and vice-principals in colleges to come into the advisory/ inspectorate service.

The need for better management

There was not only a lack of management in many services, but a lack of commitment to management on the part of many LEAs The lack of commitment was evident in the small number of LEAs (19 per cent) having a chief inspector/adviser who was able to concentrate on managing the advisory service without being deflected by other work. A number of LEAs combined the chief inspector/adviser's job with an officer's post or with other work as an inspector/adviser. This left little time for people in these posts to organise the work of the team. There was a need not only for a leader for the service but, in a large authority, for leadership at other levels. The need for management is particularly evident at a time when the work of the service is changing and there is a need for strong leadership to direct the team's work in a situation when there is a large amount of work to be done.

The lack of leadership led to a lack of structure and weakness in the organisation of the service. Where there was no chief inspector/adviser, there was a tendency for everyone to work in isolation from each other and for there to be little teamwork in areas where this would be highly beneficial. There was a connection (Stillman and Grant 1989) between the position held by the head of the service and the overall status of the service within the LEA, with the service having higher status where there was a full-time chief inspector/adviser.

Communication was not good, within the services themselves, with the schools and colleges or with the administration. A further effect of the lack of leadership was lack of communication. Schools and colleges appeared to be uncertain of the role of inspectors/advisers in some cases and of how best to use their services. There was also a lack of communication within services, so that some people felt out of touch. One effect of this was that some inspectors/advisers did not feel themselves to be part of the authority. In some cases this feeling was so strong that inspectors/advisers gave advice to schools which was contrary to the LEA position. There was also insufficient attempt to bring LEA priorities and advisory service priorities together so that everyone worked to agreed ends.

Subject inspectors/advisers without other responsibilities, women, and those on the lowest scales appeared to lose out in a number of ways Stillman and Grant (1989) found that these particular groups of inspectors/advisers appeared to do less well on a number of facets of their work. They were involved in fewer meetings and working parties, had fewer opportunities to express ideas to the LEA, were more likely to be based outside the main office and had less scope for working contact with inspectors/advisers outside the LEA.

The specialist nature of advisory work was often not properly appreciated It was assumed that someone with a good teaching background could become an adviser without further training. Stillman and Grant (1989) make the point as follows:

We are also suggesting that advisory work is a separate and different professional role from teaching and headship and that to consider it as anything more than a very vague extension of these areas is to do it no justice whatsoever.

The discrepancies in salary between heads and inspectors/advisers made it very difficult for people at headship, deputy headship, principal or vice principal level to come into the advisory service except at a senior level, when they would come in without advisory experience. This has happened in some places, where it has been assumed that there were no skills particular to advisory work which were not part of the work of the senior teacher. It was very hard on more junior members of advisory teams to be given a leader who was less familiar with the job to be done than they were themselves and it was often difficult for senior inspectors/advisers in this position to offer the help needed by their more junior colleagues.

New inspectors/advisers needed, and often did not receive, substantial induction training The move to advisory work can be somewhat traumatic, and new inspectors/advisers initially needed information about the system and how to get things done. They then needed training in the skills of the job. Many inspectors/advisers in these studies commented on the value of working with experienced colleagues.

Advisory work tends to be the final career step for many, who then spend twenty years or more in the same post. There was therefore also a need for training for experienced inspectors/advisers, who needed to keep up to date and might need to learn new skills as the job changed.

Inspectors/advisers were inadequately supported by clerical assistance and technology The waste of the time of comparatively well-paid officers left to do tasks like filing was commented on in both these studies. They also pointed out how much more effective inspectors/advisers might be with adequate technology to keep them up to date with information about schools and colleges and deal with some of the problems of communication.

The role of advisory teachers

The overall numbers of advisory teachers have increased substantially in recent years as a result of various government initiatives and, while numbers vary considerably from one LEA to another, there are currently nearly as many advisory teachers as there are inspectors and advisers. They undertake advisory work in a variety of different circumstances. Some are appointed to full-time permanent posts. Others are seconded from a teaching post for a period of time, usually between one and three years. There are also some who are appointed for two or three days a week, working in their own schools for the remaining days.

Generally the advisory teacher posts are filled by good teachers whose strength is that they bring recent and first-hand school experience which makes them highly credible to teachers. Stillman and Grant (1989) and Harland (1990) both found that although the idea of seconding people from schools for a limited period seems attractive it was actually leading to a number of problems:

1 Schools and colleges were often not willing to lose a good teacher, and advisory teachers were sometimes unhappy about returning to the classroom. They felt that they had gained advisory experience which should be used.
2 The advisory teacher service lacked management. In many LEAs the advisory teachers were responsible to individual inspectors or advisers and this added considerably to the inspector/adviser's work. There were similar problems of organisation of work to those of inspectors/advisers, although the advisory teacher generally had acquired fewer extra tasks.
3 Advisory teachers lacked career opportunities and it was not clear where they could look for promotion. The advisory teacher service generally lacked promoted posts.
4 There was an assumption that advisory teachers, like inspectors/advisers, would be able to move from work in a classroom or as a head immediately into advisory work. There was a need to train them for the work that they were expected to do.

None of the comments coming from government or from the two studies described above gives any hope of less work for inspector/adviser. It will require some firm handling of the use of time to enable the service to cope with all that is being demanded of it.

In looking at the value-for-money aspect of the service, it is interesting to note the figures in the Audit Commission survey that overall there are 10.1 institutions per inspector/adviser, 3,210 pupils, and that the cost per pupil is £8.05. Stillman and Grant (1989) found that there were 44.1 inspectors/advisers per million adults. The minimum ratio was 23.8 per thousand and the maximum ratio was 109.2 per thousand.

More recent surveys

A survey was undertaken for the Education Management Information Exchange (EMIE) in September and October 1990 (Dean 1991b) to discover how far LEAs had moved towards the changes suggested above. All LEAs were circulated and there was an 85 per cent response.

This survey and information contained in papers from a number of LEAs demonstrate that almost all authorities have reorganised their advisory teams. It should be noted that we actually know very little about the most effective way to undertake the different aspects of advisory work and some authorities have reorganised into the patterns which others have abandoned.

Inspectors and advisers

The results of this survey generally showed a very substantial move to meet the criticisms in the earlier studies described above.

The management of the service We have already noted from previous studies that there were some LEAs where there was no leadership of the advisory/inspectorate service. All authorities showed in their replies to the EMIE questionnaire that they had someone with overall responsibility for the service and in 79 per cent of cases this person had a background of advisory work. Thirteen per cent were from the administration, 4 per cent from headship and 2 per cent from HMI.

In general the service now appears to have a higher profile. Sixty-five per cent of chief inspectors are now at second-tier level in the hierarchy, 32 per cent at third-tier and only one at fourth-tier level. Eleven have deputy director or the equivalent in their title.

A small number of authorities (10 per cent) have separated inspection and advice and have officers with either title. At least one authority is planning to make advice something which can be purchased by schools and it seems likely that, with the pressure on LEAs to get all the money into the schools, others will do likewise. This is likely to change the nature of the relationship between advisers and schools and to make the service more one of consultancy. A possible cause for concern is that it may be the schools which most need help that will be least likely to seek it.

Most authorities appear to have developed a middle management structure, although it is not possible to tell from the information received how far those in senior posts are responsible for the work of their colleagues. Eighty per cent of authorities have specialist/general posts in which inspectors/advisers play both adviser and inspector roles. Twenty-five per cent have some inspectors/advisers with a general role only and 26 per cent have inspectors/advisers with a specialist role only.

Another small survey of thirty authorities (Dean 1990) showed 10 per cent of teams organised on a phase basis, with 29 per cent organised with phases plus themes (e.g. evaluation, curriculum) and a further 14 per cent having an organisation which incorporated phase plus area plus themes. Fourteen per cent had an area organisation and a further 10 per cent had an area organisation plus themes. Fourteen per cent had themes only and 19 per cent involved officers as well as inspectors and advisers in the overall organisation.

Themes included evaluation, monitoring and assessment, staff development and appraisal, computers, review and development, training and development, operations, planning, resources, headteacher management development, headteacher appraisal and community education.

The training of inspectors/advisers The studies quoted at the beginning of this chapter noted a lack of training for inspectors/advisers and it was also evident from the Audit Commission study that training would be needed to enable many teams to fulfil their rather different role. The (Dean 1991b) survey suggests that this too has been taken very seriously by LEAs and that a great deal of training has taken place, although comments on some questionnaires suggest that some of it may be rather superficial, a matter of very short courses together with some training on the job. Sixty-five per cent of authorities provided for appraisal of inspectors/advisers.

Advisory teachers

Establishment The establishment of advisory teachers in all authorities is funded partly by grants and partly by LEAs. Many of the grants run out in the near future and it seems likely that a number of posts will disappear. This was stated in notes on several of the questionnaires in the EMIE survey.

It is evident that, even allowing for differences in LEA size, there are considerable differences in the number of advisory teachers employed by different authorities. This may reflect the overall views of the LEA on the importance of having teachers working in this capacity or it may be that some advisory teachers are providing a specialist skill missing from the inspector/adviser team. The numbers were currently substantial – an overall total of over four thousand.

Management of advisory teachers Dean (1991) also found that there had been some movement on the management of advisory teachers, with thirty authorities with a senior adviser in charge of the advisory teacher team, three with administrators in charge and four with a senior advisory teacher. Forty-eight involve the appropriate inspector/adviser, but this was often in addition to other patterns of management. In twenty-seven cases this was the only form of management.

Responsibilities of advisory teachers Advisory teachers cover a very wide range of responsibilities – 115 responsibilities were identified overall. There was great variety in the posts held by advisory teachers and they clearly provided LEAs with the opportunity to support particular aspects of the work of schools relevant at a given time. This was evident from the existence of posts like those held for assessment, child abuse, LMS, as well as all those relevant to the National Curriculum.

The training of advisory teachers The studies of advisers/inspectors and advisory teachers described above noted that both groups lack training for the work in hand. Dean (1991b) suggests that a good deal has been done to deal with this problem. Seventy-nine per cent of LEAs overall have provided an induction programme for advisory teachers, 65 per cent have a compulsory in-house programme, 86 per cent gave the opportunity to attend other courses and 34 per cent provide appraisal.

Overall Dean (1991b) suggests that, in spite of the pressures on them, LEAs have given a good deal of priority to reorganising their advisory/inspectorate teams to meet the changes required. It remains to be seen whether the reorganised teams are in a better position to meet the new demands.

The overriding responsibilities of LEAs are clearly articulated in legislation, DES circulars and publications of the Audit Commission:

> It shall be the duty of the local education authority to contribute by securing that efficient education shall be available to meet the needs of the population of their area.
>
> (1944 Education Act, Section 7)

> It shall be the duty . . . of every local education committee as respects every school maintained by them to exercise their functions including, in particular, the functions conferred on them by this chapter with respect to religious education, religious worship and the National Curriculum, with a view to securing that the curriculum for the school satisfies the requirements of this section.
>
> (Education Reform Act 1988, para. 1.1)

> Within the overall requirements of the Act, the LEA will articulate policies for the service, including its curriculum policy, and co-ordinate national and local specific grant initiatives. It will continue to have the main responsibility for the professional development of its teachers, including appraisal and in-service training. Its monitoring role will be particularly important in ensuring that its overall responsibility is met.
>
> (Circular 7/88, para. 19)

The LEA retains key responsibility in seven key areas. It must:

- issue a policy statement on the curriculum, showing how the National Curriculum will be implemented, and help schools to prepare development plans;
- prepare a curriculum policy for pupils 5–17 and students 15–19 and contribute to the implementation of the National Curriculum;

- inspect LEA maintained institutions and monitor their performance and schools' delivery of the National Curriculum;
- evaluate the success of local management schemes in improving the quality of teaching and learning;
- define educational grounds for withdrawal of governors' delegated management authority and ensure that monitoring systems are adequate to detect where there are grounds for withdrawal.

(Audit Commission 1989a)

Chapter 2

The roles of inspectors and advisers

As we have already noted, there have been substantial changes in advisory/ inspectorate teams in recent months, which take account of the criticisms of the service made by the Audit Commission (1989b) and the NFER study (Stillman and Grant, 1989). It is possible that this is only the beginning of much larger changes. As the EMIE study (Dean, 1991b) showed, some LEAs are not only separating the advisory from the inspectorial function but are making the advisory part of the work something to be bought in by schools and colleges which are being given the money formerly spent on advisers or advisory teachers. This pressure to give all the money to establishments is also likely to reduce substantially the numbers of advisory teachers at a time when the original grants are running out. These changes will take time to absorb.

Since the publication of the Education Reform Act 1988 there have been a number of definitions from the centre about what advisers should be doing. The paper *Better Schools*, (DES, 1986a) stated that 'an LEA cannot discharge its functions without up-to-date knowledge of the institutions it maintains'. Hancock (1988) in a speech to the National Association of Inspectors and Educational Advisers stated that:

> The objective is that each LEA should develop a coherent inspection policy in order to monitor the quality of education, the implementation of the National Curriculum and the operation of schemes of local financial management.

Coopers and Lybrand (1988) in their study suggested that delegating more authority to schools will result in an enhanced role for inspector/advisers because of the need for greater monitoring and accountability. They suggest that under LMS the role of advisers and inspectors is likely to change in emphasis:

> There will still be an advisory task to be performed, not least to governing bodies, and there will be the additional dimension of providing advice on the overall management of the school. But the monitoring role will mean

that the emphasis will shift more towards the inspectorate end of the spectrum (as opposed to the advisory one) as the advisers/inspectors will need to act to a greater extent as the eyes and ears of the LEA in matters of educational quality and management.

The draft circular *Education Reform Act* (DES, 1988a) states:

The local inspectorate or advisory service, together with the LEA's advisory teachers, will have an essential role in preparing for, implementing and monitoring the National Curriculum and other developments arising from the Education Reform Act.

The Audit Commission study (1989b) of the advisory/inspectorate services confirms the need for more monitoring of what is happening in schools and suggests that each LEA 'should formulate a policy on the observation of teaching. This must include a view of the amount of classroom observation needed'. It also stresses that advice should be made available to three groups of people:

1   Members and officers of the LEA.
2   Those responsible for managing institutions – governors, headteachers and principals.
3   Individual members of school and college staff.

All this suggests that there will be a change of role, not only for inspectors and advisers but also for advisory teachers, who may well be expected to fill the gaps left when advisers and inspectors spend more time in monitoring and evaluation. Dean (1991b) also included information about the training of advisers and advisory teachers and it is significant that LEAs provided less training in in-service work and teacher support for advisers and inspectors than for advisory teachers.

There is apparent national support for increased inspection of schools at frequent intervals with public reports. This is likely to absorb many of the present advisory/inspection service, leaving advisory work as something to be undertaken by contract with schools. This is likely to shift the role of advisers and inspectors in the direction of consultancy.

One issue that has to be considered in the context of moving to a more inspection-based service is that of credibility. LEA inspectors/advisers are well known to the schools and colleges in their authority and heads are often aware of the previous experience of members of the service. Hellawell (1990) describes a small study of primary heads' views of who should undertake their appraisal. It was very evident from their replies that very few of them felt much confidence in their local inspectors/advisers as appraisers of the head's work. It was not that they lacked respect for what some of their advisers offered but rather that they felt that an inspector/adviser who had spent all his teaching life in secondary schools was not an appropriate person to assess the rather different job of being head of a primary school. Likewise principals and lecturers in adult and further education will be doubtful about people who have not had similar experience to their own.

If this problem arises over appraisal, it will also arise over inspection. Schools accept HMIs without too much concern about their background, but because local authority inspectors and advisers are so much closer to the schools they have to work much harder to achieve acceptability. This will be even more of a problem in adult and further education. This is a strong argument for substantial training for inspectors and advisers as well as an argument for appointing more people who have been heads of schools and more people who have had experience of teaching in the primary sector. Inspectors have to prove their worth to schools.

The pressure at the present time is on inspection. It is important to remember that inspection and advice are closely linked. Inspection without advice is a somewhat sterile activity which is unlikely to be acceptable to teachers. Effective advice must involve inspection, since anyone offering advice must know the situation in which he or she is offering it. If these two functions are separated, the people concerned must work closely together.

The changes coming about will require some new skills – those of marketing the service and analysing and advising on business plans, for example – but in the main the skills and knowledge called for are much the same as they have always been, although the recipients may be different. In particular, inspectors and advisers will be called upon to advise governing bodies. Advisory teachers will be called upon more frequently to run in-service courses and to support teachers. It is evident from the study by Harland (1990) that advisory teachers in some authorities are concerned about the lack of intensive training before they start work. The main problem for all three groups is how to spread the team's skills so that the service is effective.

The aims of the advisory/inspectorate service

Most LEAs have now defined the aims of their service. Many of the definitions of aims include the following:

1 To monitor, evaluate and report upon the quality of educational provision and the standards of learning and the implementation of local and national policy objectives.
2 To provide the LEA with the information and advice needed to shape policy.
3 To provide a coordinated programme of advice and support for all schools and other institutions, particularly in the implementation of the National Curriculum and in the management of resources.
4 To promote the professional development of all teaching staff.

5 To promote curriculum development, particularly in those areas not covered by the National Curriculum.
6 To offer advice and guidance to governors and headteachers on teaching appointments.
7 To provide support and advice for the appraisal schemes of schools and colleges.
8 To develop the work of the service and the individuals within it.

Influencing schools and colleges

How do inspectors/advisers and advisory teachers influence? The effectiveness of any individual inspector/adviser or advisory teacher has in the past depended upon the extent to which he or she can influence teachers. This remains true but it is now becoming evident that many of the areas where advice will be sought and given come within the Education Reform Act. There is a greater pressure on institutions and their governing bodies to use advice, particularly that arising from inspection, because advisory/inspectorate services now quite clearly have power delegated from the LEA, which could, in the ultimate case, withdraw funds. This is the hard end of the service. A soft end remains in which advice may or may not be used according to the value set upon it by those receiving it. If the trend towards consultancy continues, with a consultancy service separated from inspection and requested and paid for by those who use it, schools and other institutions will feel some pressure themselves to consider seriously advice that has cost them money. In any case, if consultancy is really to work, it will be more a matter of working with teachers and others to reach a solution than one of handing out advice, although there will still be a place for this.

Some advisers/inspectors and advisory teachers have always been better at offering acceptable advice than others. This has not always been a matter of the quality of the advice but of the way in which it has been presented. It is worth considering where an inspector/adviser's or the advisory teacher's influence comes from. Margerison (1978), writing about advisory work in industry, lists a number of kinds of influence:

Force influence The influence that arises from power to make things difficult if the other person does not do as the adviser wishes. In the LEA situation there is an element of this because the inspector or adviser is the representative of the authority. This will be more evident in the new situation in which monitoring and inspection are playing a larger part. It is less a form of influence for advisory teachers, who are more often seen by teachers as colleagues rather than representatives of the LEA. It is a comparatively easy way to influence but not a very satisfactory one for the work inspectors and advisers do, which requires understanding and commitment on the part of teachers if it is to have long-term effect. A person may do as someone else wishes from fear of the consequences, but the results are often superficial. Inspectors, advisers and advisory teachers need to win hearts and minds if they are to be effective.

There are, however, situations where force influence is useful. Where a teacher is failing, it may be necessary to insist that certain things are done if unpleasant consequences are to be avoided. There may also be an element of force influence in getting some teachers to try new ideas which they afterwards adopt and become committed to. The changes which have come about as a result of the Education Reform Act may be of this kind. Many teachers started work on the National Curriculum because they were forced to by legislation, but already many have made some of its thinking their own and are working happily within it.

Knowledge influence   Influence arising from that fact that the inspector, adviser or advisory teacher is expert and has valuable skills and knowledge. Most inspectors and advisers use this particular kind of influence a great deal and advisory teachers even more so, and research suggests that this is much appreciated by teachers. The difficulty comes in situations where the inspector or adviser is not expert, as, for example, where a person with a secondary background is responsible for advising a primary school. In this situation it is important for the inspector or adviser to work to become expert and to seek out common principles and practice so that he or she has something to offer teachers as well as skill in observation.

Reward influence   Influence arising from the ability of the inspector, adviser or advisory teacher to reward the other person for doing what he or she wishes. In the past many inspectors/advisers have had sums of money available which they could use to encourage teachers to move in certain directions and more recently advisory teachers of IT have had the chance to help in the distribution of hardware. These opportunities are disappearing. Inspectors and advisers also had considerable influence on promotion in the past and still have some influence, which will have an effect on the way teachers regard their advice. People are also rewarded by approval, encouragement and praise and this can be an important part of the influence of an inspector, adviser or advisory teacher.

The problem about reward influence is that it is a little like force influence in not necessarily carrying teachers' thinking and commitment.

Positional authority influence   An inspector or adviser may have influence from the position he or she holds. This will be particularly true for the chief adviser and senior members of the advisory team. Advisory teachers will also have positional influence. It is useful as an incentive, but there is a need to go further if understanding is to be developed and commitment won. Winkley (1985) gives a depressing quotation about the dangers of positional influence

Last week our inspector lectured us for an hour and a half without stopping. After that he asked for questions. We're not in a position to offer real questions – to discuss questions honestly – because he's got such enormous powers of patronage, and although he's a very nice, competent man he doesn't realise the problem. There's no possibility of a fruitful dialogue.

Personal friendship influence   The influence which arises because the inspector, adviser or advisory teacher is trusted as a personal friend who ought not to be offended. There is a sense in which this too is a form of force, but generally this kind of influence is wholly beneficial and represents the best relationship which inspectors and advisers can form with the establishments for which they are responsible. However, just as teachers, particularly teachers of young children, must be careful not to make children over-dependent, so inspectors and advisers must be careful to use good relationships with teachers to help them to develop their thinking and autonomy. The move to inspection on a large scale may make this kind of relationship much more difficult because the fact that someone is judging work militates against the formation of a trusting relationship. Although, in the past, there was always an element of judgement in the work of advisers and inspectors it was not all that evident in many authorities. Teachers have always been ready to accept constructive criticism more willingly if the 'critical friend' is prepared to support development afterwards.

The way inspectors, advisers and advisory teachers use their influence will depend to some extent on the way they see their job and their views of teachers.

Advisory style

There is a style in the way advisory/inspectorial work can be undertaken. Winkley (1985) describes this very clearly. He suggests that the context in which the inspector or adviser works in the LEA as well as his or her personal views is an element in the style developed. He gives seven possible views of advisory work:

1 *The line management view* which the inspector or adviser is seen as part of the line management structure of the authority. In the past inspectors and advisers who worked in LEAs where this view was prevalent were likely to have had a good deal of influence over what happened in the schools and colleges. Although this influence will diminish under the Education Reform Act, there is a sense in which the legislation supports this style, since in the inspection role the inspector is clearly acting on behalf of the LEA in helping to fulfil its responsibility for what happens in its institutions.

2 *The personal development view* where the inspector/adviser is basically concerned about the personal development of teachers and the overall attitudes and sensitivities which will lead to or limit development. Advisory teachers will be in a better position than inspectors/advisers to develop this view.

3 *The management-by-objectives view* which needs no explanation and might be seen to link with work on appraisal.

4 *The subject specialist view* which can be described as 'handing down knowledge' rather than exploring knowledge with teachers.

5 *The career-control view* where some authorities' inspectors and advisers have had considerable influence over promotion. This has changed as a consequence of the Education Reform Act (1988) whereby the appointments are in the hands of governors, although inspectors and advisers may still be influential in some LEAs.

6 *The system-facilitator view* where the inspector or adviser is concerned with assessing the needs of schools and other establishments and responding to them. It might perhaps be termed the organisation development view.

7 *Analytical-observer view* where the inspector or adviser is reflecting for teachers what is happening and helping them to analyse in order to move forward.

Most of these styles will be used by inspectors and advisers at some point and some will be used by advisory teachers but the emphasis for any particular inspector or adviser will be determined partly by the context and partly by personal preference. Some of these styles are also more likely to emerge in the current climate, since inspectors and advisers will now have less time for working with teachers. As we have already noted, some of the work previously done by inspectors and advisers may now be done by advisory teachers who also develop personal styles. Winkley (1985) points out differences in LEA styles and expectations of inspectors and advisers.

Style in any aspect of work is something one develops over a period as one becomes confident in what one is doing. People come into advisory work confident in their previous experience and with a definite style of their own, but need to adapt this to the new situation and to the exercise of new skills. It is helpful if those new to advisory work can visit with more experienced colleagues in order to see different styles at work.

An adviser or inspector will also to some extent match style to establishment and to teachers and to the particular task being undertaken. The style an inspector or adviser adopts will also change with the way in which contact with the school has came about. An adviser or inspector invited into the school, is unlikely to work in the same style as when he or she has come in order to inspect, although the differences may be comparatively minor. The task of observing a teacher in order to assess performance is different from that of observing in order to help, although one hopes that the assessment will also lead to help. It is a matter of which task is taking priority. Style can also influence the processes of inspection, in the way in which reports are presented for example.

The tasks of inspectors and advisers

This chapter sets out to cover as many as possible of the tasks of inspectors and advisers. It will not be possible for any individual to undertake all of them all the time. Each team and each inspector or adviser must select tasks to undertake from those which are possible. An inspector or adviser may also choose to concentrate on a number of tasks each year and thus cover ground over a period.

It is clear from many recent publications that the inspection in some form of the establishments maintained by an LEA is now the major task of its advisory/inspectorate services. The possible ways of tackling this task are discussed in chapter 5. It is also clear that advisers and inspectors are expected to operate in other roles, supporting schools and other institutions and providing advice to a variety of people. The support role is described in some detail in chapter 6. This chapter is concerned with identifying the tasks which inspection and advisory work needs to cover.

The tasks of an inspector or adviser might be broadly described as general, specialist, phase or management. The Society of Chief Advisers and Inspectors (SCIA 1989) suggests that the advisory/inspectorate service of an authority should provide the following range of expertise and support:

1 A 'general' or 'link' adviser for each institution, as advocated by the joint DES/LEA working paper (DES 1985).
2 Specialist expertise on each phase of the educational process, including further education, community education and training, early years and special needs as well as management expertise for schools and colleges in those phases.
3 Specialist expertise in each major subject and aspect of the curriculum, including cross-curricular themes and issues, with greater provision for the vocational curriculum than usually exists.

In many LEAs, the general adviser, who has a responsibility for a number of establishments and may be called a pastoral adviser or a link adviser, now plays an important role in both support and evaluation. It will be essential to ensure that the support role is given sufficient time and attention in view of the pressure for inspection, but the general adviser is in a very good position to contribute to the evaluation of the establishments for which he or she is responsible. Advisers and inspectors in managerial roles will need time allowed for this work and should have job descriptions which define the work in some detail.

The job description

The general adviser's job description is likely to cover the following:
The general adviser should:

1 *Be involved in inspection* according to the arrangements agreed locally and by the advisory/inspectorate team
2 *Have a good knowledge* of the group of establishments for which he or she is responsible, including knowledge of:

- their philosophy
- their development programme and planning
- management, including finance and resources
- organisation
- curriculum
- staff deployment
- teaching approaches
- standards being achieved
- methods of evaluation
- staff development programme, including appraisal
- relationships with governors
- relationships with parents and the community

3 *Advise the staff and particularly the head,* on the items above
4 *Advise the LEA and governors on:*

- education in these establishments
- the work of their teachers
- the standards being achieved
- general trends emerging from groups of schools
- policy
- the selection and appointment of staff
- their particular needs
- specific problems concerning them

5 *Encourage continuity* between phases and cooperation between establishments.

Some inspectors/advisers have specialist responsibilities only; some have both general and specialist responsibilities. Both arrangements have their problems and advantages and these are discussed in a later chapter. Whatever the form of organisation it is important that the relationship between these two aspects of the work should be well-established and that there should be clear lines of communication and consultation when they are undertaken by separate people. The specialist inspector or adviser's job description is likely to cover the following.
The specialist adviser should:

1 *Be involved in inspection* according to the arrangements agreed locally and by the advisory/inspectorate team
2 *Know the state of the specialism* for which he or she is responsible, including knowledge of:

- the overall philosophy
- the National Curriculum and other curriculum guidelines
- appropriate teaching approaches
- the way work is organised in the schools and other institutions
- the standards being achieved
- the methods of evaluation, both those used by schools and other establishments and appropriate methods for inspection
- current developments at a national and international level

3 *Advise teachers and particularly the head,* on the items above
4 *Advise the LEA and governors* on:

- education in the specialist area of curriculum or other work.
- appropriate forms of approach and organisation
- the requirements of the National Curriculum where appropriate
- the work of their teachers in this area of curriculum or other work
- the standards being achieved
- current developments nationally and internationally
- the selection and appointment of staff
- their particular needs
- specific problems concerning them

5 *Encourage continuity* between phases and cooperation between establishments.
6 *Supervise the planning of the staff development programme* in this area of work.

If the specialist is also a general adviser then the job description will include elements of both the job descriptions above.

Taking part in inspections

LEAs are adopting a variety of approaches to inspection and many are using information from visits to schools and other establishments and their self-evaluation as part of a total pattern, augmented in most cases with a certain amount of more formal inspection. Some authorities are separating the roles of inspectors and advisers but in most places people are undertaking both roles. The advantages and disadvantages of different forms of organisation are discussed in more detail in chapter 11.

Knowing and supporting the schools and colleges

Some LEAs have abandoned the idea of attached or link advisers, but in most places the point originally made in the DES (1985) working paper on advisory services that 'it is essential that each institution is known as a whole and known well by at least one adviser' is accepted. In this context the following might be expected.

The adviser should help the head and staff by:

1 *Working with them to help to formulate and implement the development plan and monitoring its progress.* The way the general inspector or adviser does this will depend a good deal on what is in the plan and what he or she has to offer. Support may involve inviting colleague advisers, inspectors or advisory teachers to contribute to school-based INSET or provide support for teachers in the classroom. It may involve helping staff to identify specific targets, develop plans and implement them. It may involve encouraging staff to make desirable changes and helping to evaluate what has happened. The specialist inspector or adviser will be able to offer a particular contribution in the area of his or her specialism.

2 *Providing support to the staff in dealing with the outcomes of inspection.* This is related to providing support for the development plan, since inspection must involve looking at how the school is managing this. Initially it may involve drawing up action plans to tackle problems revealed by inspection and following these up with the staff, keeping them involved and active and working towards agreed dates by which action will have taken place. The general adviser may need to involve appropriate specialist colleagues. Providing support may also involve helping people to regain their enthusiasm after an inspection which has uncovered a good deal which needs development.

3 *Advising the head and senior staff in their management role.* This may involve:

   • assessing aspects of management such as communication or decision-making
   • advising on the relationship between the budget and the curriculum offered, and obtaining advice on budgetary issues from specialist officers within the authority as necessary
   • advising on timetabling and staff deployment
   • encouraging the head to make a personal action plan and monitoring its progress

A head needs a personal action plan which may include the development of particular members of the staff and personal intentions to achieve particular goals. A general adviser can do much to provide material for this plan in making the kinds of observations listed above. The general adviser can also provide an opportunity for making such a plan, perhaps by gathering together a small group of headteachers from his or her schools and spending time with them working on action plans. The members of such a group can also support each other. Groups of schools can work productively together on such issues as curriculum development and policy formation under the guidance of the general adviser.

The general adviser can then talk through the implications of the action plan with each head and monitor its progress, assisting with any problems and eventually evaluating the outcomes. This may link with headteacher appraisal.

4 *Contributing to the professional development programme.* Almost every activity has possibilities for the development of staff. The general adviser and the specialist adviser can do a great deal to help the head and staff to be aware of these possibilities. Inspections and visits may also identify issues for professional development. The general adviser can also help the teacher responsible for professional development to consider the needs of each member of the staff as well as to organise in-service days.

5 *Monitoring the work of teachers, particularly probationers and any who are failing or are looking for promotion.* The general adviser and the specialist should see as many teachers at work as possible, but he or she will have a particular responsibility for teachers who need extra help or are looking for promotion. A teacher who is failing is likely to be a cause of concern to head and governors, who may wish to dismiss him or her. The specialist may be called in to help and to advise both the teacher and the head and governors. The advisory/inspectorate team needs to have a policy about the way they work in this situation, but the general adviser and the specialist will both play an important part, in trying to help the teacher and also in providing evidence on which a decision can be made.

6 *Reviewing specific aspects of the work of the establishment,* for example, record keeping. The general adviser can be of particular help to the school or college in evaluating particular aspects of its work which may not be part of an inspection programme. This is also a useful way to get to know an establishment. Specialist advisers can also be helpful in looking at a particular aspect of a school, probably by request of the head or governors.

7 *Contributing according to the needs of the establishment.* Much of the help both general and specialist advisers give to an establishment will be in response to particular needs. Many heads find it helpful to talk over aspects of their work and try out ideas with a general adviser. Heads of department and specialist teachers will want to talk over work with the appropriate specialist adviser. The general adviser will also have particular strengths to offer the establishment and will call in the specialist colleague when necessary.

Advising governors and the LEA

The general adviser should be the most important professional outside source of general information about the school or college. He or she should be:

1 *Involved in presenting inspection reports to the governors and the LEA.* Each advisory/inspectorate team will have its own system for writing and presenting reports of inspections. This may be similar to that of HMI, or a cooperative venture with the school or college, or a gathering together of information from those inspectors/advisers who have visited the school. At some stage the report will need to be presented to the school governors and the general adviser must play an important part in this as the person within the advisory service with the most knowledge of the particular establishment.

2 *Prepared to advise on the follow-up to inspection and its effectiveness.* We have already noted that part of the task of the general adviser is to see that inspections are followed up. He or she must advise the governors on this and explain what is planned and by what date. It will then be necessary to let the governors know how effective the follow-up has been. The follow-up may well involve the specialist adviser, who may be asked by the governors to report on his/her particular area of work.

3 *Prepared to comment on the standards being achieved, including the quality of management.* At any stage, the general adviser will be an important source of information about standards for the governors, as will the specialist. There must be a readiness to comment on the quality of the management of the establishment, which will be a difficult task in view of the relationship of the general advisor with the head. However, the general adviser is the only source of such information that the governors can call on. Such a report should be discussed with the head, probably on a number of occasions, before information is given to governors. The head should be aware of what the general adviser might say at a governors' meeting. Generally speaking, the governors are unlikely to ask for such information if things are going well.

4 *Ready to advise on the selection and appointment of staff.* The appointment of head and staff is now the responsibility of the governing body. While there will be some governors who are experienced in staff selection, the majority will not be and will rely on the professionals to advise them. The head will, of course, play a major part, but the general adviser and the specialist will also be important, both in advising on the selection process and also in advising on and taking part in interviews.

5 *Advising on the work of teachers who are posing problems or are seeking promotion.* We have already noted that the general adviser should be involved in these cases and that the governors will look to the general

adviser for advice. The general adviser is likely to look to the specialist where appropriate.

6 *Ready to advise on the needs and problems of the establishment.* Governors may wish to turn to someone who knows the school or college and has a wider view of what is happening to see their own particular problems in perspective. Officers also need to be able to turn to someone who knows the establishment.

Encouraging continuity and cooperation

The general adviser is in a good position to bring together teachers, schools and colleges, both of different phases and also those of the same phase. This is particularly the case where he or she has responsibility for a family of schools in which pupils move from one to the other.

There is a great need to improve continuity between schools, and the National Curriculum provides a good incentive for doing this, since it should make curriculum continuity rather easier. There is also much to be said for getting heads and teachers of the same phase to work together, so that the emphasis on competition is balanced.

Professional support

The Audit Commission (1989b) states what every adviser has been aware of for many years, that the extent of professional support for advisers 'varies enormously from place to place and in some cases is quite inadequate'. The SCIA paper (1989) quoted earlier notes that:

The changing nature and increased load of advisory work will place a high priority on effective and efficient use of time. That renders the provision of an appropriate administrative and professional support team indispensable. . . . The following areas of support are essential:

1 Management of a range of budgets which underpin aspects of advisory and curriculum development work
2 Personal assistant support to the team
3 Project management and monitoring
4 Administrative and clerical support
5 Statistical, research and development back-up for inspection
6 Office management services
7 Database and IT facilities
8 Educational development facilities (such centres may currently include writers, graphic designers, reprographic specialists and corresponding equipment)

Reporting

Each advisory/inspectorate team will have its own arrangements for reporting on inspections and these are discussed in detail in chapter 5. Most authorities are also now requiring advisers to report on all visits in some form. At least a section of a visit report should be formulated in such a way that the information it contains can easily be entered into a database and made available to others who need it. The following information might be included in this section of the report: establishment visited, date, name of adviser, teachers seen, teaching seen (subject or topic, age group, time spent), discussion with the head, time spent altogether, type of visit, specific topic, curriculum discussion, newly qualified teachers seen.

Advisers and inspectors will need to record more than this if they are evaluating what they have seen, particularly where the visit reports will eventually form part of a report on the whole establishment. The Audit Commission (1989b) suggests that records should:

> make plain the status of the information they contain. Particularly in relation to any piece of judgemental information advisers should be clear whether:
>
> - the judgement was made 'on the fly' during a visit to an institution for a purpose other than that of making that judgement
> - the judgement was made during a structured visit of formal inspection
> - teaching staff whose work was observed were notified of the potential uses of the information
> - immediate feedback was given after the observations were made

Conclusion

The general adviser's role is a privileged one which allows him or her to get to know an establishment well. In a number of authorities advisers and inspectors now have specific areas to evaluate in visiting schools and colleges. When this is not the case it can be helpful to select some aspect to study or some problem to tackle and it is usual to find that, in the process of undertaking these tasks, an adviser learns a great deal about the establishment and absorbs much of the atmosphere, as well as offering something useful to the staff.

An adviser or inspector whose own background is secondary, coming to work in a primary school, may, find it helpful to select a particular aspect of the curriculum and follow it through the school, learning how the staff tackle it. As a person coming with fresh eyes, he or she may well have some useful comment to offer the school at the end of the study.

Another approach is to spend most of a day in a classroom with a very good teacher (if time can be found for this!) and to select particular aspects of the work to observe, perhaps looking at what happens to a particular child for a period, then observing how the teacher operates, then noting the extent to which children are on task and what they are doing and so on. Here again, it is possible that, by the end of the day, the adviser will have a number of useful points to offer the teacher.

The specialist role is also privileged in a different way. The specialist sees many schools and a great variety of work. This places him or her in a strong position to advise schools and to keep others informed the about the state of the specialism in establishments across the authority.

Chapter 3

The role of the advisory teacher

LEAs have been appointing advisory teachers since at least the early 1960s but it is only in the last few years that these posts have begun to be established on a large scale. According to Stillman and Grant (1989), 82 per cent of advisory teacher posts were created after 1974 and 37 per cent were brought in between 1984 and 1986. Further posts have been added since then and there are now about as many advisory teachers as advisers, although the number varies considerably from one authority to another. As we have already seen, Dean (1991b) found that there were currently over 4,000 such posts. The largest team had 169 posts and the smallest six. The sizes of teams generally bore only a superficial relationship to the size of the authority. Stillman and Grant also found that very little thought had apparently been given to the management of this part of the service.

Dean (1991) also found a very large range of specialisms among advisory teachers, with 115 different ones identified overall. Most LEAs had advisory teachers for English, mathematics, science, technology and information technology but the rest of the posts were extremely varied, with 40–9 per cent of authorities having posts for health, modern languages, physical education and religious education and 30–9 per cent art, assessment, humanities, multicultural education and special educational needs.

The development of the advisory teacher role has been supported by government grants, so that there are now some advisory teachers with LEA appointments and some who have been appointed to the LEA because of a grant. There is also considerable variation in the terms under which such teachers are appointed. Some have permanent full-time posts, some are seconded for varying periods and some spend part of their time as teachers in schools and part advising other teachers. The additional salary for these posts ranges from an A to an E allowance, with some advisory teachers on other scales earning even more.

Advisory teachers have generally been welcomed by schools. Petrie (1988), writing of his experience with science advisory teachers, says:

It is possible to report an overwhelming acceptance of advisory teachers in the schools, and of the classroom support of the teacher. It is also possible to say categorically that advisory teachers have been instrumental in catalysing science experiences for children in many instances where one suspects that otherwise they would not have occurred.

Max de Boo (1988), who worked as a science advisory teacher in Haringey, speaks of the advantages of school-based support as follows:

- working alongside teachers on their home ground;
- adapting to the individual teacher's level of experience, expertise and needs;
- relating the science teaching directly to the teacher's own class of children;
- relating the response directly to the conditions pertaining in the school;
- being a positive influence for science in the staffroom;
- being an opportunist and incorporating other cross-curricular activities into the science programme;
- being a guide through the difficulties, if any, of policy development and documentation.

He also lists what he has learned about supporting curriculum change:

1 The headteacher must give active support to the project.
2 There must be a curriculum leader for science, with at least two other supportive colleagues.
3 The whole staff must feel involved and able to contribute to the project.
4 The project must be a long-term commitment (minimum one year).

The work of advisory teachers

It is very much more difficult to provide a generic job description for advisory teachers than for advisers or inspectors. Harland (1990) made a study of a small group of advisory teachers in three authorities. He notes:

It is easy to make the mistake of discussing 'advisory teachers' as though there was a commonly agreed definition of what such a person is, or as if there was a uniform image of what their work entails. Such conformity does not exist in reality and thus it is important to base any deliberations on this occupation on the recognition that advisory teachers are not a homogeneous group.

He suggested that there appeared to be six different roles:

1 Class teacher trainer, with the advisory teacher promoting staff develop- ment by working alongside the classroom teacher.
2 Presenter of INSET sessions and workshops.
3 Researcher, with the advisory teacher undertaking surveys of practice in schools in aspects of curriculum or management.

4 Developer of curriculum or related activity.
5 Coordinator of teams of advisory teachers.
6 Administrator for specific tasks, for example training requirement for GCSE, appraisal.

These were not separate tasks and one person might undertake more than one set. This is borne out by the definition of tasks given by the Micro-electonics Education Support Unit Course Materials (MSU 1988), which describe the role for the posts for information technology as:

− advising staff about policies, and/or about roles of responsibility
− supporting teachers who are:
  • using new hardware
  • trying out new teaching methods
  • introducing new software
  • developing materials to supplement software etc.
− leading staff meetings or workshops
− supporting a school/department on an INSET day
− advising about provision for individual children (e.g. SEN, E2L learners)

Max de Boo (1988) identifies four areas in which he saw himself offering support to teachers:

1 Support at a basic level in providing practical ideas.
2 Teaching support given in the classroom, through demonstration, general teaching, alongside the classroom teacher, team teaching and assisting in a debate or dramatisation of a science/moral issue.
3 Personal support for teachers, increasing their confidence, being a personal ambassador for science.
4 Helping teachers to change the way they taught science.

The Cockcroft Report (DES, 1982) made several comments about advisory teachers and clearly recognised the part they could play:

Advisory teachers commonly work alongside teachers in the classroom. They may spend a period of several days in the same school or visit each of a group of schools on a regular basis. They may perhaps help with drawing up or revising a scheme of work or assist with the in-service programme of the LEA or school. We believe that advisory teachers can play a valuable role in providing in-service support in a school. This is perhaps especially the case in a primary school which lacks a member of staff who has mathematical expertise.

Straker (1988) abstracted data from diaries of eleven advisory teachers of mathematics in five LEAs to discover the nature of their work throughout the week. The figures shown in table 1 give the lowest and highest percentages of time spent in each area of work.

Table 1 Time spent by advisory teachers

Topic	Activities	Highest time	Lowest time
Teaching	School-based inset – working alongside teachers Running in-service courses or workshops Specific planning of lessons or workshops	80	28
Administration	General administration	22	–
Meetings	With other advisory teachers With LEA mathematics adviser Committee meetings Attendance at workshops/user groups etc With visitors	25	–
Advisory	Specific discussion with heads and teachers Giving specific advise to individuals	25	–
Curriculum development	Producing materials/creating resources GCSE training role Visits to HE institutions relating to curriculum development	30	–

These statements are not untypical of the work of advisory teachers of many specialisms.

It is possible, in spite of the variety of posts, to define some aspects of the job description in broad terms:

1 It will involve working closely with teachers, supporting and advising them in their work.
2 It is likely to involve some form of staff development activity, whether within the school or as part of INSET or workshops.
3 The majority of time for people in most of these posts will be spent in schools.
4 It will involve working closely with one or more advisers or inspectors.

The work of advisory teachers differs from that of advisers in that most posts are more school-based and they have no element of inspection in them except in so far as inspection is needed to assess the situation so that help may be given. This means that they can work in a more relaxed way than inspectors and advisers in that teachers do not see them in a judgemental role and many are in a position to spend time working alongside teachers. As advisers become increasingly involved in inspection, it seems likely that advisory teachers will undertake more of the work of supporting teachers and schools which was formerly the province of advisers.

An article in the ILEA magazine *Insight* (Jane and Varlaam, 1981) notes that the advisory support teams working in school 'saw themselves as helping teachers develop particular aspects of the curriculum by discussing and examining with them how children learn'.

Problems of work as an advisory teacher

Whitaker (1990), in a paper written for the Centre for Adviser and Inspector Development (CAID), notes that there are a number of problems about the employment of advisory teachers:

- confusion about allowances and the rate for the job;
- inadequate and sometimes non-existent job descriptions;
- confusion about terms and conditions, especially in relation to temporary and permanent posts;
- lack of clear line management structures and absence of regular contact between individual advisory teachers and their designated line manager;
- lack of information about LEA developments;
- a sometimes elitist differentiation between advisory teachers and inspectors and advisers.

If the intention is to ensure that those giving advice to teachers in classrooms have recent classroom experience themselves, the permanent appointment does not seem to be the ideal. Furthermore, as we have seen, seen there is now some hesitation about making permanent appointments, since money for them may not continue to be available. Permanent appointments also make it difficult to vary the responsibilities covered by these teachers as demands change. On the other hand, seconded posts also bring difficulties. Schools do not want to release their best teachers and the teachers themselves tend not to want to return to a teaching post when the secondment is over because they feel that they have acquired skills which should be used. It is also a fact that advisory teachers require training and may be becoming most competent at the work just as they are due to leave it. Working part-time in a school may seem to be a good way of ensuring that the person concerned is in close touch with the classroom, but the demands that this duality makes are considerable, especially as the post in school is likely to be at a senior level. These are problems which no LEA appears to have managed to solve satisfactorily.

Harland (1990) also found a great deal of dissatisfaction over salary and status. The practice of seconding people on their existing salary meant that different people were doing the same work for different remuneration, which was naturally a source of dissatisfaction. They also felt that the rise in status that the job gave them and their commitment to it deserved financial reward. In addition when the secondment was over they were finding difficulty in getting jobs which matched the skills that they felt they had now acquired. Governors and heads appeared to think that two or three years away from the classroom were a disadvantage rather than a source of new thinking and new skills and advisory teachers had difficulty in obtaining more senior posts in schools. They had at one time thought that the natural progression might be to a post as inspector or adviser, but were much less enthusiastic about this possibility in the light of the new emphasis on inspection.

Harland also noted that there were problems about office space, the loss of routine and need for self-discipline, the size of the task and the business of sorting out priorities as well as a certain culture shock in finding themselves working with people 'higher up the ladder'.

The management of advisory teachers

While there is evidence from Dean (1991b) that a great deal has been done to reorganise the inspectorate/advisory service for its changed role, it appeared that much less had been done for advisory teachers. This group is at present as large as the adviser/inspector group although the likelihood is that it will diminish in spite of the need for the work to be done. As we saw in chapter 1 some work has been done to meet the demand for proper management and training of the advisory teacher force. Thirty authorities now have a senior adviser in overall charge of the advisory teacher team, three have an administrator in charge and four have a senior advisory teacher. Forty-eight involve the appropriate inspector but in twenty-seven cases this is the only form of management.

Most advisory teachers are responsible to individual inspectors or advisers who meet them regularly to plan and evaluate their programme. Usually the visits they make to schools will be carefully planned with particular objectives in mind which have been negotiated with the head, sometimes by an inspector or adviser and sometimes by the advisory teacher. Advisory teachers also need a certain amount of time each week to plan and organise their work and to evaluate what has happened. They need to keep records of each visit and what was achieved and these should be part of the overall records of the advisory service. It is helpful if they have a standard visit form comparable to that of inspectors and advisers but one which allows them to make notes of their own as well as recording agreed information.

One of the particular contributions of advisory teachers is that they can often plan their schedule so that they have a series of visits to one school in which they work with teachers in the classroom to achieve particular objectives. This may be a follow-up to inspection or to other visits by inspectors or advisers or it may result from a request from the head. It is therefore important that advisory teachers are not so laden with work that they are unable to do this. There is therefore advantage in planning the programme with an adviser or inspector who can support the advisory teacher in saying 'no' if too much is being required. As with advisers, it is important that advisory teachers define priorities and balance them carefully. They also need to analyse their diaries regularly to see whether they are maintaining the priorities they have established and whether the balance of their work is satisfactory.

The paper from the MSU (1988) on advisory teachers suggests that the following points about time management be considered:

- deciding what needs to be done;
- establishing what the real priorities are;
- keeping a sense of perspective;
- identifying any constraints;
- saying 'no';
- being punctual;
- allowing realistic travelling time;
- not going to schools 30 miles apart on the same day;
- starting/stopping meetings at the scheduled time;
- preparing thoroughly;
- keeping a file of useful addresses and telephone numbers;
- being equipped with useful resources/information lists;
- devising ways of using each other's strengths;
- responding as quickly as possible to letters/ phone calls;
- meeting other people's target dates;
- letting people know if an appointment can't be kept;
- phoning the day before to confirm arrangements;
- maintaining a duplicate diary to be kept at the office base showing the week's appointments;
- keeping well organised files/notes on school visits;
- planning time for the things which the advisory teacher wants to do as well as those he or she has to do;
- marking in the diary well ahead:
  - fixed points like meetings
  - regular time each week for planning and preparation
  - unplanned time to deal with the unexpected;
- not taking work home every day of the week.

Training for advisory teachers

The skills described in the next chapter are needed for advisory teachers as well as advisers and inspectors. Just as training is important for inspectors and advisers, so it is for advisory teachers.

Max de Boo (1988) identified the qualities and abilities he felt he needed as an advisory teacher and these give some guidance on what is needed by way of selection and training:

- ability to create an atmosphere of trust;
- credibility as an ordinary class teacher;
- adaptability and flexibility;
- being sure and clear about my own aims – setting achievable objectives – having realistic expectations;
- ability to supply ideas and information.

There is evidence from (Dean 1991b) that much more is being done to train this group than was formerly the case. Training offered in different authorities includes not only an introduction to the LEA and to advisory work, but also training in interpersonal skills, in-service education, supporting teachers, management, personal organisation such as time management and updating. Suggestions for a training programme will be found in chapter 10.

Jane and Varlaam (1981) describe the training needs which emerged when teams of support teachers went to spend a term in different schools. They concluded that training was needed in classroom observation techniques, group dynamics, effective questioning and ways of promoting adult learning. These teams met weekly and topics discussed at their meetings included confidentiality, accountability, how to analyse and identify INSET needs, how to report to head and staff and obtain feedback on their work.

Chapter 4

Skills with people

An adviser or inspector or advisory teacher may have many skills and be extremely knowledgeable about many aspects of education, but that will be of little value if he or she is not also skilled in relating to other people. Advisers and inspectors constantly need to form new relationships and to do so quickly because first impressions may affect the readiness of other people to accept what is said later. They need to be seen as people who have something to offer and people who can be trusted.

Advisers, inspectors and advisory teachers also need particular skills in dealing with people. Advisers and inspectors will often be talking with heads and teachers in a one-to-one situation, tackling problems and counselling. They may be involved in the appraisal of heads and others. They sometimes have to tell teachers that their work is not good enough. They may be negotiating with teachers and governors, with administrators and LEA members to get ideas adopted or resources provided. Advisory teachers will often be persuading heads and teachers to try new ways of working. Advisers, inspectors and advisory teachers are frequently expected to lead discussion groups and meetings and to talk to groups of people. These are all skills which can be learned.

Common features of interpersonal skills

Starting points

The beginning of any interpersonal activity is important in setting the scene for what is to follow. The start of a talk may capture the attention of the audience or lose it. The first comments by the leader of a discussion may encourage people to be ready to contribute or silence them. The opening words of a one-to-one discussion may help to determine how it goes subsequently. The strategy is to make others believe that they are important, that their contribution is valued and that their point of view is understood. This can be done in many ways. In a one-to-one situation some general chat which reveals knowledge of the person concerned may be a good starting point. A talk may start with a story which reveals knowledge of audience interests. A discussion leader may start with encouragement to group members to contribute in some already familiar area.

Body language

It is important to be able to read the body language of other people because this tells how they are reacting to what is being said. The following are frequently evident both in working with a group and in talking to individuals:

Eye contact   Human beings signal their readiness to start and end conversations with eye contact. A person makes eye contact at the beginning of a contribution to conversation and looks away as the end is reached. Eye contact is also important in retaining trust.

Interest and involvement   People signal their involvement or lack of it by the use of their bodies. For example, active listening is signalled by nods and smiles and sounds of agreement and often by sitting forward. Lack of interest and involvement is shown by sitting back, losing eye contact, fidgeting and more obviously by looking at the clock or a watch. People also signal impatience or disagreement with what is being said by fidgeting or changing position.

Tension   This is shown by rigidity of the body, facial expression, clenched hands, feet wound round chair legs, frowning, swallowing frequently, licking the lips.

Emotional involvement   In the course of a discussion an individual may feel hurt, upset, embarrassed and may signal this in similar ways to tension. In particular, eye contact tends to be dropped when a situation is emotionally charged. It is important to recognise this quickly in order to act appropriately.

Views of relative status   People convey views about their relative status by the way they behave in a one-to-one or group situation. An adviser or inspector is generally seen by teachers as superior to them and most teachers will show this in their behaviour. The adviser or inspector thus exercises control over the discussion, whether with an individual or in a group. It is very easy in this situation to talk too much and listen too little, or to talk down to people. This is less likely to happen with advisory teachers, who are more often seen by teachers as colleagues. Another danger is to use status to dismiss rather than encourage other people's ideas.

For the other party in a discussion, the reverse may happen. They do not like to interrupt, back down easily if someone talks them down, may put ideas forward very tentatively and withdraw them quickly if the climate seems unfavourable. Of course not all teachers act in this way, but some will, and it is the adviser/inspector's responsibility to ensure that all are happy to contribute, feeling confident that their ideas will be well received.

Discussion with individuals

Advisers and inspectors spend a lot of time talking to heads and teachers about their work. Sometimes they are gaining information, sometimes dealing with a problem, sometimes being critical of the work seen, sometimes making a request, appraising a situation or the work of an individual. It is also probable that advisers and inspectors will play some part in the appraisal of heads. They may also find themselves acting as adjudicators where a teacher is unhappy with the appraisal provided by the school. There will also be occasions when they are talking to individual governors, parents and administrators. Advisory teachers also work with individuals and need similar skills.

The interview

All these situations require skill in conducting what might be regarded as a form of interview. Interviews need to be managed. The following points are common to all discussions with individuals

Environment   Advisers and inspectors can rarely choose where they talk to people and have to make the best of whatever environment is offered. There may be some choices, however. Privacy is often important if a person is to feel free to talk frankly, and if the conversation is likely to be a difficult one it may be better to take a walk outside if the weather is good or sit in a car than to talk in a corner of the staff room where others can overhear the conversation. It is usually better for the interviewer to sit on a level with the person he or she is talking to and the comfort of the chairs and the room can make a difference. If a person is too hot or too cold or generally uncomfortable, this prevents full concentration on the subject under discussion.

It is also important for the interviewer to sit where he or she can see the other person full face in a good light so that facial expression and body language are easy to observe. It is equally important for the other person to be able to see the interviewer clearly.

Note-taking   It is very often sensible to take notes of a discussion, but unless this has been agreed it can seem threatening to the other person. It is a good idea to explain that note-taking is needed so that the discussion will be remembered, but that the notes are purely for personal use. Of course, when a person is known in a school, everyone will be aware that his or her usual practice is to take notes and it will then need no comment.

Starting points It is usually best to start with some general conversation and lead on to any positive points that can be made before tackling more difficult issues. It is also wise to explain the purpose of the interview at an early stage.

Active listening The task of listening should be an active one and most conversations should involve a great deal of listening on the interviewer's part. In active listening, the listener demonstrates that he or she is actually taking in what is said by nods and smiles and sounds of assent. It is also demonstrated by follow-up questions and probing to know more and to check what is said.

Response The interviewer's task is to create a situation in which the other person gives information freely. This is most likely to happen if the interviewer responds well to the information given initially. Comments like 'That's useful' or 'That's very interesting' encourage the other person, as does nodding and smiling. As the conversation continues it is useful if the interviewer sometimes responds with a statement or question which demonstrates that the information given has been understood and absorbed.

Types of interview

The various different kinds of discussion with individuals require different treatment and the exercise of different skills.

Interviewing for information Advisers are often interviewing for information. It is, in any case, a necessary beginning to many interviews for other purposes. The strategy is to get as much accurate information as possible in the shortest possible time compatible with maintaining good relationships. The 'shortest possible time' will vary according to the person with whom the discussion is being held. Some people take a lot of time to give information and need encouraging to avoid bypaths and anecdotes. Others can give information quickly and directly, especially if led through appropriate questions.

It is also important to check what is being said by asking questions and by offering summaries for comment. In some situations it is wise to go beyond the factual information and try to find out how the other person feels about what is being said. This is likely to throw some light on the accuracy of the information being given because people tend to misinterpret situations when they feel strongly. Discussion of how people feel often provides clues to what action may be acceptable.

Problem-solving interviews   Many of the discussions with individuals are concerned with solving problems. The starting point for such discussion is to get information about the problem. It is particularly important to find out how people feel about a problem, since this affects the solutions which might be possible.

It is essential to be sure that the real problem has surfaced before going on to discuss what might be done. People often raise a comparatively simple problem as a way into discussing a much deeper and more difficult problem about which they have strong emotional views.

People trying to help others with problems often fall into the trap of assuming that what worked for them in a similar situation will work for someone else. It may, but it is unwise to make this kind of suggestion at too early a stage before the problem has been fully explored. It is usually better to try to lead the other person to his or her own solution.

An adviser or inspector needs to preserve some professional detachment in trying to help people with problems. Problems are often emotionally charged and the adviser needs to be seen as sympathetic, yet calm and able to see the problem in perspective. It may also be necessary to speak frankly but supportively from time to time.

Once the facts about a problem have been established, solutions can be generated. It is a good idea to try to think of as many solutions as possible and then to go through them, looking at the implications of each. It is particularly important to think how others will feel about particular solutions.

Some problems seem to defy solution or are not soluble by schools and advisers. If, for example, a problem of accommodation cannot be solved, then the only way forward is to use the space available as well as possible.

It is important to view problems positively. Teachers in schools for children with severe learning difficulties often succeed in teaching their children to undertake a task which on the face of it seem impossible by breaking it down into very small steps. Most problems will yield to this process but some do not warrant this kind of expenditure of time. Sometimes the best solution that can be offered is to live with a problem.

Criticising someone's work   An adviser or inspector is sometimes in a position of needing to be critical about someone's work. The most satisfactory way of dealing with this is to make the person involved feel that he or she must do everything possible to improve because of the trust shown. The strategy is to criticise in such a way that the other person feels committed to improvement.

Criticism should be given in private if at all possible. Sometimes a head or a senior member of staff will be prepared to given up his or her room for this purpose for a period. Time is also important. A person may need time to come to terms with what is being said and will find this difficult if he or she has to dash back to a class after a short conversation during a break. If the teacher can be released from the class for a short time this is helpful; otherwise it is best to use lunch time or after school, when there is less pressure.

The first task is to try to get the other person to recognise that there is a problem. This may be done by asking him or her to comment on a lesson seen or on problems encountered in teaching. This may bring out all the points necessary and the adviser or inspector can then summarise the problem and go on to discuss what might be done about it. In some situations, however, the person concerned is not prepared to recognise that there is a problem. In this situation it may be necessary to spell out the problem and try to get the the person to accept it. If this proves to be difficult, it may be best to go on to discuss a course of action. This should be well within the person's capacity. For example, a teacher whose organisation is leading to a disorganised class might be asked to provide notes of the way in which the work might be organised for at least a proportion of lessons and to discuss them with a senior colleague each week. A teacher with control problems might be introduced to the thinking in Wheldall and Merritt's *Positive teaching* (1984), which makes concrete suggestions about class-room control which a teacher can actually carry out.

Throughout the discussion the adviser or inspector needs to demonstrate that he or she is genuinely concerned and anxious to help. Problems should be treated positively, stressing that a solution is possible and short steps to improvement should be sought.

When the problem is serious it is wise to follow up this kind of interview with a letter stating the nature of the problem as the adviser sees it and the steps which must be taken to achieve an improvement. A date should be set for a further visit by which improvement should be expected. A letter of this kind may become evidence at a tribunal, so it is important to check that it is as accurate as possible, that any critical statements made are supported by evidence and that it includes suggestions for improvement.

Cases of this kind may lead to informal and formal warnings and eventually to dismissal. It is therefore very important that detailed notes are kept of every step taken. Both the advisory/inspectorate service and the school will be expected to show that they have done everything possible to support a failing teacher if the case comes to a tribunal. The adviser or inspector should not only offer help him or herself, but ensure that the school sets up a support and monitoring programme and records what happens. It is also wise in a serious case to involve advisory colleagues so that more than one person has observed the teacher in question and judgement does not rest on one adviser's opinion and that of the school. The help of a specialist colleague may also be needed in helping a specialist teacher. It is sometimes useful for a more senior member of the service to take on the critical reviewing of the teacher's progress, leaving the general or specialist adviser to support the teacher.

Initial discussions in this situation will be with the teacher alone. As the case becomes more serious, such discussions need to involve the head, both as a witness and also because he or she is the person who should deliver informal and formal warnings if and when these become necessary.

Where the head is the person who is failing, much the same pattern applies. The problem needs to be spelled out, either by the head him or herself or by the adviser. Steps to be taken must then be agreed and a check made later to see whether they have resulted in any improvement. Every advisory/inspectorate service needs a policy for dealing with failing heads and teachers so that each case is dealt with in a similar manner and so that advisers/inspectors are fully covered if a case comes to a tribunal.

Dealing with complaints Advisers and inspectors often find themselves asked to deal with a complaint from a parent. Many of the parental complaints which have come to LEAs in the past may now be dealt with by governors, but it seems likely that there will still be occasions when an adviser is asked to look into a problem arising from a parental enquiry. There may also be expressions of concern from governors which need investigation.

Heads may, not unreasonably, be disturbed to learn of a complaint which has gone directly to the authority or to the governors. Inexperienced heads, in particular, may find this situation upsetting and the adviser/inspector may need to be very supportive in investigating the complaint and helping the school to deal with it.

The first task, in dealing with any complaint, is to talk to the head about it and find out what he or she knows which is relevant. It may come from a parent who complains a great deal and is a thorn in the side of the school, or it may come from someone who has never complained before. The parent who complains a great deal may not be satisfied with the answer he or she is given and may go on to complain to a local councillor, an MP or the DES and this makes it particularly important that any investigation is thorough and that the answers given are based on firm evidence.

The next task is to look into the substance of the complaint. This may be a matter of looking at the performance of a teacher or questioning people about an incident which has given rise to parental concern or one of many other possibilities.

Once all the evidence is collected the adviser or inspector needs to discuss with the head and anyone else concerned whether anything should be done as a result of the complaint. This may be a matter of putting right something which is not satisfactory or it may be a matter of the head seeing the parent to explain what has happened. The evidence may also show that there is no substance to the complaint and that nothing needs to be done except to explain this to the parent.

The adviser/inspector will need to report his or her findings to the administrator who is dealing with the problem or to the governors and this should normally be done in writing, so that there is a record of what has been done, written in such a way that, if a complaint is taken further, the report holds water.

Negotiation

Advisers, inspectors and advisory teachers are constantly negotiating and require a good deal of skill in undertaking negotiation. Negotiating involves an adviser in attempting to understand the frame of reference from which the other person is working and looking at where it matches his or her own. This gives a basis for arguments towards any particular end.

Fisher and Ury (1983) describe negotiation as *getting what you want from others*. They suggest that what is required is what they call *principled negotiation*. This involves looking for mutual gains and then making decisions about areas of conflict by agreed standards. For example, a governing body is concerned and doubtful about the methods by which reading is being taught. The head and staff feel passionately that their way of working is right for their children. It may be possible in this situation to get both groups to agree that, if the results of reading tests show that the majority of children are reading at the appropriate level for their ability, then the staff are probably right in their view. If, on the other hand, such tests show that there is an agreed proportion of children reading at a level below their ability, then the staff should think again. Fisher and Ury argue that taking positions should be avoided and that discussion should be concentrated first on the areas of agreement and then on the criteria by which decisions about the areas of conflict should be decided. They suggest that the more one knows about the views and feelings of the other party the more chance there is of resolving the conflict in a way which is satisfactory to everyone.

The following kinds of negotiation are likely to be part of every adviser's work:

Negotiation of role

Although advisers, inspectors and advisory teachers are generally accepted by teachers in the various roles which they are required to fulfil, each has to negotiate his or her own acceptance by teachers by showing a sympathetic approach and demonstrating that he or she has something to give. The changes following the Education Reform Act may mean that some advisers will be expected to undertake a different role, that of inspector rather than adviser, and this will need tactful handling with teachers. It is more likely to be accepted if teachers feel that they are getting good advice and help as a result of inspection. It will be very important for advisers changing their role to talk in a supportive way to teachers whose work they have observed, praising what is good and treating less good areas as possible growth points. Teachers will hope for ideas and suggestions they can use as a result of this exercise and the more inspection can lead to development in thinking about teaching and learning the more successful it is likely to be in raising the level of classroom work and and in becoming acceptable to teachers.

Negotiating philosophy

Advisers and inspectors are now in a position where they will be trying to persuade, not only heads and administrators but also school governors that one philosophy is likely to lead to better results than another. There will be many situations where advisers are involved in decisions with governors where the frames of reference of individual members of the group will differ considerably. This is one of the situations where it will be particularly important to look at where frames of reference come together and provide a common basis for discussion. It is also one of the areas in which the idea of principled negotiation most clearly applies.

Negotiating resources

There are several situations in which advisers, inspectors and advisory teachers are negotiating resources. While there will be few of the opportunities which have obtained in the past for advisers to make money available to schools, some advisers and advisory teachers will still be engaged in initiatives which qualify for government grants and may need to negotiate the spending with administrators and teachers. Generally speaking it is wise to involve a team or group in working out how such money should be spent.

This again is a situation where the idea of principled negotiation comes into its own. The best way out of a dilemma about how much should be spent in a particular area is to devise the criteria for making a decision about it. This might involve agreeing that the decision should be made on providing so much per school or per teacher. Or it might be a matter of agreeing that the decision should rest on a survey of comparable spending of a group of neighbouring authorities, taking the average amount spent.

Negotiating work

Advisers, inspectors and advisory teachers negotiate their work with senior members of their team and also with heads and teachers. The new situation in which the work of the advisory team is more closely managed means that they do not have the same choice of ways of working as they had formerly. Nevertheless, there will be scope for discussion about particular tasks and how best to do them.

Although advisers, as representatives of the LEA, have certain rights in schools, such as the right to observe teaching, an adviser and in particular an advisory teacher may want to work in a particular way, and this needs to be negotiated with the head and teachers. This will be particularly important for advisory teachers wishing to work with teachers in the classroom. They will need to negotiate their own role and work out with the teacher the role that he or she will be playing in this situation.

Giving a talk

Advisers and inspectors will probably find themselves giving talks less frequently than in the past since their involvement with in-service work has been reduced by the need to monitor what is happening in schools. However, they will still be asked to talk from time to time and it is important that these occasions are used well.

The nature of this task varies according to the size and composition of the audience, the subject matter and the venue, the context and the state of the audience. Subject matter and presentation need to be matched to these variables. A talk given to a small audience differs from one given to a large audience. A talk given to professionals will differ from one given to a lay audience. An audience listening at the end of a busy working day will be less receptive than first thing in the morning.

In preparing a new talk, thinking round the subject can be helped by using a sheet of paper with the topic in the middle and then jotting ideas about the page as they occur, linking them with lines and arrows, rather as primary teachers plan topic work with children. This can then be translated into a linear plan, which puts the points in order.

It is usually wiser to aim to make a few points clearly and give several illustrations than to attempt too much. It is particularly important to prepare the beginning and the end of a talk well. At the beginning of a talk the speaker needs to capture the attention of the audience and make them feel that he or she is with them. A story or an anecdote which brings this out is often useful. It is also helpful near the beginning of a talk to outline what it is intended to cover. A good ending sends people away with something to think about. A planned ending also enables a speaker to skip to it if he or she is running out of time, although a good speaker should be able to time a talk well so that everything is covered in the time agreed.

Advisers and advisory teachers often find themselves giving similar talks on different occasions. It is therefore worth preparing notes on cards or overhead projector transparencies in such a way that they can be combined with other cards or transparencies on other occasions. This means using one card or transparency for each particular aspect of a topic.

Once the outline of the talk has been prepared, visual aids and handouts can be considered. These should add to what is said and should be of high quality, since they are setting a standard for teachers and others. Desk-top publishing programs are now widely available and these provide excellent opportunities for making good transparencies. These should be made with at least 18 point type if they are to be seen from a distance. Handouts are also enhanced by the use of desk-top facilities.

A speaker arriving to give a talk needs to check that all the facilities he or she needs are available. Visual aids should be checked and the focus adjusted if necessary. It is a good idea to check sight lines and any need to draw curtains or blinds. In a large hall, a check on acoustics is wise. A speaker should also check that drinking water is available.

At the start of a talk it is wise to look at the audience, scanning them, making eye contact with some and looking for behavioural clues as to their reactions. It is helpful in maintaining the attention of the audience to vary the voice, both in pitch and in pace, and to use pauses effectively.

Most talks end with opportunities for questions. These can often be tricky. There are occasions when members of the audience work to catch a speaker out. A wise speaker is generally prepared to admit ignorance and ask the questioner for information. There is also the person who is looking for the support of authority for a pet idea, such as the parent who wants the speaker to say something which supports him or her against the school. Speakers have to be on the lookout for this and answer such questions tactfully, perhaps trying to give both sides of a question.

Leading groups

Advisers, inspectors and advisory teachers may find themselves leading groups from time to time. Some of these may be formal groups with an agenda and minutes, but many will be informal discussion groups looking at some particular aspect of education and perhaps trying to produce ideas or materials or the solution to a problem. There are a number of skills involved. Some vary with the kind of group, but many are common.

Preparation

All meetings require some preparation, whether they are formal or informal. It may be necessary to give some preliminary thought to problems which could arise from the size and composition of the group. Very large groups usually require more direction from the chair than small groups, and groups which contain both very senior and very junior people need careful handling if the more junior people are to play a full part. It is a good idea to start by considering the object of the meeting and what needs to be put in writing in advance. Is there a need for an agenda or a discussion outline? Should there be a list of members' names? Are background papers needed?

Possible starting points and ways of presenting items should then be considered and possible directions of discussion, noting points and questions which need to be covered, particularly where there may be problems. It is important to consider what should be achieved by the end of the meeting and to have a plan for drawing the meeting to a close. It is also useful to make a time plan for discussion, particularly if there is an agenda. It may not always be possible to keep to this, but it is a useful way of becoming aware when the group is spending too long on one item.

Seating is something to watch in group discussion. People need to be comfortable if they are to concentrate on the discussion. They also need to see each other. Seats in a circle are better than seats in a straight line, since people tend not to talk to people they cannot see properly.

Preliminary thought should be given to the matter of note-taking. Someone needs to take notes in most meetings. The chairperson may wish to take notes him or herself, although most people find that this makes it difficult to concentrate on the discussion. It is better to ask someone before the meeting to do this than rely on volunteers at the meeting itself, since it gives the note-taker a chance to think about the task.

The working session

The first task in leading a discussion group is to put people at ease. If the group is one where people do not know each other, some time needs to be spent on introductions, each person giving some information about him or herself. The next step is to outline the purpose of the discussion and what should be achieved by the end of it. It is then a good idea to invite everyone to make a short contribution about some aspect to which all can contribute. For example, the leader may ask each person to describe how he or she deals with the particular issues under discussion. This helps those who are shy about talking in public and gives the leader a chance to demonstrate that he or she will receive contributions in a positive way, perhaps simply smiling and nodding, or making some comment about the value of what has been said in forwarding the discussion.

During the discussion, the leader's tasks are as follows:

Setting and maintaining the rules of discussion   When the meeting is a formal one, the rules are normally assumed, and the leader's task is to see that they are followed. In an informal discussion the leader has to establish such matters as how far the discussion should be allowed to stray from the task in hand, whether recounting of anecdotes is acceptable, whether discussion between two or three individuals in the group can be allowed to continue and so on. An informal group may diverge from the matter in hand more than a formal one, but still needs to be kept on task.

Rewarding of contributions   The leader sets up a relationship with each member of the group by the way he or she reacts to the contributions people make. A good group leader rewards contributions by acknowledging them, praising them, asking questions and extending what people say, perhaps weaving it into the overall thinking of the group. The leader's reaction to contributions does much to determine the readiness with which others speak and the degree of frankness they show. The leader also needs to guard against talking too much, although an adviser or advisory teacher may be in something of a teaching role in leading a group and in this circumstance may legitimately say more than someone whose only task is leadership of the discussion.

Scanning the group   A leader needs to be constantly scanning the group, looking at how people are reacting and noting those who wish to speak. Usually people make the leader aware of this by trying to catch his or her eye or by leaning forward. A person trying to break into discussion will draw breath ready to speak and this is noticeable. The leader may need to make an opportunity for people who are trying to get into the discussion but are finding it difficult.

Analysing and classifying   As the discussion proceeds the leader needs to be looking for patterns in what is being said, so that the discussion can be kept moving.

Summarising and moving on   The leader needs not only to be aware of the direction of the discussion but to make others aware of it too. This means summarising from time to time and then moving the discussion in a further direction. There is considerable skill in knowing the moment to do this. If the group is not ready to move, people will go back to the previous topic regardless of what the leader says and continue until they feel ready to move. Where there is a formal agenda the leader will need to sum up the findings of each item. This makes things a good deal easier for the note-taker.

The discussion should end with a full summary and a statement of any action plans. Time needs to be allowed for this.

Problems in discussion

There are a number of problems which may occur in any discussion:

The silent member   The group leader needs to be on the lookout for people who are not contributing. There may be all sorts of reasons for this and, where a group meets regularly, it may be a good idea to seek out anyone who does not contribute and discuss this. In general, however, a silent member may be drawn in most happily by asking for a specific contribution on a topic on which the leader is sure the person can contribute.

The over-talkative member A group may have someone who has so much to say that other people do not get a fair share of the discussion. This requires tactful handling. Sometimes the talkative member can be pre-empted by asking a particular person to contribute. On other occasions he or she may need to be interrupted with some comment like 'May I stop you there so that we can see what other people think about that point?'

One useful way of coping with this problem is to run a group on discussion leadership with someone as observer noting the extent to which different people contribute. This can often provide the opportunity to give factual information about someone who habitually talks too much. A statement like 'Don made 72 contributions. No one else made more than 30' may bring home to Don in a way which is non-threatening the fact that he talks too much.

Conflict or emotional tension Sometimes people in a group get into a conflict or at least create emotional tension. In this situation the leader has to choose whether to talk the conflict through or change the direction of the discussion if the group will allow it. It is often a good idea to postpone the resolution of a conflict until later in the meeting, when people have calmed down and can see the problem in better perspective.

Interruptions and late arrivals Sometimes people arrive late. When this happens the leader should choose a suitable moment to welcome them and bring them up to date on the discussion so far. If there are interruptions, it may be helpful to summarise before moving on.

Attempts to avoid the group task Sometimes a group will demonstrate that it does not want to work at the task in hand. People do not say this directly, but introduce red herrings, spend time blaming other people, act negatively or helplessly and refuse to think constructively. The leader has to work through this stage, looking for the right moment to get people working. It is difficult to cut short the expression of frustrations. If the leader suspects that task avoidance is likely to happen it may be possible to pre-empt the situation by asking everyone to write down something positive about the topic and to use that as a starting point.

Continued pairing Sometimes two people will start a discussion between themselves, leaving out the rest of the group. This may be dealt with in a similar way to the over-talkative member, by a tactful interruption and invitation to others to contribute.

Leadership roles in different groups

All that has been said so far has a general application to many different kinds of groups. Different groups require rather different leadership, however, and a leader needs to know the style that comes most naturally to him or her and to be able to match it to the work in hand.

If the group is an exploratory one in which the primary aim is the learning of the participants, the leader's skill in making relationships is of considerable importance. He or she needs to be encouraging, to extend people's thinking and draw contributions together and build on from them. People will also need time to work through their own thinking. Where the group has a specific task, the leadership may need to be firmer, with people being kept to the point and being brought back to the task if they stray from it.

Problem-solving groups are somewhere between these two. They require firm leadership but also need people to think widely and contribute as much as possible. This may mean letting people wander from the point occasionally. The leader's skill in drawing together the points of agreement and finding a way forward is crucial.

Dealing with relationship problems

Advisers and inspectors sometimes find themselves trying to help a school to reconcile differences between people. Head and deputy may be at odds with each other or a teacher may not get on with his or her head of department or with the head. When this begins to affect the working of the school an attempt needs to be made to resolve some of the differences.

There are three main kinds of conflicts between people. Some conflicts are over territory, where the boundaries of one person's job overlap those of another. Others are over ideology where one person does not agree with another's handling of a situation because it does not conform to his or her frame of reference. A third category of conflict arises when people just do not like each other to the point where they find it difficult to maintain a professional relationship.

Each of these forms of conflict requires rather different treatment. Conflicts over territory can best be resolved by defining the boundaries between different people's work. Conflicts between head and deputy are often of this kind. The deputy's role is not clearly defined and head and deputy both have different ideas of what the deputy should be doing. This sort of problem often arises when a new head takes over from someone who has run the school rather autocratically, leaving comparatively little for the deputy to do. The new head may then expect the deputy to be doing far more than he or she did previously, but not appreciate the change this involves for the person in office, particularly if he or she has been a long time in the post.

In this situation the adviser or inspector may be able to help both parties to define and agree the deputy's role. The deputy may then need help in undertaking the kind of role expected, which the head should be encouraged to offer. The deputy may also find it helpful to attend a course of training for deputies and perhaps to visit other schools and talk to other deputies who have a similar role to the one suggested.

This kind of situation also arises with postholders in the primary school. People are given responsibility for a particular area of curriculum, but not always given the delegated authority to carry out the necessary tasks. The problem can often be resolved by clarifying the job description and persuading the head to make sure that the whole staff know that authority has been delegated to an individual to carry out particular tasks.

In secondary school conflicts may arise because the organisation is large and it is easy to miss the fact that some boundaries are ill-defined, especially where posts have been held by people who have got on well together. A change of staff may throw up a problem where two people disagree about within whose role a particular task may fall or who has the right to particular facilities. This again can best be resolved by discussion with the people concerned and agreement about the issue causing concern. The points made earlier about negotiation are relevant here.

A variation of conflict over ideology is the conflict which can arise over procedures. Some people find it extremely difficult to keep to rules, even when they have been involved in creating them or have agreed that they should operate them. When a teacher behaves like this, it is likely to lead to conflict between that teacher and the head and, to some extent, to conflict between that teacher and colleagues who resent the difficulties which the person causes by not following agreed procedures. This problem is one which a head must tackle directly, but with some sympathy, appreciating that some people find rule-keeping difficult. Dealing with the problem may mean making checks at frequent intervals to keep the teacher concerned in line. The adviser's role here may be to support and reinforce the headteacher's ruling.

Conflict over ideology is more difficult. People often do not realise at first that they are working with different frames of reference and act on the assumption that the other person has a philosophy similar to their own. Differences over what is important gradually emerge and begin to sour the relationship. Here the task of the adviser or inspector may be first to try to make clear to both parties that they have different values and then to look for the places where their values come together. If people are willing to accept that there can be points of view other than their own, the situation can be a developmental one for everyone concerned.

Where conflict over ideology leads to disagreement about how something should be done, it may be possible to reach a compromise decision or to try out both ways of working if the situation lends itself to this.

The most difficult conflict of all is when people simply dislike each other for no apparent reason. Everything they do then appears to conflict and their problem intrudes into anything planned. There would seem to be two possible ways of dealing with this. The first is to keep them apart as far as possible. The second is to insist on professional attitudes and behaviour, which means that people who dislike each other should try to overcome or ignore this fact when the working situation demands it.

Assertiveness

People in most jobs will, from time to time, meet situations which make them angry or frustrated or in which it is likely that other people will be made angry or frustrated. A teacher may feel that the head is asking something unreasonable. A headteacher may have to deal with an angry parent who is attacking the school unreasonably or take a decision which is known to be unpopular with the staff. In these situations it is easy to become defensive or aggressive and this usually makes the situation more difficult to handle. Ideally such situations should be handled assertively so that everyone concerned finds the outcome acceptable.

Back and Back (1982) describe *assertion* as behaviour that involves:

Standing up for your own rights in such a way that you do not violate another person's rights

Expressing your needs, wants, opinions, feelings and beliefs in direct, honest and appropriate ways

They stress that being assertive does not mean ignoring the rights of others, but encouraging them to state their views as well as stating one's own and then seeking a solution which meets the needs of both.

For example, an adviser might be asked to visit a particular school which urgently needs help on a day when he or she already has an important programme. In such a situation being assertive involves stating clearly that what is asked is not really possible, perhaps adding that it would be possible to go the following day.

A more tricky situation might be one where a teacher is failing but does not accept that this is the case. Being assertive in this situation might involve the adviser or inspector in stating clearly how he or she sees the situation and suggesting that, even if the teacher disagrees, an action plan which improves the work would be a good idea.

Another situation sometimes encountered is where a headteacher makes it clear that he or she does not welcome advisers and does not feel a need for anything they may have to offer. In this situation being assertive might involve raising this problem with the headteacher, expressing concern about the lack of welcome offered and explaining that this makes it difficult to offer anything useful.

Consultancy

Gray (1988) describes consultancy as follows:

Consultancy is a helping relationship provided by people who have a particular range of skills for helping managers and others in organisations to understand more clearly what their business is about and how it might become more effective.

Margerison (1978) enlarges on this view:

Our job is to facilitate improved relations between people in the work which brings them together. In this, our job is to get alongside those engaged in operations activity and provide them with information, support, ideas, training or whatever is concerned with the organisation of work.

Lavelle (1984) describes the consultant role as follows:

a facilitator, helper or objective observer; as a specialist in diagnosing needs and the means of meeting these needs. The consultant concentrates on the *how* of problem-solving in contrast to the conveyor who tells *what the solution should be*.

Schmuck (1973) suggests that there are three roles a consultant may perform. These are:

- consultative assistance – providing technical assistance to an organisation in respect of a specific problem
- content consultation – attempting to bring about changes in the attitudes, understanding or skills of members of an organisation in terms of some specific concern rather than in terms of the development of the whole organisation
- process consultation – leading to significant organisation change by focusing on organisational features such as communication, decision-making, stress on members of the organisation

Havelock (1975) provides five characteristics which distinguish consultancy from teaching (and from most advisory work):

- the client initiates the consultancy
- the consultant–client relationship is temporary and specific to the immediate problem in hand
- the consultant and client come from different professional disciplines
- the consultant is advisory only
- the consultant has no administrative relationship with the client (i.e.he is not a superordinate or able to assess the client)

The devolution of budgets to schools has resulted in some authorities handing over the advisory function to be purchased by schools as they feel a need for it. While much advisory work differs at present from consultancy in being a briefer matter and requiring a concern with LEA policy, an advisory service which is purchased by schools may become something rather different in which its members are one of a range of people acting as consultants.

Consultancy as defined by Gray (1988) also differs from advice in being much more a matter of helping organisations to find their own way forward with assistance from the consultant. The consultant needs to be more neutral than the adviser who normally and quite properly has a picture of where he or she feels that schools and colleges ought to be going. The consultant, on the other hand, is much more concerned with where the school or college itself wants to go. Sayer says of this process:

> By being drawn into consultation we may well enable others to clarify their own needs and intentions, but if we take over the thinking and clarifying for them, we have become arbiters and have dispossessed them of decision-making responsibility.

Margerison (1978), on the other hand, sees the process as something much nearer to the normal role of the adviser. He makes the following points:

> Clients usually come to the personnel and organisation adviser because they wish to relieve pressure. They are looking for a way out of the complex web in which they feel locked. The main job of the adviser in such situations is to help the manager to discover his way out of the maze. In this sense the adviser plays more of a counselling, catalytic and process-oriented approach.

The business of working through the thinking of the school is a long one and a school may not be able to afford a consultant for very much of this. In this case the best use of the consultant is to train internal consultants so that the process can take place over time.

Consultancy may be a more detached process than advisory work as we have known it. The adviser with a pastoral role normally identifies with the schools for which he or she is responsible and knows a great deal about them. The consultant, on the other hand, comes in cold and develops his or her own overview, staying outside the school or college.

Advisers are likely to function more as technical than as process consultants, since they have particular technical knowledge of aspects of the curriculum which schools and colleges will wish to use. They may also be asked to act as process consultants. The task here is one of helping others to think through problems, probably discovering in the process that problems are seldom what they seem on the surface and need resolution at a deeper level than is at first apparent.

A school or college employing a consultant on a paying basis will need to provide a contract for the work to be done. This should include:

1 The consultant's area of activity.
2 The time the consultancy will run for.
3 The fee and costs agreed.
4 The work expected for the fee.
5 What the process of reporting will be.

This means that the team which works in this way needs to cost its time carefully, not forgetting the overheads such as accommodation and secretarial support.

Gray (1988) gives some details of the kinds of background knowledge and skill required by a consultant. Educational consultants:

> should understand the ethos of the various educational systems and should work from a coherent and academically respectable base and through a valid intellectual perspective; they should understand how individuals actually behave in the educational system; they should have appropriate interpersonal counselling skills; they should be expert in any technical areas in which they are working.

Conclusion

The skills described in this section apply to all members of the advisory and inspection services, including advisory teachers. Many of them are skills which will have been learned and exercised in previous posts because interpersonal skills are essential in all posts which involve people. There is, however, a strong case for ensuring that advisers, inspectors and advisory teachers entering the service have training in these skills. Without them they cannot be effective.

Chapter 5

Inspecting and monitoring

The Education Reform Act has changed the role of local authorities and inspection services as well as that of schools and their governors. The Act and other pronouncements from the Secretary of State and DES suggest that the LEA needs to keep the work of its schools under continuous review, including a review of the management. This must be largely a task for the inspection service, who already maintain an overview of educational establishments, although there will be aspects in which other officers may need to be involved. In some LEAs teams for inspection are now made up of officers and inspectors, with officers looking at such issues as finance and some management issues and inspectors looking at curriculum issues and other aspects of management. The difference from past practice is partly that this overview will need to be more systematic so that it covers all establishments over a period.

LEAs have had the right to inspect schools since the 1944 Act which stated:

Any local authority may cause an inspection to be made of any educational establishment maintained by the authority and such inspection shall be made by officers appointed by the local education authority.

(Section 77(3))

This is confirmed in various ways with the Education Reform Act and DES circulars. The Act states that:

It shall be the duty . . . of every local education authority as respects every school maintained by them . . . to exercise their functions . . . with a view to securing that the curriculum for the school satisfies the requirements [of the Act].

(Section 1(b))

DES Circular 7/88 emphasises that 'the LEA's monitoring role will be particularly important in ensuring that the overall responsibility for the service is met' (DES, 1988a, para. 19).

The same circular states that:

In general, the Secretary of State expects that, in discharging their responsibilities under the schemes, LEAs will build on existing arrangements for monitoring the efficiency and effectiveness of their schools, and accord an increased monitoring role to their officers and inspectors/advisers and provide advisory and associated support to schools that give cause for concern.

(para. 151)

Elsewhere it requires that 'inspectors/advisers will report on the performance and achievement of schools both to governing bodies and to LEAs'. (para 20).

The Audit Commission (1989b) lists a number of the benefits of inspection and the percentage of respondents mentioning them in the questionnaires used in the study by Stillman and Grant (1989).

Inspectors get to know and understand individual schools	26.5
Provides full objective information and reference points for the LEA (CEO, members, governors, parents)	23.6
Promotes inspector collaboration, encourages team ethos	19.2
Identifies teachers' strengths/weaknesses/INSET needs	18.4
Assists management and organisation of school/department	16.5
Identifies good practice in schools	15.4
Promotes curriculum development	13.5
Helps schools to identify needs and determine their goals	12.6
Improves school standards and is generally beneficial	10

Before considering what is involved in inspection it is perhaps necessary to consider what inspection is and to look at some definitions of monitoring and evaluation. Rhodes (1981) classified inspectorates into those concerned with enforcement and those concerned with efficiency. Enforcement inspectorates are concerned with the application of the law and this would include such inspectorates as those of mines, health and safety and industrial inspectorates. There is now an element of this in the work of LEA inspectorates, but they themselves do not have the power to enforce the law, although their evidence may play an important part in law enforcement upon occasion. They are concerned with efficiency in education.

Wilcox (1989) identifies some of the main general elements in educational inspection as follows:

- the involvement of experienced professionals with some independence from the institution or programme being inspected;
- the observation of various aspects through formal or informal visits involving one or more inspectors;
- the preparation of a report on a formal visit for the institution or programme and those responsible for it;

- the expectation that inspectors have intimate knowledge and continuing experience of what is inspected;
- the inspectoral function of not only pronouncing judgement but also encouraging and developing the institution or programme.

Nebusnuick (1989) quotes papers from Cheshire and Buckinghamshire which define a number of the words connected with inspection, as follows
Monitoring:

The regular checking against a set of criteria and performance indicators of aspects of the processes of education. Monitoring is carried out through observation and analysis of each establishment's own documentation and processes. The County criteria will form the framework within which performance indicators will be developed by schools in partnership with the County.

(Buckinghamshire)

The systematic consideration of data gathering according to norms.

(Cheshire)

Evaluating:

The process of conceiving, obtaining, analysing and communicating information and forming judgements for the guidance of educational decision-making with regard to specified aspects of education.

(Buckinghamshire)

a description of any activity by the institution or the LEA where the quality of provision is the subject of systematic study. Its function is to secure or improve the functioning of an institution in order to produce a better quality of education and experience.

(Cheshire)

Stephens (1989) suggests that inspection may be to prove or improve quality and that if the purpose is mainly to improve quality then it is essential that there is full involvement of the establishment being inspected.

Inspection is not the only source of information about the performance of schools and other establishments. The Audit Commission (1989b) lists tests, student attendance patterns, student records of achievement, curriculum information, budgetary and other financial information, reports by vocational examining bodies on courses, further education efficiency indicators, national testing and assessment following ERA. This kind of information should be collected by the LEA and recorded on computer so that it is available for inspectors and others as part of the information which is known about schools. Inspectors should be able to draw on this kind of information before undertaking inspection.

It must be stressed that the whole purpose of inspection is the improvement of the establishment concerned and this needs to be kept in mind whatever is planned. However, as the list given above suggests there are also advantages for the members of the inspector team, who benefit from working together and sharing each other's view of what is seen. This is particularly helpful to inspectors new in post.

Inspection is an extremely delicate task and all inspectors need to develop the skill of making critical comments in a supportive way. The credibility of the inspection service depends upon the ability to be honest but supportive. The relationship which an inspector forms with teachers in the course of an inspection does much to determine whether they gain from the experience or not.

Inspectors going into any establishment need to be sensitive to its needs and to what is happening at that particular time. They should know enough about its history to be able to recognise its progress or lack of progress as well as the stage it has now reached. In this, LEA inspectors differ from HMIs, who can only take a snapshot of what is there at the point in time when they visit. This may prove difficult under the suggestions now being made.

The ability to listen in an open-minded way is important as is the ability to observe, taking into account the objectives of the teachers concerned as well the inspector's own views of what the school should be doing. An inspector should be aware of how inspectors are perceived in the particular establishment and the effect this may have on the acceptability of any advice offered.

Advice needs to be positive, looking for what is good and attempting to help teachers develop from this. At the same time it needs to be honest, with doubts clearly stated in the positive context of looking for what might be done to create improvement. Teachers should be treated as professional peers who have important experience to offer. Inspectors generally need to be aware of the effect of people's prejudices over matters such as gender, race and subject status.

Perhaps the most important thing an inspector can do, whether as part of an inspection or at some other time, is to communicate to teachers something of his or her vision of education so that they are stimulated and excited by the subject under discussion and thus find the energy to travel further.

The suggestions given in this chapter and the skills required apply to inspections whatever the nature of the team undertaking them and whatever the conditions under which they are undertaken.

Performance indicators

Many authorities are either defining performance indicators or asking schools and colleges to define their own. Performance indicators might be defined as 'evidence of something done'. Performance simply refers to actions completed. Judgement is then required to assess the quality of the action. The Audit Commission (1989b) also stresses the importance, not only of having performance criteria, but of telling staff what these are in advance. A performance criterion should be a statement which can actually be checked or measured or seen to be achieved. Some performance criteria for communication among staff, for example, might be as follows:

1 There are regular staff meetings for information and discussion.
2 There are well-kept notice boards which give good information to staff.
3 There is a good system for seeing that all staff are informed about children with particular problems.

These will not give information about the quality of communication, which will become evident only from discussion with those concerned.

Some LEAs are going further and defining not only the performance criteria, but also standards within them, so that there can be comparable grading for each item. HMIs adopt a not dissimilar practice in assessing areas of work as satisfactory, more than satisfactory or less than satisfactory. This has advantages for making comparisons but demands very careful judgement. There would seem to be some advantages in doing it for a limited range of topics but an attempt to use grading widely would be very time-consuming and might lead to other, less tangible, aspects of work being missed.

The Society of Chief Inspectors and Advisers (SCIA 1990) makes the following statements:

> What we really want to evaluate is not the inert data that describes the performance of a system, but the living aspirations, endeavours and achievements that characterize the work of schools, colleges and their students.
> From the LEA's perspective, the evaluation of schools and colleges needs to draw on a wide range of evidence or 'indicators' of achievement. The system for determining such indicators should be dynamic and flexible and should relate to the institution's and the LEA's objectives. Indicators may be expressed in terms of quality and quantity and should be openly declared and negotiated with the institutions.

The Society of Chief Inspectors and Advisers (1990) also suggests some useful ways of looking at performance indicators. It identifies a number of dimensions of performance indicators. The most important of these are location and power. Location differentiates the proximity of the indicator to the core target being assessed. Within the dimension of location it identifies direct indicators, which immediately reflect the target behaviour, indirect indicators, which occur close to or in support of the activity, and contextual indicators, which are more distant from the activity. Within the dimension of power it identifies high inference, which are indicators having a high correlation with the target behaviour, medium inference and low inference. These

LOCATION

		Direct indicators	Indirect indicators	Contextual indicators
POWER	High inference	Students' adjustment/ security	Curriculum time Priority for pastoral work	Staff INSET for pastoral work
	Medium inference	Student/student behavour (e.g. bullying)	Sanctions/reward systems	Parental support
	Low inference	Students' work levels	Form of pastoral system (house, year)	Post-school leaving; offending levels

Figure 1   A performance indicator grid

are represented diagrammatically in figure 1, which outlines performance indicators needed for assessing pastoral care in a secondary school.

Types of inspection

In their programmes for monitoring the progress of schools and other establishments many LEAs are employing a mixture of methods, using recorded visits and self-evaluation alongside inspection. The actual balance of these elements varies from authority to authority.

An advisory/inspectorate service planning to keep its schools under systematic review starts with a given number of schools and a given number of inspectors, not all of whom will be able to operate at every level. The first task is to decide how much time each inspector can give to this aspect of the work and calculate it as a total number of inspector days available. The number of days which will be needed for each inspection, however it is carried out, is then calculated. This calculation must include the time needed for report writing and presentation and for follow-up work with the school. These calculations then make it possible to work out how many schools can be inspected in the course of a year. If this number is too low the team will need either to devote more time to this work, or revise the time for each inspection. There is no agreed figure for the frequency of inspection of schools, but once every five years would seem to be a minimum figure to aim for. The pro-forma in figure 6 is intended to help inspectors to calculate the time that inspection is actually taking both for teachers and for inspectors.

There are eight possible ways of reviewing schools. The one chosen will depend upon the preferences of the LEA, both officers and members, the needs of the particular school, and the strength of the service and the amount of time which can be devoted to this activity. The cost of the different forms of inspection must also be taken into account, whether calculated in terms of the time used by inspectors and teachers or in actual cash terms.

Full inspection

A visit by a group of inspectors to inspect the whole school. A full inspection has the advantage of concentrating attention, both of the advisory team and of the school. It gets the inspection part of the process over quickly and from this point of view may interrupt the work of the school rather less than more extenuated forms of inspection. It is, however, the most threatening and probably the most demanding from the teachers' point of view and it is often the case that an inspection turns up so much to be done that the school can only select those issues which seem to the staff to be most urgent. This is particularly the case in a secondary school.

Specialist inspection

Specialist inspectors visit to look at work in their particular field. This has the advantage that the school can give attention and resources to a selected department or area of concern and can probably do a more thorough job of following up the inspection than is possible when everything is looked at. It is also less threatening to teachers. Over a period, it is possible for the whole school to be looked at, including a study by inspectors with appropriate experience of the management.

A specialist inspection requires much the same preparation and follow-up as a full inspection but each stage can be briefer.

Long-term inspection

A full inspection carried out over a period according to the availability of inspectors. This has the advantage of being easier to arrange, since members of the team can have choice about when they visit. It is also less disruptive in some ways. However, it is likely to make less impact because the time between the inspection and the report will be considerable and much that was noted at the time of the inspection will have changed by the time the report is made available to the governors. It requires the same stages and tasks as a full inspection and may be rather more expensive in time because inspectors will do a good deal of work individually.

Substantial visit or dipstick inspection

A brief but detailed look at some part of a school or a brief survey of different aspects. These are useful in that they cover more establishments in the same amount of time as would be used for full inspections. They are also less threatening to the teachers and provide a smaller and more easily assimilated amount of information. It is important, if this form of inspection is used regularly, to ensure that the ground covered in the long term is comprehensive.

Collaborative inspection

Inspection as a shared process between inspectors and the institution. There are various ways in which this can be done. The establishment can be part of the process throughout, joining in the planning, identifying the evidence and assessing it. A variation on this theme is for the advisory/inspectorate service to draw up its plans and then discuss them with the establishment, modifying them if necessary. The establishment may also select from a range of possible inspection possibilities those which it feels are most relevant and these can be added to those which the inspectorate feel to be relevant. The school can also add possible evidence.

This approach has a great deal to recommend it. In many ways it will be felt to be more professional and teachers are more likely to be committed to the exercise and to learn from it. However, there are three difficulties. The first is that of time. Preparing for an inspection is very time-consuming and it may be very difficult to find enough time for teachers and inspectors to work together. From that point of view consulting the school about possible plans is probably the more economical approach. Inspectors will in any case have some form of check list and it would seem uneconomical of time to rewrite this with teachers. Much more time in meetings will be needed both by teachers and inspectors. Teachers will also need to spend time on various kinds of reporting.

The second issue is that of convincing governors and the public of the validity of an inspection which has involved those being inspected. The difficulty of this will vary from one area to another and this will have to be taken into account in planning the programme.

The third issue is that of the school or college which is satisfied with an inadequate level of work. This tends to be the case in areas where the pupils are able and appear to reach good standards with little effort. In this context the pupils are often not being extended although they are apparently learning satisfactorily. Parents are often satisfied and staff see little wrong. An inspection from outside may bring home the need for more demanding work.

Monitored self-evaluation

A self-evaluation scheme is the basis of the inspection process. Many LEAs have schemes for self-evaluation for schools and are using these as the starting point for inspection. This is the most usual way of collaborating with teachers. The task of the inspectors is then to act as moderators checking on the validity of the self-evaluation.

On the face of it this looks as though it might combine happily the merits collaborative inspection with more formal inspection; and in a situation where the school really works at its self-evaluation and is properly self-critical there is much to recommend it. In practice, many institutions do a very limited job of self-evaluation, particularly when there are other more pressing demands upon them, and in this context the inspectorate needs not only to mount a complementary inspection, but to see that adequate self-evaluation actually takes place. Some of the LEAs that are using this system are making considerable use of performance indicators and are relying on these to overcome some of the problems

A paper by Turner (1987) describes a self-evaluation/inspection exercise in a secondary school. Although this was in many ways successful, there were problems. He lists some of them as follows:

1 For many teachers the self-appraisal failed to be a major event, either because they were not required to participate in any review activities or because they were unwilling to devote much time to it.
2 Some of the self-evaluation was merely descriptive. It seems that most staff were unwilling to produce anything more than a public type of document, providing little more than factual information.
3 It was apparent that staff needed much more guidance from advisers in implementing [their] recommendations. Identifying weaknesses is a far cry from facilitating their solution.

At least one LEA is asking its teachers to produce self-report schedules with lesson plans and lesson evaluation and also asking pupils to complete a schedule which reviews their experience. These would seem to be useful additions to other forms of self-evaluation.

Visit record

The normal visits of inspectors are used for assessment. Some LEAs are using these as a way of reviewing their establishments. Each inspector has a detailed list of checks to make and these reports are put together to make a total picture, which is set alongside work on performance indicators. This is really using monitoring for inspection purposes. The overall involvement of the inspector places him or her in a good position to make judgements about effectiveness. This approach tends to go with some full or dipstick inspections.

The advantages of this approach are that inspection and monitoring appear as one activity and this would seem to save time. In practice checking on all the detail normally looked at in the course of an inspection may take as much time as a full inspection. There is also the disadvantage that the establishment is not seen by a group of people and the judgements arrived at are those of one person, although this problem could be easily overcome by involving other people at various stages.

Review

This involves looking at particular aspects of work across a number of establishments. The word 'review' is somewhat differently used in different LEAs and this is only one definition among several. Whatever it is called, there is a case from time to time for looking at particular aspects of work across a sample of institutions. This may be a review of a curriculum or cross-curricular area or it may be an issue like equal opportunities or parental involvement. It can be difficult to fit this in, but planning should include reviews of this kind which will provide information needed by administrators and committees as well as inspectors.

Inspection policy

The inspection policy of an LEA needs to include statements of the following:

1 The aims of inspection.
2 The methods of inspection chosen.
3 The way institutions for inspection should be selected and the frequency of inspection.
4 The people to be involved in inspection.
5 The relationship to be established with the institution being inspected.
6 The aspects of the institution to be inspected and the evidence which might be sought.
7 The preparation required for inspection, including the information which should be available within the office or required from the institution.
8 The way inspection and monitoring should be carried out, including the way time should be spent.
9 The arrangements which should be made for verbal reporting immediately after an inspection.
10 The discussion which should take place following an inspection.
11 The writing of reports.
12 The presentation of reports to the institution and to the governors.

The full inspection programme

Once the pattern of inspection has been decided, the programme of establishments to be visited can be drawn up. A year's programme should contain a mixture of establishments, spread across the authority. Space should also be left in the programme for any institution which poses major problems in the course of the year and needs careful study as a prelude to help.

Work on performance indicators has tended to concentrate on what can be measured and counted. An inspectorate is concerned with exercising judgement about the evidence available whether it is quantifiable or not. An inspection team needs to ask 'What do we want to find out?' The first and most important answer to this question is 'the quality of pupils' learning'. All the other issues are subservient to this, which is the purpose for which schools exist. There are, however, a number of other areas to which this question can be applied and these generate further questions which can guide observation. They are as follows:

Ethos	Staff selection and deployment
Behaviour/relationships	Staff development
Environment	Forward planning
Resources	Continuity
Curriculum	Relationship with governors
Quality of teaching	Parental relationships
Organisation	Relationship with the community
Discipline	Multicultural education
Management	Equal opportunities
Administration	Special needs
Communication	Head's personal organisation
Evaluation and records	

The evidence available for making judgements about schools is finite but extensive, and an observer needs to select from what is available. Here again the most important evidence comes from observation of pupil learning but there is much else which affects this. Careful thought should be given to the need to sample representative evidence.

Sources of evidence

In looking at a school or college an inspector has a range of items of evidence from which to work. They are as follows:

Basic data Schools and other establishments are asked to provide basic data and these will be very valuable to inspectors. Most authorities are getting this material on to computer and this will make it easily accessible.

This could form the basis of the general inspector's record of each individual school. Details on computer usually include staffing, curriculum data and examination results.

Written material by head and staff   This might include: the prospectus; the current development plan; the professional development plan; any policy statements; any curriculum statements; timetable; schemes of work; staff lists with details of responsibilities; staff handbook; governors' reports to parents; head's reports to governors. It is helpful to have a written list of what is required which can be handed to the headteacher in advance of the inspection.

Pupils' work   There are various ways in which one can make judgements about pupils' work. One can look at its appearance, its content, level of accuracy, appropriateness for age and stage; the quantity, the quality, the extent to which it is original work; the teacher's contribution in marking (this may not be relevant at the primary state, where teachers may avoid making marks on a child's work and will talk to him or her instead.) A good deal can be learned by talking to pupils about their work.

One can sample work by looking at (say) that of every fifth person in the class; or the most able, the least able and the average; or one can sample the work of a department by looking at all the books of a particular group. One can also make assessments of work from a display.

Observation of teacher performance   There are a great many observations one can make about teachers' performance and it is sometimes a good idea to look for a limited number of points at any one time. An observer can look at preparation and planning; organisation; the environment; teaching methods; teaching content; the match of the work to the class; provision for the most and least able; continuity; exposition and explanation; questioning; discussion leadership; use of resources; control; relationships; concern for equal opportunities; evaluation used; records kept.

Observation of teacher behaviour   Teacher behaviour is part of teacher performance but it may be useful to look separately from time to time at the way the teacher behaves towards pupils, the reception given to ideas and suggestions; the extent to which praise is given and how far it is used to encourage particular behaviour; the way misbehaviour is dealt with; how far independence is encouraged.

Observation of pupil classroom behaviour   Looking at pupils' work will given some idea of their level of achievement, but a good deal more information will come from observing how they perform in the classroom.

One can observe their skill and knowledge in answering questions or undertaking practical work; the way they settle down to work; the extent to which they remain on task; the existence of genuine group work in which they actually work together to an agreed end; the extent of independence; the way they move about the classroom; their ability to speak to a purpose, their ability to listen. One can gain further information from questioning them about the work they are doing.

Observation of pupil general behaviour Behaviour can be observed other than in the classroom: the way pupils move about; greet or ignore a visitor; speak to others; behave in the dining room. Their appearance may also be noted.

Observation of pupil/teacher interaction The attitudes of teachers and pupils to each other will be evident in what they say about each other and the way they speak to each other. A great deal can be learned about the way teachers regard pupils in observing how misbehaviour is dealt with. The balance of statements of encouragement and praise and statements showing a negative reaction is also important in assessing attitudes. Teacher expectation of pupils can also be observed, particularly with very able and less able groups.

Pupil/pupil interaction The behaviour of pupils to each other can be seen in the playground, about the school and in the classroom: the way they speak to each other, their reaction to points made by other pupils in discussion and the extent to which they are prepared to help each other; attitudes towards the opposite sex and towards racial differences.

Curriculum in practice Part of the task of the general inspector will be to check on the progress the school is making with the National Curriculum and to see how understanding, knowledge and skill are being built up as pupils move through the school. It can be valuable to follow work in a particular subject through the school, looking at how it is developed and the extent to which teachers are building on what went before. This can be a useful way of getting to know the work of a school or of finding out about an unfamiliar subject. It is also important to look at the work going on in areas which do not form part of the National Curriculum.

Management systems If a school is to run efficiently, it needs good systems for many aspects of its daily life. These are worth checking to see if they work as the headteacher thinks they are working. Systems to check might include discipline, pastoral care, arrangements for decision-making, communication with staff, governors, parents and pupils, arrangements for professional development, provision for the most and least able.

Progress with the development plan The development plan provides a yardstick for assessing how well the management of the establishment is going forward. There should be evidence of the different developments it lists.

School events Most schools like to invite their general inspector to plays and concerts and other events and there is a good deal to be learned from such occasions. The choice of work for performance, the extent of student involvement and the standards achieved give interesting information about the views and expectations of the staff.

Environment The environment of a school or a classroom says a great deal about the teachers and pupils who live in it. On entering any establishment one receives an immediate impression of the quality of caretaking and cleaning and the care for the environment. Flowers and plants make a good impression if they are well arranged and cared for but probably the most impressive evidence is the display of work.

One might also look for any safety hazards, the provision for the different activities the school undertakes, the existence of litter and graffiti, the quality of provision for the staff and the particular problems of the building.

In a primary school the classroom should be a workshop, with well organised facilities for the activities to be carried out. Display should be well arranged and include a range of work, not merely the best. There should also be items about the room which would stimulate children.

In a secondary school this is more difficult, since teachers are not always in their own rooms. Where they do have base rooms and are teaching in them, much the same standards as those in primary schools should be expected, appropriately differentiated for the age group in question.

The outside environment is also important and one might look for a cared-for environment, the absence of litter, the separation of boisterous and quiet activity, the provision and quality of areas for physical education and other areas of interest and the general appearance of the ground around the school.

Discussion with headteacher Discussion with the headteacher is important because of the need to know the head's perceptions of what he or she is trying to do. The inspector will want to find out about the overall philosophy of the school, its organisation, its curriculum plans, arrangements for decision-making and consultation, plans for staff development, the state of finance, the discipline system, provision for the most and least able, the record-keeping system, homework policy.

Discussion with teachers Discussion with teachers sheds a valuable light on the way the establishment works. It can be useful to meet a small group of teachers and ask them about the institution. What do they think its strengths and its problems are? Where are the growth points? How satisfactory is the communication and decision- making? How good is discipline? Does the curriculum provide for the whole range of pupils, including the most and least able? Does the record-keeping system work? Do they use the records? Are there opportunities for professional development? What evaluation do they do?

The outcome of this kind of discussion may be the identification of issues which should be discussed with the headteacher and become part of an action plan.

Discussion with pupils Pupils have a unique view of their establishment which is not always sufficiently considered. With very young children at the infant stage, finding out their views will be a matter of talking to them as they work in the classroom and asking questions about their views of the work they are currently undertaking, their favourite activities, the things they think are good about their school, the things they like, what they would do with the school if they could wave a magic wand and change it in some way.

At the junior stage, there is a lot to be said for gathering a group of children to talk about their view of the school. Questions may be like those asked of the younger children, but it will be possible to pursue them further and perhaps ask questions about their view of the National Curriculum and the testing involved, what they think about discipline in the school, their views about assemblies, what they think about the way lunch is organised, the way they like to work in the classroom.

At the secondary stage different questions might be asked of a group of pupils according to the level they are at. First-year pupils might be asked about problems of transfer, whether they have found it difficult to settle and whether they are repeating work they did in the primary school.

With older pupils it is useful to know how they view what has happened to them in the school and how they view the school after several years as pupils. Sixth-formers often have useful things to say about transfer to the sixth. They also have views about the opportunities they have for being involved and about the need to make their voice heard. It is useful to know pupils' views about the implementation of equal opportunity policies.

Discussion with governors Inspectors will have many opportunities for talking to the governors because they will be expected to take part in some meetings. These will give the opportunity both for getting general impressions about the governing body's views and also for talking informally to different governors. An important question to discuss with governors, which may need to be approached obliquely, is that of how they view the relationship with the headteacher and the opportunities governors get to be a real part of the establishment. It is also valuable to get an impression of how the governors view the school and where they see its strengths and weaknesses. This will be particularly important where the governors' views differ from those of the head and staff. In this situation, the general inspector may need to play the part of mediator and try to reconcile the differences.

Discussion with parents Finding opportunities to talk to parents is not easy, but they may occur at parents' evenings and similar events. It may also be possible for a group of parents to be gathered for inspectors to talk to, since they may provide different views from those of the head and staff. It will be helpful to know how the parents view the school, what they consider its strengths and weaknesses to be, what are their concerns about it, whether they feel they are getting enough information, whether they are happy with the teaching methods. It will be important to remember that any group gathered for this kind of discussion is only a small sample of the total parent group and their views may not be typical.

Results of tests and examinations The general inspector should study carefully the results of examinations and tests and discuss with the head and staff any results which give cause for concern.

Timetable The timetable in the secondary school provides a great deal of information about the way the school is organised and the choices available to pupils. It is one of the basic pieces of information which the general inspector should study.

At the primary stage the timetable is less useful, since in most schools it is mainly a timetable for facilities. However, it may give some useful information about provision for those with special needs and it may also give information about the amount of physical activity taking place, including dance and drama and the amount of broadcast material being used. In some schools it may give information about other aspects of the curriculum.

Other details of organisation The way a school is organised tells a good deal about the school philosophy. The extent of streaming or setting or mixed-ability grouping reflects different philosophies. The size and the duties of the management team also say something about the views of the headteacher on sharing responsibility.

Records of staff and pupil absence Absence can often be an indicator of the health of the organisation. People are sick more often when they are under stress or not very happy at work and there are often significant absences among pupils on certain days of the week, which may coincide with certain lessons or with events outside the school.

In looking at the type of evidence listed above, an inspector needs to consider similar issues to those in other kinds of research. In particular, he or she should consider:

1 *The validity of the evidence observed.* It is easy, in looking at someone else's classroom, to draw conclusions which are not entirely valid. It is therefore important to talk to the teacher about what is observed, to check with him or her whether the inspector's impression is a fair interpretation of what happened. Similarly, conclusions about the school need to be discussed with the head.
2 *The reliability of the evidence observed.* One of the problems about making a visit to a school or a classroom is that what is seen may not be typical of what normally happens. This needs checking with other people.
3 *Sampling.* Anything seen in a school is no more than a sample of what normally happens there. The samples an inspector sees may not be representative and the inspector must recognise this.

All judgements about a school should be tentative and be offered to the head and staff as possible interpretations of what has been observed. It is valuable to observe with colleagues from time to time so that observation can be made a little more objective.

Before the inspection

The flow chart in figure 2 itemises the tasks to be undertaken prior to an inspection. They are as follows:

Select establishment The school or college selected will be part of an overall pattern but there are a number of reasons for selecting one school rather than the next within the pattern:

1 There have been complaints which give rise to a need to investigate.
2 The establishment appears to have problems which need investigation and help.
3 It is at a point of change or has recently experienced change.
4 It has asked for help in evaluating its work.
5 It is doing outstandingly well in certain ways and a closer understanding of how this is happening may be valuable to other places.

Decide pattern of inspection The pattern chosen in an individual case will depend upon the overall plan. Whichever pattern is chosen, however, it will be necessary to work through the stages given above in some form. Even when regular visits are used for inspection, the school will need information about this and its documents will be needed. The reporting inspector will

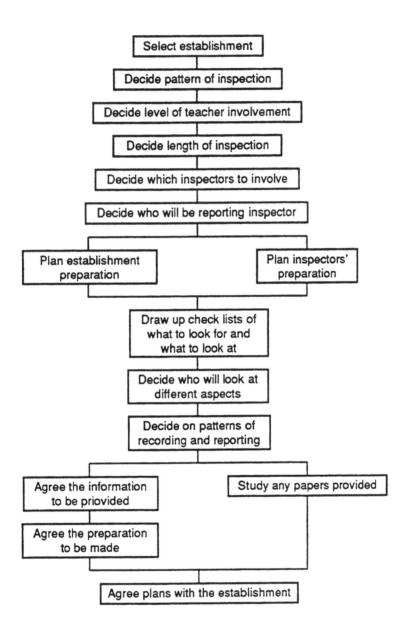

Figure 2   Preparing the individual inspection

also need to consider a check list of the school documents needed and this will require preparation on the part of the establishment.

Decide level of teacher involvement At one extreme, teachers can be totally involved, at the other they can be simply the recipients of an inspection. Many LEAs are developing a policy about the extent to which teachers should be involved so that there is a common pattern.

Decide which inspectors to involve Building a team to undertake an inspection requires careful thought. In the case of a full inspection of a secondary school, this will be more or less dictated by the specialist skills and knowledge required, although it is valuable occasionally to include a person whose interest is mainly primary who may see with a fresh eye. At the primary stage there will be some inspectors who are primary specialists but in many teams there are not enough of them to undertake all the inspection needed. In this situation it will be necessary to train some other inspectors to work with the primary specialists. This may also be necessary at the further education stage.

Richmond upon Thames (1989b) notes in its paper on inspection that:

In assembling teams for the inspection schedule, the inspectorate may wish to add to its own resources by inviting the attachment of consultants who have expertise in the relevant area. These may include as appropriate:

a) senior staff in local schools
b) senior staff in local F/HE
c) senior professionals in the education or other departments
d) advisory teachers
e) external 'consultants'
f) observers e.g. a school governor

Consultants may be attached to the inspectorate for a particular exercise or for a longer period of time.

Decide who will be the reporting inspector Each inspection requires someone to be the key figure who coordinates all that the team is doing and, in particular, coordinates the report. In many teams this will be the person with a pastoral responsibility for the school being inspected. In others there may be a deliberate policy to select someone else on the grounds that the link inspector is too close to the school to undertake this task. The difficulty of collating an appropriate report should not be underestimated and there should be some built-in check with the chief or a more senior inspector before any report goes to the chief education officer or the governing body.

Plan establishment preparation   The school needs to be well briefed about what is planned and a visit should be arranged by the reporting inspector at an early stage to explain what will happen. It is helpful to have a document setting out all the information which can be left with the school. The inspector who makes this visit should have a clear list of matters which need to be discussed and arranged.

Plan inspectors' preparation   Whatever the pattern of inspection, the inspectors concerned will need to meet together to discuss the degree of teacher involvement, the overall plan for the inspection, the evidence they will use, the kind of reporting which is required from them and what will happen to it, the reporting processes in which the teachers are involved, and reporting to the governors. They will also wish to hear about the arrangements the establishment is making for them and the dates and times involved in the inspection and the follow-up meetings.

Draw up check lists of what to look for and what to look at   Check lists may be drawn up mutually by school and inspectors working together, by the inspectorate but incorporating comments from the school, or by the inspectorate which may or may not share with the school the check lists they are proposing to use. Whichever of these patterns is used, it is helpful to have a group of people working on a check list which should not be too complicated or long. An inspectorate may wish to make a standard list, since it is time-wasting to have to make new lists each time. This might be drawn up by a mixed group of teachers and inspectors and items selected from it for each inspection, by the inspectors or by the teachers or by both.

Decide who will look at different aspects   The work of the inspection needs to be carefully parcelled out among those concerned. If the teachers are to be involved in the actual process of inspection this will require some detailed planning. If possible all teachers concerned with the aspects under consideration should be seen at work, preferably for more than one lesson.

Decide on patterns of recording and reporting   This will be dealt with in greater detail later in this chapter but at the preliminary stage there must be agreement about the format of the report, so that notes can be made under similar headings. Attention should also be given to 'house style', for example that teachers should not be identified by name, the avoidance of sexist language. It is also important to remind people of the need to avoid jargon, bearing in mind that much of the language we normally use to talk about education is regarded by the layman as jargon.

Agree the information to be provided   Most establishments have a great deal of useful information already on paper including:

1 Number on roll.
2 Prospectus.
3 Plan of the school and map of how to get there.
4 Development plan.
5 Policy statements.
6 Staff list, giving groups taught and responsibilities.
7 Details of organisation of teaching groups.
8 Timetable.
9 Staff handbook.
10 Head's last report to governors.
11 Curriculum guidelines.
12 Arrangements for directed time.
13 Staff development programme and arrangements for training days.
14 Test and examination results.
15 Information about provision for special needs, including that for the very
   able.

It is helpful for an advisory service to have a standard list of papers they
would like to have from the school. It is unwise to impose on a school
excessive data collection. The emphasis should be on having copies of what
is already available.

Agree the preparation to be made   While most inspectors would wish to
disturb the establishment as little as possible, it is inevitable that a group of
people coming in to observe what is happening will affect its running.
However good the relationships between teachers and inspectors, and however much the teachers are involved in the inspection, the element of
judgement in the situation means that there will be tension, and inspectors
need to be sensitive to this. It will also be necessary to arrange space for the
inspectors and, make domestic arrangements.

Study any papers provided   Inspectors will need to study in advance of
the inspection whatever papers are provided.

Agree plans with the establishment.   Whatever the pattern of inspection
proposed, the inspectorate needs to agree plans with the school, so that the
head and staff are fully informed about what is happening.

Carrying out the inspection

The major observation task is within the classroom and there are various
ways of undertaking this. It is very important for anyone acting as an
observer to be as sympathetic and unobtrusive as possible. The presence of
another person in the room will to some extent affect the way the pupils
behave and will certainly affect the teacher.

It is important to be clear about what is being assessed and the kind of evidence being sought. If a teacher's performance and pupil learning are to be fairly assessed, it is important to know in advance what the teacher is intending to do and his or her aims for the particular work observed. In practice it is often difficult to get sufficient information of this kind before observing, but where possible it should be sought. This enables an observer to make judgements in terms of the teacher's aims and how far the pupils are succeeding in the intended learning. It will also be necessary to make judgements in terms of what the observer feels the teacher ought to be doing.

The list of evidence given earlier applies to the individual classroom as well as to the school. The following are the main areas to be studied:

1 Written material by teacher.
2 Pupils' work.
3 Organisation.
4 Teacher performance and behaviour.
5 Observation of pupil performance and behaviour.
6 Pupil/teacher interaction.
7 Pupil/pupil interaction.
8 The environment.
9 Discussion with teacher and pupils.
10 Results of tests and examinations.
11 Records of pupils.

There are several basic ways of recording classroom observation:

The use of a check list   Provided it does not become too rigid it is helpful to have as a prompt a list of what might be observed . The check list in figure 3 may be useful.

The use of a rating scale   In this situation the observer goes into the classroom with a list of what to look for and rates the extent and the level at which they are found. This requires a pro-forma and a sample is given in figure 4. The advantage of the rating scale is that the observer has a clear basis for making observations and for the conclusions reached. The disadvantage is that the observation is dictated by the list and other important matters may be missed.

Within this category of observation there is quite a wide range of possibilities. The items for rating can be very straightforward, with little scope for personal judgement (low inference rate) or they can be fairly broad and vague categories which allow a lot of latitude to the individual (high inference rate).

It is often best to select out an area of the work for rating rather than trying to make observations of everything.

CLASSROOM CHECK LIST

School ....
Teacher ....
Class(es) seen ....
Duration of visit ....
Lesson topic(s) ....

Date ....
Post ....
....
Inspector ....
....

Preparation and planning
(Objectives, clarity of planning, continuity, work on National Curriculum)

Organisation
(Beginning and end of lesson, changes of activity, differentiation, extent of independent work, grouping)

Pupils' work
(Match of work to ability, ground covered, appearence, quality of marking)

Figure 3 A classroom check list

Teacher performance
(Appropriateness of teaching methods, skills in questioning, pupil participation, clarity of instructions, discussion, leadership skill, use of resources, control)

Teacher/pupil interaction
(Relationship, the way the teacher speaks to pupils, teacher expectation, concern for equal opportunities)

Pupil/pupil interaction
(Behaviour of pupils to each other, their readiness to help each other, the extent to which they work together)

Environment
(Overall attractiveness, layout for work, quality of display, safety)

General comments

Signed ....

CLASSROOM RATING SCALES

School ....
Teacher ....
Class(es) seen ....
Duration of visit ....
Lesson topic(s) ....

Date ....
Post ....
....
Inspector ....
....

Preparation and planning

Teaching objectives clearly set
Clear planning
Continuity taken into account
Clear relationship with National Curriculum

Organisation

Organisation of beginning and end of lesson
Organisation for changes of activity
Provision made for pupils of different abilities
Development of ability to work independently
Appropriateness of pupil grouping
Control of pupils

Pupils' work

Match of work to pupils' ability
Ground covered in pupils' work
Appearance of pupils' work
Quality of marking

Rating scale

X	Demonstrates above average skills
P	Meets performance standards required
I	Needs to improve
U	Unsatisfactory
N	Not observed or not applicable

Figure 4   A classroom rating scale

Pupils' performance

Extent to which pupils are on task
Performance in discussion
Ability to answer questions
Concentration
Quality of group work
Degree of independence in learning

Teacher/pupil interaction

Teacher/pupil relationship
The way the teacher speaks to pupils
Teacher expectation of pupils
Evidence of concern for equal opportunities

for race   for ability
for gender   for social class

Pupil/pupil interaction

Behaviour of pupils towards each other
The way pupils speak to each other
The readiness of pupils to help each other
The ability of pupils to work together

The environment

Overall attractiveness
Suitability of layout for work
Safety
Quality and appearance of display
Frequency of change of display

The use of timed observation   Here the observer notes what is happening at carefully timed intervals in certain parts of the classroom. This method is often used in classroom research and is a matter of noting what the teacher is doing or what particular children are doing. It is too time-consuming to use to any considerable extent in inspecting schools, but it may be useful to make a small number of timed observations of such matters as the number of children on task. It is also useful to note the time it takes for the class to settle down to work at the beginning of a lesson or the proportion of time a teacher spends in talking to the class.

The use of specific observations   It can be valuable to identify a number of important aspects of what is being observed and to spend some time looking for these alone. Montgomery (1984) looks for the teacher's concern with three issues:

1 The extent to which the teacher 'rewards' pupils who are doing the right things (Catch them Being Good or CBG).
2 The occasions when the teacher does something which develops the pupils' thinking (Positive Cognitive Intervention or PCI).
3 The management strategies a teacher uses (3Ms or Management, Monitoring and Maintenance).

The use of a narrative   Montgomery's work is allied to keeping a narrative of what is being observed in the classroom. There are occasions when inspectors will wish to feed back to teachers evidence of what they are observing, and the narrative is very useful for this. It involves noting everything of interest which happens, setting this alongside a note of the time taken by each part of the lesson.

The classroom is probably the most important place for observation but there are other areas which should be considered:

Pastoral care   A good deal of energy in most schools is expended on the care of pupils. In a secondary school the form tutor is likely to have specific tasks to undertake for the care of pupils and may also have a programme of work designed to help pupils personally and socially. In a primary school the children are with their own teacher all or most of the time, so that personal and social education are worked into the day's programme, but there is still a great deal done in this area of work. An inspector may wish to find out whether the establishment has any policy on or agreement about how pupils should be treated and how they are expected to behave in different situations. It is useful to discuss this with teachers first and then talk with a group of pupils about what they think they are expected to do. The inspector may also want to know how much planning of the work has been done by the tutor or class teacher and to what extent there is a programme which has continuity.

Management   This is a very important area and there is probably a case for one or more observers spending time with the head and senior staff studying how issues of management are dealt with. It is also very profitable to spend time with a number of groups of staff questioning them about how they see the school at the present time.

The discussions with staff and pupils will give a feel for the management style of the school. It will be clear if the head is one who works autocratically or democratically. The extent of delegation may also be clear from questioning. Teachers who are dissatisfied as a group, usually make this evident though they may try to disguise it. New teachers and probationers often have useful contributions to make, since they see the organisation with fresh eyes.

An interview with the chairman of governors may also be helpful. He or she will have a view from the outside but with considerable information about what is happening. The paperwork should also give a good deal of information about management. The following issues should be explored:

1 Aims, objectives and policies.
2 Organisation of pupils.
3 Organisation of staff.
4 Staff meetings.
5 Decision-making.
6 Finance.
7 Communication.
8 Staff selection.
9 Professional development.
10 Evaluation.
11 Discipline.
12 Administration.
13 School and community.
14 Head's personal organisation and use of time.

Check lists and observation schedules should be linked to the headings which will be needed in the final report. It is therefore important to prepare check lists carefully so that the information gathered is the information required.

The activities of the governing body

As yet there has been no suggestion that the way a governing body is working should be the subject of inspection. Yet the working of the establishment can be supported or impeded by the governors. The LEA has the right to remove financial management from a governing body and this will presumably require inspection of the way they have dealt with the school's finances:

> Where it appears to a local education authority, in the case of any school in respect of which financial delegation is required for the current year under a scheme, that the governing body of the school
>
> (a) have been guilty of a substantial or persistent failure to comply with any requirements under the scheme; or
> (b) are not managing the appropriation or the expenditure of the sum put at their disposal for the purposes of the school in a satisfactory manner;
>
> the authority may suspend the governing body's right to a delegated budget by giving the governing body (subject to subsection (3) below) not less than one month's notice of suspension.
>
> (Education Reform Act 1988, para. 37)

Some evidence about the way governors are working with the head and staff will emerge looking at the management of the school and it may be that, in reporting, inspectors need to comment on how the action of governors has affected what is happening.

After the inspection

Most inspectors like to give teachers some feedback. It is essential that the inspection team should meet at the end of the inspection and put together their thinking about the main impressions coming through for brief meetings both with the staff and with the head. The difficulty about this is that the impressions may be widely differing and the team needs time to sort them out. It is also difficult if the overall impression is very negative, in which case the team needs time to work out the best way of putting its thinking across. Each advisory/inspectorate service needs to come to a conclusion about how to do this. It is normally helpful to the school to get some feedback immediately after what may have been a threatening experience. The head and teachers are also usually very ready to receive advice at this point.

One way of planning this is to list first of all observations about good points. This sets the scene positively and makes it easier to discuss those things which need attention. These can then be presented as growth points. It is also helpful for each inspector involved to give the head an account of what he or she saw in the classroom. Where growth points are concerned, it will be valuable to discuss some of them in a fair amount of detail, looking at what has already been done by the school and what might be done next.

This advice should be treated as a starting point only and a more detailed discussion should take place as part of the follow-up (figure 5).

Many inspectors find it difficult to give feedback on issues which need

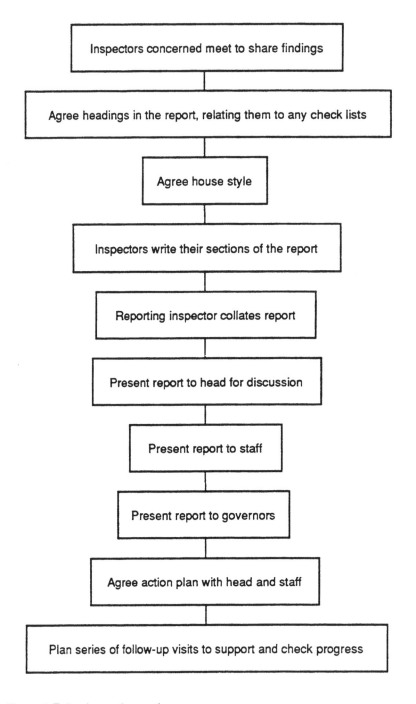

Figure 5 Following up inspection

attention. This has been dealt with in chapter 4. It is essential to state problems clearly and unequivocally, following this by discussion of what positive steps can be taken.

Inspectors concerned meet to share findings This is an important meeting in that it gives everyone a chance to explore in more detail what he or she thought about the establishment. It should be held as soon after the inspection as possible, preferably within a week. Probably the best way to run such a meeting is to go round the group, letting each person report on his or her experience and then to identify common threads. It is unusual to find that people differ completely and it should be possible to find a number of themes which can be discussed with the establishment with evidence from a number of people which will form the basis of the recommendations of the report and also provide a starting point for introducing the report to staff and governors.

Agree headings in the report, relating them to any check lists Some LEAs provide both a working paper for the head and staff and a final report for the governors. The working paper contains a much more detailed account designed to help teachers. The final report is more a summary of findings. The working paper in a secondary school can very often be more or less a collection of the reports as individual inspectors wrote them, each teacher receiving only that part which applies to his or her area of work. The final report really needs to be of a single style throughout and to draw conclusions across the whole of the work.

Whatever the form of the report the meeting of inspectors should reach agreement about its final shape. If a working paper is also to be produced, agreement also needs to be reached about that. Although headings may have been planned before the inspection, they may turn out to be inappropriate. It is also important that everyone follows the same pattern in writing his or her section of the report so that there are no difficulties in putting it together. It should contain an introductory section describing the way the inspection was conducted and a final section of recommendations. It is wise at this stage to stress that judgements should always be backed by hard observational evidence. Those writing reports should also be made aware that it may be necessary to change what they have written in order to gain consistency over the report as a whole.

Agree house style Decisions should be reached about the following:

1 The overall format, including the way the following are stated:
  • headings chosen
  • order of parts of the report
  • statement of facts

- observation of evidence
- recommendations

2 The length of the report
3 The use of terminology for curriculum, organisation, management and ideology.
4 The 'ownership' of the report, i.e. is it to be written in first person singular or plural or the passive voice?
5 The naming of teachers.
6 Such textual detail as:

- use of capital letters – will 'head' have a capital letter and if so, what about 'teacher'?
- treatment of abbreviations and acronyms – GCSE or General Certificate of Secondary Education?
- treatment of headings
- numbering of paragraphs
- should numbers be written as words or numerals?
- paragraph layout
- standard spelling of words where there is an alternative, e.g. judgement, judgment; organisation, organization
- use of hyphens in words such as 'co-operation'
- use of contractions, e.g. 'doesn't' or 'does not'
- use of full stop after contractions e.g. 'Mr'
- style of date
- use of inverted commas

An early deadline date for finished reports should be given.

Inspectors write their sections of the report People vary in their skill in report writing. It may be helpful to pair an inexperienced inspector with a more experienced one known to be good at this task and to suggest that they come together at an early stage in writing the report so that the experienced person can help the inexperienced.

There is much to be said at this stage for individual inspectors discussing with the teachers concerned what they are proposing to put into the report. This provides an opportunity to check detail and ensures that the final report does not come as a shock. It also helps the inspectors concerned to anticipate the kind of reaction their reports will receive. An inspectorate may decide that their practice should include adding a passage to the report about the views of the teachers concerned.

Reporting inspector collates report The task of collating the report is not an easy one, even when all the constituent reports are good. They are frequently very varied in quality and style, however carefully the planning has been done and it is important that the reporting inspector is free to make necessary changes in order to give the overall report a similarity of style. It may be necessary to shorten some reports and possibly to lengthen others if there is material to do so. It is also usually necessary for the reporting inspector to consult each colleague over any points and it is useful to take this as an opportunity to let him or her see what is proposed as the final report.

At this stage some inspection teams will build in other checks such as submitting the report to the chief inspector or even the chief education officer. This is generally a wise move. Inspection reports are to some extent public documents and the more checking they receive, within reason, the better.

Present report to head for discussion Once the report is finished it should be discussed with the head so that any details which are incorrect can be corrected and so that the reporting inspector can get a first impression of the likely reactions. It also provides an opportunity to start talking about a possible action plan and to discuss ways of presenting the report to the staff and to the governors.

Present report to staff A meeting of the inspectors and staff together is needed to present the report to the staff. There are various ways in which this may be done. The written report may be given to the staff in advance and, after a brief introduction bringing out the main points, it may be opened to questions and discussion. Alternatively, the reporting inspector may present the report in rather more detail before the discussion or each inspector may present his or her part of the report. Whichever format is chosen it will be important to time carefully the contributions made by inspectors so that there is sufficient time for discussion. The meeting should be advertised to finish at a given time and this should be strictly adhered to.

Present report to governors The report should be presented to the governors by a small group or a pair of inspectors. Those chosen should be noted for their tact and ability to present information well. It is also helpful to discuss with the head beforehand the likely reactions of members of the governing body.

As for the staff, the written report should be distributed well in advance of the meeting, and it must be remembered that the governors have as yet had no chance of hearing officially the outcomes of the inspection. The governors will need a fuller introduction than the staff, since they have not been involved and it may be that each attending inspector presents a section of the report. This should be followed by discussion and concluded by a summary of what needs to be done, with an assurance that discussion about action has already started and progress will be reported to the governors. It may be helpful to the head to give some idea of how long some of the tasks facing the school are likely to take. Again it is wise to agree in advance the length of the meeting and how long each inspector will take to introduce his or her section of the report. Time for questioning and discussion is essential.

Agree action plan with head and staff   Different people may be involved with the head and staff over action plans, depending on the organisation of the inspectorial team. If it includes a general or link inspector for each establishment then this is the person who might be expected to work with the head and teachers to follow up the inspection, drawing on colleagues' specialist expertise as necessary. In a primary school the general inspector might draw on primary specialists or on whomever appears to be necessary. In a secondary school the general inspector might be expected to deal with management issues and specialist inspectors with their own subjects. This will vary according to the practice of the team and the skills of those involved.

Whoever may be involved, one inspector needs to ensure that there is an action plan and that it is carried through with whatever support is necessary. The action plan should contain statements in specific terms of what is to be done and the action steps should be time-bonded. This plan will need to become part of the school development plan. A concern about the general appearance of the establishment, for example, might involve a series of statements such as the following:

1 Use one staff development day to brainstorm and agree what might be done to improve the environment.
2 Establish a small environment committee involving both staff and pupils, the main task of which is to take the ideas generated by the staff and turn them into an action programme.
3 Investigate the possibility of spending some money on redecoration in some parts of the building.

Dates for the completion of each activity need to be incorporated in the plan. Furthermore, the inspector concerned will need to agree with the head the dates by which information about each of these tasks will be sent to him or her or, alternatively, a date for another visit to discuss progress.

It is sometimes not possible to deal with all the problems thrown up by an inspection at the same time. The most important ones and those easiest and least time-consuming should be selected for implementation in the first instance and others built into the development plan and discussed as part of the follow-up procedure. The detail of these plans will not be part of the inspection report, so it may be a good idea to put them on paper in a letter to the head.

Plan series of follow-up visits to support and check progress This should be planned within the time allowed for the follow-up of the inspection. Each school inspected should have an entitlement of a certain amount of advisory time as part of the follow-up process. Some time should be devoted to checking whether problems identified in the inspection have been overcome and some to dealing with problems which were not included in the original action plan. It may also be necessary to set up a staff development programme.

Cost of inspection

Inspection is an expensive process, taking a good deal of time of both inspectors and teachers. It is valuable to cost inspections so that the time put in can be weighed against the results. The pro-forma in figure 6 identifies the various meetings and observations which may be needed for primary and secondary schools, either by inspectors or by teachers. In any inspection there is time which is fixed, because the activities are necessary whatever the size of the establishment. There is also time which varies according to the size of the school because it is related to the number of teachers. These are listed separately and together these two elements make it possible to calculate how much time any particular inspection is likely to take. It is valuable to consider the time needed by teachers as well as that needed by inspectors. Time is probably best calculated in days and fractions of a day, but may also be calculated in hours.

This exercise makes it possible to calculate roughly how much time is needed for inspections overall.

Calculation of adviser time:

(number of schools x fixed time) + (number of individual teacher days x number of teachers)

Calculation of teacher time:

(number of schools x fixed time) + (number of individual teacher days x number of teachers)

Tasks to be done	Inspectors				Teachers			
	Primary		Secy		Primary		Secy	
	Fixed	Var	Fixed	Var	Fixed	Var	Fixed	Var
Insp preliminary meeting								
Preliminary visit								
Other visits								
Headteacher preparation								
Teacher preparation								
Observe teachers								
Observe pastoral care								
Observe middle management								
Observe senior management								
Observe headteacher								
Observe building/resources								
Talk to groups								
Sum up with head								
Sum up with staff								

Figure 6   Identifying the cost of inspection

Report writing									
Collating reports									
Inspectors' report meeting									
School study of report									
School meeting to discuss report									
Inspector/teacher meeting									
Governors' meeting									
Follow-up action									
Review									
Totals									

Chapter 6

Supporting and developing the work of teachers

The changes in the way that advisers and inspectors are working in some authorities have resulted in a more limited amount of time and responsibility for supporting and advising teachers than was available to the service in the past. There will, of course, be advice stemming from inspection, but follow-up help may be limited or may be given by a different group of people, perhaps advisers who do not inspect or advisory teachers. In other authorities the idea of a right of each establishment to a certain proportion of adviser time has been pursued. Yet others are moving towards the idea that establishments should purchase the advisory help they need. There are also LEAs where the role of the pastoral adviser is very important and is built into the review process.

Whatever the pattern of advisory work it is probable that there will be a need for some members of the service to be working to provide advice and support for teachers. This was envisaged in the unpublished paper (DES 1985) on advisory services drawn up by the DES and a group of administrators and advisers which stated that every establishment should be known well by at least one adviser. This is quoted in the Audit Commission Report (1989b). The then Secretary of State, in a speech to the Society of Education Officers emphasised the need for 'support to schools and teachers to help them find their way through the uncertainties and anxieties which change so often brings in its wake'. This statement was reinforced by Hancock (1988) who in his speech to NAIEA said that 'advice and support will, in large measure, need to be provided by local inspectors'.

He continued:

> This does not imply that I believe your advisory functions and support to schools on curriculum development, in-service training and curriculum organisation should be reduced. On the contrary I am sure that much greater calls will be made on your advice and support as a result of the government's reforms.

An article in *Education* by Crowther (1988) reported Hancock as saying that, in addition to monitoring and evaluating school performance and providing an evaluation of how the service is performing, advisers should give professional advice and encouragement based on first-hand observation and help to manage innovation and change.

The Society of Chief Inspectors and Advisers (SCIA 1989) listed a number of the areas in which advice and support are needed:

- advice and support for heads, groups of teaching staff and individual teachers
- advice and guidance to governors on staff appointments;
- curriculum development;
- staff development;
- assistance to schools in preparing and keeping under review their development plans;
- assistance to schools with the National Curriculum and its assessment;
- introduction and oversight of appraisal schemes.

The report of the *School Management Task Force* (DES 1990) emphasised the need for management development to be not only a matter of external courses but an integral part of each institution, using the day-to-day life of the institution to develop its managers. It envisaged the LEA establishing a team of officers and advisers with the resources and expertise to implement this type of policy. It also expected the LEA to 'work with headteachers and help them to identify their needs and then provide for them'. These would seem to be tasks for the adviser or inspector. It is clear from all these sources that it is still important for the advisory service to provide support and help for teachers and headteachers.

The way an adviser or advisory teacher sets about the task of supporting and developing the work of teachers depends to a large extent on the philosophy held about education and the advisory work style adopted. Anyone going into advisory work needs to have a clear view of the educational process and where it should lead. The difficulty is that he or she must also be sympathetic to other views. An adviser or advisory teacher who can see only one point of view limits his or her influence to those who can be persuaded to share that view. Teachers in Winkley's study (1985) of the advisory services complained that, on in-service courses at least, advisers were inclined to offer only their own point of view and invite speakers who reinforced that view. There are many good practices in education and the good adviser acknowledges this and gradually becomes able to advise and support teachers who work in very different ways.

Chapter 2 looked at style in advisory work. The evidence from Winkley's study would seem to suggest that the most effective styles in terms of school and teacher development are those which respect the professionalism of teachers and work with them rather than as their managers. At the same time advisers are the representatives of their LEA and in most LEAs are likely to need to work in a managerial role from time to time and this is likely to be increased by the current stress on monitoring and inspection. Advisory teachers do not have this managerial role and this can be an advantage in that teachers see them as sympathetic colleagues recently in the classroom whereas the adviser may be seen primarily as the representative of the LEA. The fact that the only pressure that advisory teachers can offer is that of persuasion might be seen as an advantage or a disadvantage, according to one's point of view, but it is certainly an advantage in so far as it requires the advisory teacher to convince those he or she works with that a given change is worth making. It places great emphasis on negotiating and persuading skills.

This is the way many advisers have seen their work in the past and it should still be at the heart of what advisers do. There is now also a more directive role, in that advisers are responsible for seeing that schools are teaching the National Curriculum, teaching it well and implementing a good development plan. This requires that advisers have to assess, not just in order to advise but in order to report to governors and others on the progress of the school.

If an adviser is to influence teachers, it is essential that he or she forms good relationships with them at an early stage. One's first visit to a school or college is crucial from this point of view. Margerison (1978), reminds us that '[one] must understand the other person's position before [one] can become in any way effective as an adviser'; and again: 'the adviser should begin to understand the client's culture and the context in which he behaves'.

Advisers in the education service are in an easier position than the industrial advisers for whom Margerison was writing in that the culture of different educational establishments is probably more similar than the culture of different industries. Establishments nevertheless differ considerably in their culture and it is essential at an early stage for an adviser or advisory teacher to find out their philosophy and style and to convince the staff that he or she understands what they are about. An adviser coming new to an establishment, whether experienced in or new to advisory work, will be regarded rather as children regard a new teacher. Teachers will want to be assured that the new adviser knows something about the kind of work they are doing and will be looking at what he or she can offer them. At the same time they will be put off if the adviser or advisory teacher advertises his or her skills and previous experience too blatantly. One needs to be honest about one's limitations.

Visiting schools and other establishments

Winkley (1985) found that:

- The advisory contact acts as reassurance to teachers and may improve the image of the LEA.

- The better visited areas tend to:
  - have more confidence in the adviser's judgement in matters of promotion;
  - have more confidence in the skills of the adviser;
  - feel more positively about the advisory service;
  - be more positive about the LEA's overall consultancy.

Visiting policy

An advisory team needs to have a policy about visits, which should be available to all establishments as well as advisers and advisory teachers and should cover the work of advisory teachers as well as advisers. It might include advice about the following:

1 The pattern of visiting: frequency, nature, length.
2 The need to have a clear purpose in visiting, one which may in part be dictated by the extent to which the team is using visit records as part of the monitoring process.
3 The extent to which establishments should be warned of visits and the situations in which advisers should call unexpectedly.
4 The role of advisory teachers and the way in which the policy is related to their work.
5 The information available in the office which might be consulted before visiting: computer records, details of establishment size and composition, examination results.
6 The protocol in visiting: inform the head on arrival, give feedback to teachers seen, give feedback to the head or head of department on work seen.
7 The ways in which an adviser might be expected to spend time: classroom observation, discussion with staff and pupils, pupil or teacher pursuit, in which the adviser follows a particular teacher or pupil for the day, gathering specific information.
8 The priorities which should be observed: time with nearly qualified teachers, headteachers.
9 The reporting required, whether in terms of notes to be kept personally or written reports to be filed on each visit. This may be dictated by the extent to which visits are part of the monitoring process.
10 The need to be sensitive to internal arrangements: disrupting the teaching pattern in order to see something in particular or talking to teachers when they should be elsewhere, fitting in with arrangements for lunch and coffee, not over-doing making and receiving telephone calls.

These may seem very obvious points, but there should be a pattern across the service so that establishments know what to expect. Each of these points needs careful consideration.

The pattern of visiting

There is ample evidence from studies of advisory work to suggest that in the past visiting has tended to be haphazard, sometimes following the most immediate demands and sometimes following the individual adviser's particular interest. It is much pleasanter to spend time in a place which is receptive to your ideas and responds to the suggestions you make than in one which is complacent or antagonistic. While an adviser starting in an area of work which is new to the authority may quite properly concentrate some attention on places likely to develop good work quickly which can spearhead developments elsewhere, in the long term advisers must try to develop work in all establishments and the pattern of visiting must reflect this. Visiting by advisory teachers has often been rather more systematic particularly where it has been planned in collaboration with appropriate advisers.

Many teams now agree a pattern in which every establishment has an entitlement of advisory time and in which every school and college receives some visits in the course of a year. The visit pattern needs to be recorded, preferably on computer, so that the team can be certain that all establishments are getting their fair share of advisory time. Many teams now have an *aide memoire* for visits which details what to look for.

The pressures on advisers, especially where a small team serves a large area, may mean that visits are very infrequent. This shows up very clearly in the research by Winkley (1985) where only 10 per cent of teachers felt that they were well known by at least one adviser and about 50 per cent felt that they were unsatisfactorily assessed by the advisory service. The present move to a better managed service in which the requirements for visiting are clearly defined should help to answer this criticism, although it is still easy for advisers to be overloaded with demands.

In a situation where the time available for support is strictly limited, it may be better, particularly for specialist advisers, to take a section of the authority at a time and visit more thoroughly, spending time in each classroom and really getting to know the establishments and teachers. If establishments are aware that this is what is happening they are likely to accept that their turn will come and to feel that they will be properly assessed at that point. Winkley (1985) noted that there was a correlation between the length of advisory visits and the views teachers held of advisers. The longer the visits the more favourably they viewed the service.

More thorough visiting of this kind will also make it easier to deal with emergencies cropping up in the periods between visits. To some extent the present emphasis on inspection will help advisers to know establishments more thoroughly, but this will be of value to teachers only if time can be spent in relating inspection findings to their situation and to action.

The visiting patterns of advisory teachers will depend upon the way the LEA has decided to use them.

Warning establishments of visits

It is evident from discussions with heads and from Winkley's study that heads and teachers much prefer to know in advance the purpose of an adviser's visit. This enables them to plan time so that it is used profitably. It must be remembered that schools and colleges today have many interruptions in their work and need to use time efficiently. An adviser calling unexpectedly is yet one more distraction even when the visit is really useful. The adviser needs to be clear about his or her purposes and tell the establishment of these in advance by telephone or letter setting out the particular aspects of work which will be looked at. If the school or college knows that an adviser wants to look at mathematics, for example, teachers can have information ready and make the visit more profitable. It is also helpful from the adviser's point of view to be clear about the reasons for a visit. It makes for a more efficient use of time. At the same time, it is important not to be inflexible, adhering to the original purpose when, on arrival, it is evident that advisory help is urgently needed in a particular quarter or there is other work going on which it would be very valuable to see.

There may be some situations in which an adviser needs to make a point of calling unexpectedly. Where it is suspected that a head is frequently late in starting school or where a teacher is failing but can put on a show if warned of a visit, it will be necessary to call to check without informing the school in advance. There will also be occasions when it is necessary to call into a school unexpectedly to give or seek some information. Whatever the views of the advisory team about this, there should be general agreement about normal practice and all establishments should be be aware of the policy.

Advisory teachers should also warn establishments of their visits and give information about what they hope to do, since they are coming into the school or college to work with teachers.

Information available in the office

Every advisory service should have access to detailed files on individual establishments. These will probably be partly on paper and partly on computer. Computer files have the advantage that specific information is more easily accessed and kept up to date. An adviser or advisory teacher visiting an establishment should know the following:

1 The size and composition of the establishment at the present time.
2 The current staffing situation.

3 Any plans for the future: reorganisation, opting out, new buildings.
4 Any relevant information about performance.
5 Any current problems or difficulties.
6 School development plan.
7 Curriculum proposals.
8 Plans for LMS.
9 Plans for TVE.

A general adviser might be expected to know these things without reference to files, but a specialist going into a school or college which he or she visits infrequently may need to make such checks.

The role of advisory teachers

It is likely that advisory teachers will have an increasing role in supporting establishments as advisers find themselves spending more time on inspection. Each team needs to be clear what their role is and how they should work. The following patterns are possible:

1 Advisory teachers work in much the same way as advisers except that their work is concerned with classroom teachers rather than head-teachers. They have general discussion with appropriate advisers about the places which need their attention and to some extent the nature of the attention, but are then free to arrange their own programmes, responding to requests from schools as well as requests from advisers.
2 Advisory teachers work within a range of establishments defined by the appropriate adviser. The pattern of their work is discussed and approaches agreed but they are then free to arrange their work as seems best to them. Requests from schools are channelled through the appropriate adviser.
3 Advisory teachers work closely with the appropriate adviser, who introduces them to specific establishments in which their work is defined and agreed.

The last of these options makes for the least pressure on advisory teachers but places greater pressure on the advisers involved.

The protocol in visiting

All advisory services should have an agreed code of practice which is known to all establishments and applies both to advisers and to advisory teachers. Although many of the details will seem very obvious to experienced advisers, people new to the work may find such a code very supportive. Going into schools or colleges for the first time can be daunting and it is helpful to know how one is expected to behave. Statements such as the following might be included:

1 An adviser going into any establishment should make his or her presence known to the head. If it is not necessary to see the head, it is still necessary to inform him or her that the adviser is in the school, perhaps by leaving a message with the secretary.

2 Wherever possible an adviser should have a prior word with any teacher whose work he or she hopes to see, in order to find out what the teacher intends doing. An adviser should also give feedback to teachers after their work has been seen.

3 Discussion about work with the head and teachers should involve positive statements wherever possible. It is usually best to start by giving positive feedback and then raising any queries.

4 Where an adviser is not happy with what has been seen, he or she should, within the context above, state this clearly to those concerned. If the problem is a serious one, it should be followed up with a letter to the teacher, spelling out what is needed for improvement and the intention to visit again after a specified period. Care should be exercised in putting this in writing, since the letter may become a document in a court case. The inexperienced adviser would be wise to check with a more experienced colleague what he or she has written. A copy of such a letter should be sent to the head.

5 The head should always be informed of an adviser's findings at the end of a visit. If the head is not available, the deputy head should be informed.

Spending time in schools and colleges

Advisers new to the work sometimes find it difficult to decide how best to use their time in schools and colleges although in many LEAs now this is fairly clearly defined with check lists of matters to be reviewed. Where this is not so, the policy statement can be helpful in identifying the kinds of activity which may be useful. They might include:

1 Observing teaching, using any of the methods described in chapter 5.

2 Pupil or teacher pursuit, following an individual pupil or group of pupils or a teacher in the course of a session.

3 Discussion with groups of teachers or pupils, see chapter 5.

4 Following a theme through the school: looking at the teaching of reading, record keeping, a particular subject, pastoral care. This is particularly useful when an adviser is new or unfamiliar with the age group. An adviser with a secondary school background, for example, may spend time finding out how reading is taught and will learn a lot in the process. Although, on the face of it, this appears to be much more for the benefit of the adviser than that of the school, in practice the school usually gains from the fact that the new adviser comes with a fresh eye. An adviser coming in a specialist capacity may choose to select something within the

specialism. For example, an English adviser may choose to pursue oral language teaching through the school; a mathematician may look at the extent of practical work.

5 An adviser might make a special point of looking at the appearance of a school. Is it a pleasant place to work? Is it clean and tidy? What is the quality of the display and how far is pupils' work evident? What sort of an impression does one have on arriving at the school?

It is important for advisers to plan so that they can see all the teachers in a department or primary school. Where some teachers are seen and others not, this gives rise to concern. Those teachers who have been seen wonder why they were chosen and those who have not been seen wonder why they were not chosen. If this is not possible during a particular visit, some explanation should be given as to the rationale for choosing particular people to see.

An advisory team also needs to consider whether there are any circumstances in which it is legitimate for an adviser to teach. The current pressures make this difficult to do anyway and the situation may vary from subject to subject, but in general it should be accepted that, since teaching styles differ from person to person, showing someone how to do it may not be the best approach. The headteachers in the NFER study (Stillman & Grant 1989) felt that advisers should teach from time to time since this was important for their credibility. Some advisers also feel that their credibility depends upon showing teachers that they too can do the job. Other advisers become highly credible without such demonstrations, because they offer teachers valuable help and help them to develop their thinking. The skills involved in teaching and those of advisory work are different and it is easy, particularly when an adviser has just come into the service from teaching, to be self-indulgent in returning to the known activity rather than tackling the new and rather difficult one.

Advisory teachers are in a rather different category, since in many cases their appointments require that they should work in classrooms alongside teachers and this will involve some teaching. They still need to be aware that styles differ and, in guiding teachers to change their ways of working, they should help them to do so within their personal styles.

Priorities in visiting

At any given time, an advisory team may have priorities to pursue. It may also have some overall priorities, such as checking on the progress of the development plan or to see newly qualified teachers. Since it is not possible to keep everything under review all the time, it is better to choose to concentrate on particular activities for a period. Thus all advisers might look at continuity and progression in schools, assessing this at all levels and in particular at points where pupils change schools or go on to higher and further education. They might pursue a particular curriculum area, checking on certain aspects within it. They might look at record-keeping, pastoral care, the appearance of schools, discipline, questioning by teachers, the use of first-hand experience and much else, depending on the particular objectives the team is pursuing at the time.

Individual advisers may also have their priorities, related to their specialist interests or to their knowledge of the particular school or college and its current plans. The school or college itself often has priorities which it would like the adviser to pursue.

A team also needs to have priorities in deciding whether most attention should be given to schools which are doing well and are able to use advice or to trying to improve those which are less successful. In the event both need attention. An adviser may decide that developing really outstanding work with one school or a group of schools may be a good use of time, because its starts to set a climate for others in the area and provides places which other teachers can be encouraged to visit for inspiration.

Schools which are doing really badly will probably demand attention because of complaints from parents and expressions of concern from governors. The most difficult situation is the school which satisfies parents and governors because it is doing what they recall from their own schooldays, but which in effect is failing its most able pupils by the limited nature of its teaching. Here an advisory team needs to work steadily, first to persuade the staff that changes need to be made and then to support them in making them.

The inspection programme will make advisory teams aware of many situations in establishments which need attention. The difficult task will be following this up in such a way that real improvement can be effected. Advisory teachers may play an important part here.

Reporting

The way advisers report their visits will depend very much on the use to which the team wishes to put their reports. If the visits are to be part of an assessment programme, then they will need to be reported in some detail and in a particular format so that material can be collated. In this situation it is particularly important that the establishment is made aware of the adviser's findings, especially if the record is to be put on computer.

An advisory team may also wish to use visit records to note the nature of each visit and the people seen. This might be regarded as part of the team's own accountability. It also provides useful material for analysis, showing the extent to which different establishments have been visited and the types of visits made. It is also a safeguard against some establishments being missed out altogether. The possible content of visit records was referred to in chapter 2. Records of this kind are unlikely to be used for analysis unless they are on computer.

Sensitivities

Any visitor to a school or college, however welcome, interrupts the work of the establishment. An adviser must be sensitive to what might disrupt and do as little as possible to disturb the way the establishment is working. This is partly a matter of knowing in advance what is happening and is to some extent an argument for making contact in advance. If, for example, an adviser comes hoping to see mathematics and finds very few mathematics lessons on the timetable for that day, this is at least partly a matter of inadequate preparation. Advisers also need to be sensitive to the ways in which different establishments make arrangements for lunch and coffee and to fit in with these.

In particular one needs to limit the use of the telephone. Very often an adviser is pursued by a string of telephone calls and then uses the school or college phone for return calls, some of which may be inevitable. Phone calls interrupt discussion and observation and this is not entirely fair to the teachers involved or to the school or college office. This needs to be remembered, not only by clerical staff within the education office, but also by administrators and more senior members of the advisory service.

Advisers also need to guard against being used by headteachers and others. Sometimes a teacher or a head will make a comment to an adviser implying 'You agree with me, don't you?' In this context it is important not to be drawn. It is probably best to make some noncommittal answer which implies a neutral stance.

The context of visits

An adviser may visit an establishment because he or she chooses to do so, because the establishment has asked for a visit or because the visit is scheduled to be done. Each of these situations provides a different context for what happens. It is easier to work when the establishment has asked for help than in the other two contexts.

Advisory work involves the delicate task of intervening in the life of an organisation. A school or college exists in a community and a neighbourhood culture and in this context develops a culture of its own. Head and teachers will have their own philosophy, their own frames of reference and methods of working, and the adviser or advisory teacher has to take all these into account in visiting. Sensitivity to what is happening is an essential advisory skill, one which it is very difficult to train. It is most likely to be developed from visiting with other, more experienced advisers, who may see and point out what a less experienced person may miss.

Part of the process of being sensitive to the culture of a school involves finding out the philosophy of the head and staff and their feelings about the developments the adviser would like to see. Early visits should involve much sympathetic listening and some questioning, including the question 'How do you feel about that?' In the process of these discussions, possible growth points will begin to emerge. Teachers will speak of the problems they see and of the things which excite them, which can be starting points for development.

Motivation

In the process of discussion, the adviser needs to sum up what might motivate a particular group of teachers. The following are possible motivators:

Pupil development and learning This is a major motivation for most teachers and is probably the major satisfaction of teaching as a profession. Teachers are likely to respond to ideas which will improve pupil learning. Advisory teachers in particular may find this form of motivation useful. Demonstrating that pupils learn better working in one way rather than another is likely to convince teachers.

Enthusiasm for subject matter This is also a major area of motivation, not only in the secondary school and further education college but also for teachers of quite young children, who may have particular strengths or interests. Such enthusiasm may be a valuable starting point for development.

Recognition, interest, praise, encouragement Very few human beings fail to respond to these and this is valuable in thinking how to motivate teachers. There is in a classroom almost always something which one can genuinely praise and a teacher is far more likely to listen to an adviser who seems approving than one who seems critical. This is not to suggest that advisers should be approving of work and practices which give them cause for concern, but to stress that, until and unless a good relationship is made with a teacher, help and advice are likely to fall on deaf ears. Advisory teachers may well score here because usually they spend much longer with a teacher than the adviser and this interest and the chance to discuss work with another teacher may in itself be motivating.

A chance to contribute and to shine Most people are motivated by the opportunity to show what they can do. Inviting a teacher to contribute to a local meeting or course may be motivating for that teacher as well as useful for the course and it is sometimes possible to ask a teacher to undertake something which may help his or her development.

A chance to take responsibility An adviser may ask a teacher to undertake certain responsibilities for a meeting or course or recommend to a headteacher that someone on the staff be given further responsibility. Either will be valuable in developing management skills, and general advisers may be able to do much to see that the next generation of senior staff are developing the skills they will need.

A challenge to professional skill Most people are motivated by challenges and a teacher asked to try out new materials or practices to help the advisory staff to assess them will usually find this stimulating. Headteachers may also be encouraged to give their staffs the stimulus of new groups to teach or new ideas to try out.

The inspiration of others An adviser ought to be an inspiration to teachers, but the ability to inspire is not something which can easily be learned. Generally speaking, enthusiasm is catching and an adviser who is enthusiastic about some aspect of education is likely to enthuse teachers. However, too much enthusiasm can turn people away, particularly if it is not sufficiently linked to practical applications. It is also possible to be so enthusiastic about particular practices, that others, equally good, are ignored. Enthusiasm in advisory teachers is particularly valuable because other teachers know that they have recently worked in the classroom and have the ability to develop work stemming from their enthusiasm.

Advisers also need to look out for teachers who are good at inspiring others and see that this skill is put to good use, both in their own establishments and elsewhere.

Career prospects Advisers are in a strong position to motivate teachers through their career prospects because of the influence they have on appointments. Although this influence is now less than it was, there are still many ways in which the adviser's view is important and teachers are aware of this.

Advisers need to be very careful that, in using this influence, they are not persuading people to act contrary to their own beliefs and style or leading people to expect promotion undeservedly.

Handy (1976) refers to exchange theory. This is the idea that people are continually bargaining with each other. One person gives another something in return for desired behaviour. This may be an obvious reward like promotion in return for good service, but exchange also operates less obviously by offering approval, support, friendship, status, inclusion in a group and so on. A teacher asked by an adviser to explore a new way of working is, in effect, saying to him or herself 'What's in it for me?' It may be helpful in thinking about work with individual teachers to consider this question.

Another aspect of the context in which advisers and advisory teachers work is the view teachers hold of the advisory service. The views held in any particular establishment are initially part of the background which has to be taken into account. They will be the outcome of the teachers' previous experience of advisers, so that a general adviser starting with a school which is new to him or her will inherit the views which have been developed by previous advisers. If the previous adviser was effective, the school will have high expectations of their new adviser.

Winkley, (1985) indicated that while 83 per cent of the teachers in his sample supported the idea of a high-powered consultancy service 80 per cent felt that their own advisory service did not offer this. Seventy-two per cent of the sample approved the idea that schools should be assessed by an external agency but many felt that general advisers did not have the skills and experience to be able to assess their type of school in depth. This study also found that 56 per cent of the sample felt that advisers were not important in keeping abreast of new ideas and 83 per cent felt that on the whole the existence of LEA advisers was more of a constraint than a stimulus in improving their performance.

These are depressing findings for advisers and it must be added that the teachers in the sample were very much aware of the extent to which the advisory service was under pressure of time. They are, nevertheless, important statements to remember in visiting schools, since every adviser is contributing to the views of the service held by teachers.

Figure 7 may be helpful to the individual in assessing his or her work, both as a self-evaluation document and also as a method of enquiring about the views of teachers.

The individual and the organisation

The adviser's task relates to the development of both the individual and the establishment. It must be remembered that any advice given to individuals affects the development of the establishment. This will be particularly true of advice given to heads and senior staff.

It is also important that all advisers are concerned with whole institution development, discussing with the head where the growth points and weak points are and supporting the senior staff in working to develop growth and eliminate weakness. It is easy, particularly for a keen specialist adviser, to try to persuade the head to give more resources to a particular area of work or subject without reference to the total picture. It is not enough for an adviser to know the mathematics department really well if this is his or her specialism. It must be seen, as the head sees it, as one department among many contending for resources.

The general adviser will also be concerned with monitoring the progress of the school development plan and looking with the head at ways in which it needs to change in the light of development completed. There is a similar

Mark the appropriate box in answer to questions A and B below. Put a tick for A and a cross for B

A How do you see yourself as an advisor? B How do you think teachers see you?	+	+	av	–	– –
General educational knowledge					
Knowledge in specialist area					
Knowledge of school management					
Availability					
Approachability					
General helpfulness to schools and teachers					
Skill in observing and assessing work in schools					
Skill in counselling teachers					
Skill in counselling headteachers					
In-service skills – planning and organising					
In-service skills – knowledge of different strategies					
In-service skills – presentation					
In-service skills – leading discussion					
Skill in persuading and negotiating					

Figure 7   Adviser evaluation

need to look at development plans within departments in a secondary school or within years in a primary school. A number of authorities make an explicit statement that advisers are expected to be involved in the drawing up of the development plan and arrangements for its implementation.

Headteachers will also need advice and help in planning the budget. LEAs vary in how they are providing support for heads in this situation. In some there are teams which include officers who have a special responsibility for helping heads with matters of budget. In others this is something which advisers have to become expert at if they are to be in a position to help heads. Even where there is officer advice available, the effect of the budget on the curriculum and work of the school must be the concern of the advisory/inspectorate service.

Strategies for supporting teachers

There are many ways in which advisers can help and support teachers, but all of them require careful judgement about the point of intervention and what can profitably be said to a teacher at any particular time.

General points

1 Any visit to a classroom is an intrusion and is likely to change the atmosphere in some way. An adviser can never know how a teacher works when he or she is not there or whether the work seen on one occasion is typical of the teacher's work in general. This is why it is important to get to know teachers and see their work on a number of different occasions if judgements are to be valid.

2 However kind and approachable an adviser may be, there is still an element of threat for the teacher in having an observer in the classroom, particularly someone from outside the school who may have influence on the teacher's career.

   There is also the feeling, current in the teaching profession, that inspection makes teaching a less professional activity. Winkley (1985) makes the point that an adviser may see himself as either the responsive consultant or the father figure handing down knowledge. While advisers may be expected to have knowledge to hand down, all the evidence suggests that the responsive consultant is more likely to get results in terms of teachers developing and thinking for themselves than the father or mother figure who may make other people dependent. It would therefore seem sensible, wherever possible, to treat advisory work as working with teachers rather than doing something to them.

3 Work must first be judged in terms of whether the teacher is achieving what he or she set out to do. This may not be what the adviser hoped to see, but is the starting point. Other goals can be part of later discussion.

4 It is wise to start any discussion with a teacher with positive comment about what is good in the work seen. It is rare to find nothing which can be commented on in a positive way. This helps to dispel the fears of the teacher that he or she is being found wanting. It is then often helpful to introduce as growth points, issues which need attention, a more positive approach which is much more acceptable to the teacher and therefore more likely to be effective.

5 It is also a good idea, before giving the observer's view, to ask the teacher for his or her opinion of the lesson seen. If the teacher has identified problems similar to those observed by the adviser, it becomes easier for teacher and adviser to work together to tackle them.

Some teachers become defensive when asked this question, particularly those who are not doing very well. Such a teacher may say that the lesson went well, when the adviser feels that it went badly. This is particularly likely to happen where the teacher is in good control of the class but not teaching them effectively. In this situation it may be a good idea to go on to ask about what the most able or the least able children got out of the lesson and try to lead the teacher to see that there are problems to be solved. Another possibility may be to suggest that the teacher is given time to observe similar work elsewhere, perhaps in another establishment, in the hope that he or she will recognise the need for help. In the end it may be necessary to spell the problems out clearly before going on to make suggestions.

6 When helping a teacher or headteacher on a longer-term basis it is best to start with what the teacher or headteacher sees as the problems. It may take time to get away from problems about which little can be done, such as salary and resources, to problems on which teacher and adviser can work for improvement; but a teacher is more likely to accept help and support to solve problems which he or she accepts exist than those which the adviser sees and the teacher does not.

7 An adviser would be wise to offer a teacher definite suggestions for action. This enables the teacher to make use of the adviser's advice immediately and the adviser can see on a subsequent visit whether the suggestions were useful.

8 It is important to take into account a teacher's natural style and what a teacher feels about a situation. To be asked to take a large step into more modern methods is unlikely to help a teacher whose approach is very dated. Even if he or she agrees to attempt the change such a teacher is likely to feel deskilled and to lack commitment to an alien way of working. Change needs to be gradual in such a situation to ensure that the best of the past approach is maintained as more modern methods are introduced.

9 We are all aware that children do not learn simply by being told and that it is the learning process which engenders thinking. The same applies to adults. Successful advisory work involves helping teachers to think their way through what they do. In some respects the pressures on teachers make it difficult to find the time for thinking, but the changes being demanded of establishments themselves offer many developmental possibilities.

10 Teachers should not feel obliged to accept unthinkingly suggestions made by advisers. The way a suggestion is made should leave the teacher free to use it in the way he or she thinks best. The ideal situation is where

more than one suggestion can be discussed and the teacher is then in a position to choose the route to take.

There will be situations, such as that of the teacher who is failing, where an adviser has to insist that something is done. Even in this situation, however, the teacher needs to have freedom to move within the ideas suggested if he or she is to use them intelligently.

11 Teachers learn by seeing other teachers at work. Arrangements for staff to see each other at work or visits to another school are often fruitful forms of in-service training, particularly if they are directed to looking at particular issues, perhaps with a brief to report findings to other members of staff.

12 An adviser needs to be prepared to give time to teachers where this is possible. It may be necessary to find out a good deal about how a teacher thinks and works in order to give valid advice and this cannot be hurried.

13 Advice to an individual teacher may be useless if the institution makes it difficult for that teacher to follow the advice. It may be necessary to talk to the head of department or the head about what is involved in the suggestions made and what will be required of them if the teacher is to be able to use the advice given.

Advisory teachers may use many of these strategies, but in addition they may work alongside a teacher to plan a lesson or series of lessons and then assist in carrying out the plans. This is not easy because it requires sensitivity to the teacher's style and finding an acceptable way of working. The teacher concerned needs to have the opportunity to feed his or her own ideas into the planning. Initially the advisory teacher may ideas forward but there should be a gradual move towards those of the teacher. It is also helpful if the advisory teacher can offer a range of different ways of tackling something so that the teacher does not feel obliged to choose whatever the advisory teacher says but can have some flexibility to find the way of working which best suits him or her.

Part of the planning should make clear what the role of each member of the team is to be. It may be that initially the advisory teacher takes the lead but then gradually hands over to the teacher. It is important that pupils are not confused about who is in charge.

As a teacher gradually comes to know an adviser or advisory teacher the pattern changes. If a climate of trust has been built up and the help offered is valued by teachers, they will be prepared to raise their problems and be frank about their difficulties. This takes time and is unlikely to happen if the adviser is not able to get into the school frequently enough. This is why it may be best to concentrate on a group of schools at one time and get to know them really well. If the teachers in these schools build up confidence in the advisory service they will readily turn to advisers for help.

Winkley (1985) suggests that there are four main areas in which a teacher may need the help of an adviser: lack of knowledge, confidence, skill or objectivity. Most teachers will be receptive to new knowledge coming from someone they trust. A teacher may also welcome the boost to confidence that an adviser can give by encouraging the work being done. A teacher may find it much more difficult to accept that he or she lacks skill or objectivity and the adviser needs to tread carefully when these are the areas needing improvement.

Strategies for helping teachers in the classroom

1 An adviser may reflect for the teacher what appears to have happened during a lesson. This will involve taking notes throughout the lesson and going through them in detail with the teacher. They should include the good points as well as those which need attention.

2 An adviser may identify specific points which need attention. For example, a newly qualified teacher may need to work at such tasks as getting attention in order to talk to the whole class or getting pupils to settle down to work as soon as they come into the classroom. This is one of the few situations where demonstration by the adviser may be helpful.

   With a more experienced teacher, questioning or group work or any specific aspect of the teacher's work might be selected as an area for development.

3 In working with teachers it may be helpful in discussing ways forward to ask the teacher to consider the possible results of any proposed course of action. Giving some time to analysing the implications of change may help to avoid pitfalls and provides adviser and teacher with the opportunity to work together on the problem.

4 Specific problems may be identified for mutual consideration. A teacher may have problems because of the unsuitability of the accommodation, or a problem of organisation of material so that it is easily available to pupils.

5 Specialist advisers in particular may be valued by teachers for their wider knowledge of the subject and for their advice on materials and methods.

6 An adviser may ask an advisory teacher to team-teach with a teacher or teachers, the advisory teacher leading the team in a particular piece of work.

7 Coaching is a method of helping people to develop new skills which is not very often used in schools. It may be possible to identify a particular skill or skills which a teacher wishes to develop and work with him or her, observing these particularly and helping the teacher by reflecting on how the skills are developing and what might be the next step. An advisory teacher is in a particularly good position to use this way of working and may be able to spend more time with the teacher than is possible for an adviser.

8 An adviser may ask a teacher to try out ideas, methods or materials which have wider implications. This may contribute to the teacher's development but also be useful from the adviser's point of view in finding out

how successful the ideas, methods or materials are and how difficult teachers are likely to find them to use.

9 This same kind of development can be used with a group of teachers and be even more stimulating because the members of the group can compare notes. Working with a group is generally a good way of starting an innovation.

10 Group work can also be used for problem-solving. An adviser can work with a group of teachers to consider how a particular problem which they are all experiencing may be tackled or an individual member can raise a problem for the group to discuss.

11 A major way in which advisers influence teachers is through in-service training. The actual participation of advisers in INSET is unfortunately diminishing but remains an important role for advisory teachers. However, advisers will be very much involved in setting up the programme of in-service training and also in promoting school-based training. The latter is an important area for which an adviser has general responsibility and may be the one area in which he or she should make a personal contribution. Advisers may also be involved in supporting management development within schools.

In-service education is dealt with more fully in chapter 7, but it should be stressed here that to be effective it must relate to what is happening in the school. Following up an in-service course is, if anything, more important than the course itself.

Working with headteachers

In today's climate, headteachers are more than ever in need of a professional colleague who knows the school with whom they can discuss plans and problems. In most establishments the senior management team and the deputy or deputies or the chairman of governors will provide support for the head. There will, however, be occasions when the views of someone outside the school will be helpful and where a good adviser will be of considerable value.

To be of value to headteachers, a general adviser must know a considerable amount about their work and must be able to see the establishment from their point of view. Most heads would prefer that those advising them had been heads themselves and were able to speak from experience of actually having done the job. This certainly makes for credibility, but experience without the skills of advisory work is of limited value. An adviser coming into the service has much to learn and it is a mistake to think that experience is of itself sufficient to ensure success. There are many advisers who have not had the experience of headship but have spent time and effort learning what is involved in running an institution or department, and who are able to bring to discussion with a head not only appropriate skills but the vicarious experience of many establishments.

Specialist advisers will have a different contribution to make to the thinking of headteachers. Heads will want up-to-date advice on the various specialist areas of the curriculum. In the main this will come from heads of department in secondary schools and coordinators in primary schools, but there will be occasions when it will be helpful to have these views confirmed from outside. It will also be helpful to have the views of the specialist in appointing heads of department or coordinators.

When an adviser first comes into the work from a teaching post, he or she naturally identifies with the point of view of the teachers rather than that of the head. A new adviser needs to consider the running of an establishment from the head's point of view and work with more experienced colleagues, looking at the way they relate to headteachers.

Just as it is important to discover what a teacher is trying to do and to consider his or her style, so direction and style need to be considered in advising heads. Any advice offered must match the person to whom it is offered. It is therefore important to get to know a head's thinking if one is to be of any assistance.

Methods of helping headteachers

1 An adviser should have a particular contribution to make as a professional able to evaluate what is happening in a particular establishment. It is helpful to a head if someone with professional knowledge and skill in observation can reflect an impression of the establishment from the outside and help to analyse its needs.

2 Heads very often need a sounding board for ideas, some of which might create problems if discussed initially with staff. An adviser should be able to help them to think ideas and possibilities through and consider their implications. He or she can be for the head someone with whom there can be a confidential conversation.

3 In a similar way it is helpful to a head to be able to discuss problems with someone from outside who may be able to bring a fresh mind to them as well as experience of problems in a number of different establishments.

4 A head may need to discuss the development plan with someone outside the establishment. He or she may also have a personal development plan which could not be discussed within the establishment but which could profitably be discussed with an adviser.

5 An adviser may act as the head's conscience, reminding him or her of the need to keep the development plan in mind and to make and pursue an action plan.

6 An adviser should be able to help a head at various stages with long-term planning. This will be mainly a matter of bringing experience of other

establishments to bear on the plans proposed and advising on their implications.

7 A head may need the advice and support of an adviser in working with the governors, who may not understand the professional point of view of the head but may be more prepared to accept it when it is reinforced by the views of a second professional.

8 A head will need to draw on the skills of the adviser in taking action over a teacher who is failing.

9 Heads and governors will need advice in making appointments.

10 Heads and governors will need expert advice in planning new or redesigned buildings. Some of this will come from the staff of the school and some from officers of the LEA or architects; but the wider experience of specialist advisers will be valuable.

Buying in advice

There are already authorities where the advisory service is simply an inspectorate and advice is bought in. This is a situation likely to increase in future and is a very different context from that in which advisory work has been done in the past. It brings with it the problem that some schools will not recognise their own needs and some initiatives which would be of value may not get off the ground.

In the first place the service has to sell itself. This means setting out clearly what it has to offer and making it available in an attractive form to all those likely to wish to use the service. Some aspects of this process have already been discussed in chapter 4. It has to be nearer consultancy than advisory work as we have known it in the past, for it will be much more a matter of doing what the client wants than what the adviser thinks should be done.

Margerison (1978), writing in the context of industrial consultancy, suggests that one must first decide between problem-centred and solution-centred responses. He puts forward four different ways of tackling a consultancy task:

1 *Consult:* a problem-centred approach in which consultant and client have developed sufficient mutual trust to explore a problem together. The consultant asks questions and aims to 'enable the client to distinguish symptoms from causes and to consider who should be involved in developing the solution to the problem'.

2 *Reflect:* also a problem-centred approach but differing from the situation described above in that those concerned have a strong emotional involvement with the problem and are suspicious of an outsider. In this context the consultant reduces suspicion by acting as a mirror and reflecting back the feelings that the client seems to be

expressing. The consultant allows the client to control the conversation but leads him or her to think the problem through.

3 *Direct:* a solution-centred approach which is appropriate when the 'adviser has a clear understanding of the problem, knowledge and skill that can resolve the issues and an acceptance from those involved which will allow him to proceed'. Margerison feels that this is rarely the most appropriate way of working.

4 *Prescribe:* in which a consultant recommends a definite course of action. Margerison feels that this is only likely to succeed if the client feels that the course of action is relevant to the problem and possible to implement. It is best used when the client asks for a solution or when one emerges from brainstorming. The danger about this approach is that solutions are often offered before the problem has been adequately diagnosed.

Margerison goes on to look at the tasks of the consultant.

1 *Help the client to come forward.* People with problems often go round in circles trying to find a way out. The consultant's task is to help the client to find a way out of this dilemma by asking for a description of the situation as seen at present, then to discuss the way the client feels about the situation and so gradually build on what the client says, to the point where the way forward can be envisaged.

2 *Work on the client's territory.* This involves 'encouraging the client to explain the important factors which he sees as influencing behaviour within his territory which relate to his problem'. The adviser needs to give time to this and gradually lead to the point where the client can see what to do next.

3 *Work with the client you have with you.* Margerison suggests that the consultant should discourage detached discussion about other people and start with what the client has done and wants to do about the problem. He suggests that it is useful at this stage to use diagrams to represent the problem.

4 *Develop a three phase problem-solution-action (PSA) pattern.* This involves diagnosing the nature of the problem in some detail, exploring a range of possible solutions and then planning action.

Dealing with failing teachers

In most schools there will be, from time to time, teachers who fail in some way. This was referred to in chapter 3. They may perhaps be performing inadequately as teachers or in senior posts. There may also be heads who fail and this poses a much more serious problem.

LMS makes it likely that heads and governing bodies will be impatient to be rid of people who are not doing a reasonable job and there will be pressure on advisers to help in the process. An adviser may have to ensure that a teacher who is failing gets a fair chance of improving before any action is taken.

The LEA and particularly the advisory team need a clear policy on the way that failing teachers should be dealt with. It should ensure that everyone concerned is treated fairly. It should also ensure that any case taken to a tribunal can be sustained by the advisory/inspectorate service even though it will be the governors who have the responsibility for the dismissal of teachers.

A policy for dealing with failing teachers should include:

1 *The evidence on which a teacher should be regarded as at risk.* It is likely that the head will raise the problem with the adviser and there should be some agreement about the extent to which the teacher's work should be monitored before any action is taken. Such a teacher should normally be seen more than once in different situations before being regarded as at risk, although the present disposition of responsibilities may mean that the adviser is called in at a late stage when warnings have already been given.

2 *The point at which the head should be encouraged to give an informal warning.* This is the first step in disciplinary action and the head or governing body may well have taken it already.

3 *The period during which the teacher's work should be monitored and support given.* This will probably be decided by the governing body, but an adviser may be able to influence it.

4 *The kind of support programme which should be mounted for the teacher during this period.* Ideally, this should comprise an action plan agreed with the head and the teacher, and a programme of recorded observations of performance by senior members of the staff and by at least two members of the advisory service.

5 *The point at which the governors should be encouraged to give a formal warning* if there is no improvement and the period given for further improvement.

6 *The reporting needed* from advisory staff and school.

Advisers may need to inform governors that it is necessary to go through some process of this kind if they are not to run up against difficulties should the teacher go to an industrial tribunal.

Conclusion

Offering advice is a very delicate and sensitive task. Good advisory work tends not to be very visible and is perhaps most successful when people think they did it all themselves. On the other hand there are many examples of situations where whole authorities have been influenced by the work of an adviser. The role is changing with the Education Reform Act, but it is still about helping teachers to develop their work so that the experience of the pupil in the classroom is as good as it can be made.

Chapter 7

In-service education

Traditionally LEA advisers and inspectors have played a large part in in-service work. Stillman and Grant (1989) cite INSET as the only activity common to all members of the advisory service. Winkley (1985) found that it was more usual for advisers to organise and coordinate courses than run them and he found that teachers criticised much in-service work as 'handing out packages'. Advisers in his study, for their part, commented that teachers expected packages and regarded only the immediate and relevant as useful. He was also critical of the failure of advisers and inspectors to evaluate courses, a criticism which is far less valid now.

The changes in the work of the advisory/inspectorate service resulting from recent legislation are resulting in a rather different role in the in-service field. Many advisers and particularly inspectors will now have little time actually to take part in courses and workshops, but should continue to play an important part in the planning and management of in-service work and be able to advise schools and colleges on their staff development programmes. Many are also involved in the management training of headteachers. The shift towards inspection has also created a demand for in-service training to follow up an inspection. Attitudes of teachers towards this will differ according to whether the needs have been defined by external inspection or as a consequence of self-evaluation. Some advisory teachers, on the other hand, may well have an enhanced role, since they may undertake much of the work which advisers and inspectors no longer have time to do.

Patterns of in-service work have also changed. The way in which money has been made available nationally and the information required has encouraged LEAs to think carefully about their own priorities as well as national priorities. Money is now also allocated to schools and colleges to spend on staff development in whatever way seems best to them. The major changes brought about by the National Curriculum and assessment are also dictating the kind of programme on offer. All these changes result in a very different local programme from the one available to teachers ten years ago.

The report of the School Management Task Force (DES 1990) identifies six management task areas which were causing concern:

1 Local management of schools.
2 National curriculum and assessment.
3 Appraisal and staff development.
4 Working with governors.
5 Strategic planning.
6 Monitoring and evaluation.

This chapter looks at the planning and management role of the advisory/inspectorate team, the advice needed by schools and colleges and also at the tasks facing advisory teachers.

Arrangements for managing INSET

Every LEA needs to decide its aims for in-service education and then develop a policy. This may be developed by officers working with advisers, inspectors and advisory teachers, members and teachers or by any combination of these groups. It would seem to be essential to include advisers and inspectors, however, because of their close knowledge of what is happening in different establishments, the needs of teachers and their experience of INSET activities.

The statement of policy

The statement of policy might be seen as the starting point for the process of deciding the planning of needs assessment and the designing, implementing and evaluating of the programme of INSET. This might include statements about the following:

1 *The overall attitude of the LEA towards professional development.* The policy might well start with a statement of the purpose of staff development, an affirmation of the positive need for it and the commitment of the LEA to this. It might go on to include a statement about the various groups which the programme is intended to cover. Teachers will be the major group involved, but the programme needs to include others in the service, such as officers, advisers, inspectors, advisory teachers, teachers' centre wardens, psychologists, youth and careers officers and so on. This list may vary from LEA to LEA and will be affected by the way grants from central government are directed.
2 *The balance between provision to support national and local priorities and provision for the career development of individuals.*
3 *The way in which all these groups will be consulted about INSET.* The most usual way of consulting is to form an advisory group which is concerned with the broad issues of the in-service programme. Consultation must also include other providers in the area.
4 *The responsibilities of central office staff concerned with INSET.* Most

LEAs are now appointing a senior officer to coordinate in-service work, who may or may not be part of the advisory team. He or she will need to work closely with advisers and inspectors and in some cases two parallel posts have been created, one with administrative responsibility and one with responsibility for coordinating the advice from the advisory service. The officers in these senior posts are normally backed up by junior staff. Everyone involved in INSET needs to be aware of these posts and the responsibilities of the people concerned.

5 *The way in which needs will be identified.* The authority has to identify needs at individual, group, school and college and LEA levels, taking into account local and national priorities. The policy needs to state how this will be done. It also needs to state principles about the budget expenditure devolved to schools and that managed centrally and how decisions about this and other budget issues will be made.

6 *The organisation expected at school and college level* and the way in which this links with central provision. Schools and colleges may be expected to appoint an INSET coordinator and possibly an INSET advisory group who will be the focus of communication with the authority.

7 *The way in which the programme will be built up.* This statement should identify who is responsible for making decisions about what goes into the programme and the criteria by which decisions are made. Many LEAs have formed one or more small steering groups, usually consisting of representatives of all those who are covered by the programme, to deal with its actual implementation. These groups will need to meet fairly frequently. The programme planned must be linked to the resources available and must take account of the resources needed not only for the LEA programme, but also for sending people on other courses, including some long courses.

8 *The way in which participants for in-service courses will be selected.* This should include the selection methods for those who apply for courses outside the authority as well as for LEA courses.

9 *Responsibilities for the various aspects of running courses.* There should be a clear statement about the roles of advisers, inspectors, administrative officers, advisory teachers, teachers' centre wardens and other support staff, including a statement about responsibility for support during the course and follow-up afterwards. There should also be a statement about the role expected of the school or college when teachers are attending an external course.

10 *Responsibility for monitoring and evaluating courses,* both formatively and summatively. This should be clear from the beginning in planning any course, with any evaluator involved as early as possible and resource provision made for the evaluation process. Thought should also be given to ways of using what is learned from evaluation in planning future courses.

11 The follow-up activity expected in relation to any course. In planning courses, at least as much time should be allowed for follow-up as for the course itself.

The in-service coordinator

The coordinator of INSET activities for the LEA has an important role. The job description for this post might include:

1 Chairing the INSET advisory and steering committees.
2 Organising and coordinating work on the assessment of needs and presenting the findings to the INSET committees.
3 Collecting and collating proposals for courses and presenting these to the appropriate steering committee.
4 Ensuring that appropriate advisers are involved in proposals relevant to them.
5 Advising the steering committee on priorities and resources.
6 Ensuring that the programme agreed can be resourced.
7 Communicating decisions about the programme to all those concerned.
8 Ensuring that each course provider plans adequately and within the resources allocated.
9 Informing teachers about their selection or non-selection for courses and giving information about reasons for non-selection where appropriate.
10 Advising schools and colleges on their staff development programmes.
11 Communicating information to all concerned about the LEA's in-service provision.
12 Keeping the CEO and the advisory service informed about developments in in-service education.
13 Ensuring that there is adequate evaluation of each course and that this is used in planning future courses.
14 Collecting data and completing questionnaires for any agencies providing grants for in-service education.
15 Monitoring overall budget expenditure during the course of the year and ensuring virement of funds where appropriate.

The advisory committee brief

The advisory committee will also need a brief which makes clear the way in which work will be divided between this committee and the steering committees. The advisory committee might have a brief which includes:

1 Planning the needs assessment programme in broad terms.
2 Advising the authority on in-service needs, both directly and by commenting on the results of needs assessment.
3 Making broad decisions about overall priorities, taking into account national and local priorities and the resources available.

4 Deciding the overall criteria by which course participants will be selected.
5 Planning in broad terms for course evaluation.
6 Studying evaluation reports and making recommendations in the light of them.

The steering committee's brief

The steering committee is responsible for the day-to-day decisions needed for the implementation of the INSET programme:

1 Planning and agreeing the programme of needs assessment.
2 Assessing the outcomes of the needs assessment programme and its implications for the INSET programme.
3 Agreeing overall priorities.
4 Agreeing detailed priorities for the INSET programme in the light of the views expressed by the advisory committee, the outcome of the needs assessment, local and national priorities and the resources available.
5 Agreeing the overall programme.
6 Agreeing the detailed pattern of monitoring and evaluation.
7 Noting the comments of the advisory committee on the evaluation of the programme and seeing that the findings are applied to the following year's programme.

Needs assessment

Assessing needs in an area the size of even a small LEA is not easy because so many people are involved. It is made more difficult by the fact that, while there are some needs which individuals and groups recognise, there are other needs which individuals and groups do not know that they have. It is therefore important to obtain information about needs, not only from those for whom the INSET programme is being planned, but also from others who observe what is happening in institutions and may see needs which teachers themselves do not see. It is even more difficult to assess the unrecognised needs of groups within the service, such as advisers and inspectors.

Each group of people involved in the INSET programme should have the opportunity to comment on what they see as their needs. This means that every institution and service must be asked about them. It must be done in a way which makes collating the information easy. If the authority has computer links with its institutions this is comparatively simple, since the information can be entered directly into a database and the sorting and collating done by the computer. Where this is not the case, the questions about needs should be asked in such a way that entering the information into a database is straightforward and can be done by a clerical assistant. It probably means listing possibilities and asking institutions to select from these and add any further ideas. The problem about this is that of getting the information early enough to meet demands from the DES and to plan the local programme.

The advisory team will be an important source of information about the needs of teachers, particularly the needs of which teachers may not be aware themselves. A good many needs will be identified in the process of inspection and in looking at the progress of the National Curriculum. It is therefore important that every opportunity is given to advisers to feed into the information being collected and to comment on it. Advisory teachers will also have ideas, not only about their own needs but also about the needs of teachers, and they too should be consulted. Providers of in-service training within the area, such as higher education institutions, also need to be consulted.

Planning the programme

The report of the School Management Task Force (DES 1990) lists a number of tasks for local authorities:

- Provide a management development policy.
- Establish a team of officers and advisers with resources and expertise to implement the policy.
- Coordinate and deliver support to school management in the six management task areas arising from the Education Reform Act and considered to require immediate attention.
- Publish a comprehensive account of support services for schools.
- Provide a well-planned programme of easily accessible training opportunities.
- Develop succession planning policies.
- Promote external support from:
  • industry
  • higher education
  • professional associations
  • management centres and colleges
  • training companies
- Advise schools on the availability of external support.
- Provide integrated training and development opportunities for officers, heads, staff and governors.
- Work with headteachers to help them to identify their needs and then provide for them.
- Publish the LEA's use of funding and demonstrate how it secures an appropriate balance of funds devolved to schools and central support services.
- Collaborate with other LEAs to create new policies and approaches to

school management development by the establishment of voluntary regional consortia.

Oldroyd and Hall (1988) suggest that planning might start with a survey of existing provision and go on to consider:

- what activities to retain and in what form
- what gaps are to be filled and how
- how the programme can reflect LEA and school policies as well as identified needs
- what resources, including supply teachers, are required and available to implement the programme
- the balance between institutional, local and national policies
- the emphasis on innovation as opposed to existing practice
- the time required for negotiation with LEA and higher education providers of INSET
- the capacity of staff to cope with additional pressures arising from the proposals
- the impact on pupils of the absence of their teachers on INSET activities

The next task for the steering committee is to decide on priorities, both local and national, in the light of overall decisions by the advisory committee and the information coming from the needs assessment. The committee will need to decide the level of each priority in terms of the resources available. The sum to be allocated to individual establishments for their own in-service programme must be decided, as will the funding to be made available for the training of LEA groups such as advisers and inspectors, educational psychologists, librarians, peripatetic services, central Section 11 staff and so on.

In many LEAs, the practice is to allocate parts of the budget to individual advisers and small teams for them to plan a part of the programme. This usually requires a good deal of negotiating on the part of the in-service coordinator. In making this allocation, the needs of general advisers for programmes for the schools and colleges in their area should not be forgotten, although many of the topics they might choose are likely to be part of a central programme, for example, training for heads and deputies in management skills. Other parts of the budget will be allocated to teachers' centres which will have their own planning arrangements and to institutions of higher education to enable them to plan specific parts of the programme.

One of the difficulties facing those making the allocations is the conflict between leaving individuals and groups free to make decisions about their part of the budget and maintaining a programme which has overall coherence. This too calls for much negotiation by the coordinator.

In planning the overall programme, thought should be given to the different levels at which training may be needed. Some courses will be concerned with awareness and basic information; others may be at a more advanced level, providing continuation for those who are already aware and informed at a basic level. A third kind of course may be one for training trainers. Advisers will have little time for running courses themselves and may need to use and train practising teachers and advisory teachers as course tutors. Course tutors may also follow up courses by visiting the teachers concerned in their classrooms. Training for both activities will include:

1 Understanding of adult learning styles.
2 Planning courses and workshops.
3 Learning strategies, particularly those which involve active participation.
4 Skill in observing what is happening in classrooms.
5 Coaching skills.

Oldroyd and Hall (1988) argue that teachers and advisory teachers in these roles need to have someone with whom they can discuss their work and who will act as a supervisor for them. This is probably a role for an adviser. It may be that one member of an advisory team is made responsible for the training of trainers and their subsequent supervision so far as in-service work is concerned.

Thought also needs to be given to the advantages and disadvantages of different timings for courses. Some courses are more profitable when planned with time between sessions for tasks to be carried out.

The planning of in-service courses is likely to be partly a job for advisers and partly for advisory teachers, higher education providers and others. The adviser may well be responsible for stating the aims of a course, agreeing its outline with those concerned, setting the overall budget within the resources available and agreeing arrangements for follow-up and evaluation. Those running the course will then be responsible for the detailed planning, in consultation with the adviser. Detailed planning should include the following:

1 *State aims.* The statement of aims, purpose, intended outcomes and intended clients should be the starting point for planning any course. Prospective course members should know what the aims are.
2 *Decide how success will be evaluated.* Evaluation for every course needs to be built in from the beginning. Possible forms of evaluation are described later in this chapter.
3 *Collect information.* Anyone planning an in-service course needs to know the time available, the budget, the other resources available, the likely course membership, the expectations course members may have, the possible venues and the overall context of the course, for example whether it is one of a series, whether it is being put on for a very specific purpose with a particular clientele in mind and so on.

4 *Decide on the framework for the course.* A decision needs to be taken about the length of the course, the way in which the time will be broken up and the actual times of meetings. These decisions will depend on the budget available.

5 *Decide on events.* Once the framework has been decided, it is then necessary to consider how it can be broken up into a series of activities. This is equally important whether the course is a series of evening meetings or a two or three-day residential course or even a long course, meeting many times over a considerable period.

6 *State objectives.* Stating objectives for each part of a course is a useful discipline for someone planning a course. It provides a yardstick for planning and clarifies the task of the evaluator.

7 *Plan in detail.* Each section of the course needs to be planned in detail. This involves deciding on activities, speakers, group leaders, the time plan to be followed, possible groupings for different activities, the use of space available, the resources needed and any handouts.

8 *Calculate detailed costs.* Once the plan is worked out, it becomes possible to cost the course. This needs to take account of course advertising, travel, accommodation, food, materials, fees, supply cover, evaluation and follow-up. The adviser must check that the course will be within the budget available (Dean 1991a).

Course activities

A good speaker may be a useful starting point, but the greater part of a course should have some degree of member participation. It is valuable when course members can work on material from their own establishments in some form. The following may be useful:

Action learning Action learning (Revans 1980; Pedlar 1983) involves a group of people working together to study problems in their work environment. The group normally has a set adviser who acts as a facilitator.

Active listening Listening to the other person is a skill which is needed in many aspects of management. An activity which gives practice involves people working in pairs, with one as speaker and the other as listener. The speaker talks about some topic of interest for about three minutes, with the partner listening carefully. The pairs then consider whether the speaker felt that the listener was listening and what clues there were to suggest this.

Assertiveness training Assertiveness is described as the ability to express one's ideas and rights in a way which does not upset or diminish others. Training in assertiveness (Back and Back 1982) involves role play of situations and consideration of how to be assertive rather than either aggressive or failing to express one's view.

Brainstorming Brainstorming involves working with a small group to produce all the ideas its members can think of, no matter how unlikely. For this to work well there should be a feeling of pressure to produce. Ideas are listed on a flip-chart by the group leader. This is followed by a consideration of each idea in turn to identify all its positive points. Alternatively the group can work through the ideas, noting the pros and cons of each and any points of interest.

Broadcast material, audio and video tapes Radio and television produce a number of training programmes and there is an increasing number of tapes available for training purposes. Some of these include guidance notes for course tutors in how best to use them. Any tape or broadcast used in a course should be viewed in advance by the course tutor and it can be helpful to ask course members to observe specific points.

Buzz groups It is sometimes useful to follow a lecture by asking people to discuss its content in threes, where they sit. This often leads to a better questioning session.

Case studies Case study material can be taken from the experience of members or it can be specially prepared. It offers the opportunity for discussion about how best to deal with a situation which has a reality because it is taken from life. Material from the classrooms of members has the advantage that the person from whose classroom the study is taken can fill in background and may also gain from the discussion with colleagues.

Critical incident analysis Critical incidents are those which give rise to problems. By collecting examples of particular incidents and analysing how they occur, a group can often find ways in which the problem might have been avoided in the first place. For example, one group of teachers collected examples of the situations in which indiscipline occurred in their classrooms. They were then able to analyse the context in which such incidents occurred and consider how they might have been avoided.

Delphi Delphi is a technique for collecting information about how a group views various points and in particular the areas in which they think differently. It requires a series of statements issued to each person in the group, who then grades them according to his or her view of them. For example, material for a management course for headteachers might include statements like 'All headteachers should do a certain amount of teaching each week' or 'A headteacher is paid to take decisions rather than hand them to the staff'. If the grading is arranged in columns it is easy to add up the scores in each column for the whole group and then to discuss the issues on which members differ most widely.

Discussion leadership Training in discussion leadership involves working with one or more observers who record what happens in the group and look for the kind of leadership behaviour described in chapter 4. There are a number of ways of recording, but one useful pattern (figure 8) is to set out the seating plan of the group and draw lines between individuals as they communicate with each other. Each communication is then marked as a dash on the appropriate line. Communications to the whole group are recorded as dashes on the outside of the group plan. The number of contributions in each direction are counted and this gives a picture of the range and number of contributions of each member.

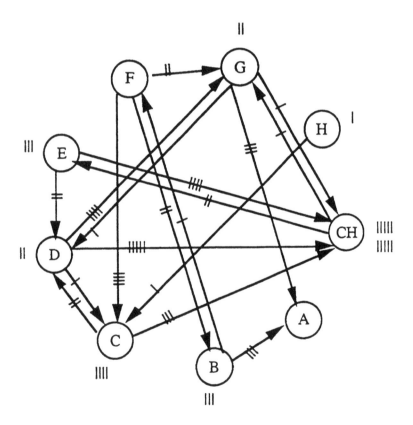

Figure 8   Recording the pattern of discussion

Group problem-solving Groups can work on the actual problems of group members or on a problem common to them all. A problem-solving group tends to work better where there is a group leader who ensures that the group keeps to the task. Problem-solving involves defining the problem clearly, brainstorming possible solutions and then selecting a solution and considering how it can be worked out and the implications it has for those concerned. The problems can be those which the members of the group are actually experiencing in their work and which have not yet been solved.

A useful technique in problem solving is force field analysis (Lewin 1951). This involves identifying the forces acting in favour of a particular solution and those acting against it. Each force is then considered, to see how the positive forces can be enhanced and the negative forces diminished.

Goldfish bowl activities This describes all those activities in which observers are used to see how a group performs a particular activity, such as that described under discussion leadership. It is particularly useful for observing a group conducting a meeting, whether this is a normal meeting at which observers are used or a simulated meeting.

Ideas collection One way of collecting ideas as part of problem-solving or any other activity in which ideas need to be generated is to select as many problems or tasks as there are group members, perhaps generating these by brainstorming. Each problem or task is then written at the top of a sheet of paper or an overhead projector transparency. These are then passed round the group and each person adds an idea. When enough ideas have been collected, each sheet can be projected or reviewed and discussed or individuals can work on the suggestions to produce collections of ideas which might be used. This technique is also useful for considering ways of implementing aims.

Information circuit Visitors may be invited to an in-service course because they have valuable experience to contribute on a particular topic. There may also be people within an in-service course who may have similar contributions to offer.

One way of making the most of this is to form as many groups as there are speakers and for each group to prepare questions which they would like to ask the speakers. The speakers spend a short specified time with each group and then move on to another group, so that over a period every group has the benefit of all the speakers. It is important in this activity to be strict about keeping to the time at which the speakers must move on to another group. The advantage of this technique is that the speakers are all contributing all the time but the preparation is done by the groups concerned.

Information exchange Course participants usually bring with them a good deal of experience which may be valuable to other course members. It is useful to ask members to bring information about a particular topic and then to provide time for very small groups to exchange information about the topic in question. This is a particularly useful device for starting a session, since people may all arrive at the same time and an activity such as this enables people to start work as soon as there are three or four people available.

In-tray activities In management training, it is often useful for small groups to consider a series of problems which might be in the in-tray of someone in a particular management role.

Making a presentation This activity has already been mentioned in chapter 4. It can be a useful part of a management course for all members to give a presentation about something of interest to the group and then for the group to consider the quality of the presentation itself.

Micro-teaching Micro-teaching involves taking part of a teaching task and using it with a small group of students in order to study a particular teaching technique. It is normally undertaken by one person while others observe. It would be useful for helping teachers to develop skills in areas like questioning and is of particular use with inexperienced teachers.

Nominal group technique This is a useful way of collecting opinions or evaluating. Each group member, individually or as a member of a small group, is asked to write down as many points as he or she can think of in relation to the topic in question. These are then listed on a flip-chart, usually by going round the group, adding points from each person in turn. Members then vote on an agreed number of points and this gives the overall view of the group.

Problem-solving interviews Interviewing techniques were also mentioned in chapter 4. They can be practised by working in pairs with an observer. One member of the pair identifies a genuine problem which he or she is encountering and the other member interviews to try to help towards its solution. It is important that the problem is real and that it has not yet been solved. This enables the interviewee to make a judgement about whether the interviewer was any real help. This is not a role play.

The observer looks for things like the way the interviewer listens and supports the other person, the extent of body language, what seems to be involved in helping people to solve problems and the extent to which the interviewee has been led towards his or her own solution rather than being given one.

About half an hour will be needed for the interview and the observer then leads a feedback discussion on which all three participants look for what makes a good problem-solving interview. This technique can be used for practising other interviews, such as that for appraisal (Poster and Poster 1991).

Quality circles A quality circle (Robson 1984) is a group convened to look at work problems. It should contain about four to six members and its task is to identify, analyse and solve problems. It is another name for the type of problem-solving group described earlier.

Self-development This involves helping people to see themselves from other points of view. For example, Johari's window is often used as a starting point for discussion and work. The aim is to enlarge what is known in quadrants 1 and 3 and to reduce what is known in quadrants 2 and 4. See Francis and Woodcock (1982).

	Known to self	Unknown to self
Known to others	1 Open	2 Blind
Unknown to others	3 Hidden	4 Closed

Figure 9   Johari's window

Team building Team-building activities are designed to help groups reflect upon the work of the teams they are in and to increase trust and openness. Almost any team task can be used for this purpose. An observer may help the team to analyse what happened. Woodcock (1979) suggests that the observer looks for points such as:

- what actions helped the group to accomplish the task?
- which actions hindered the group in completing the task?
- how did leadership emerge in the team?
- who participated most?
- who participated least?
- what feelings did members experience as the task progressed?
- what suggestions could be made to improve team performance?

Video recording Video recording can be used in two main ways. A tape can be produced and watched as a starting point for discussion. Video can also be used to record what is happening so that it can be watched and discussed by a group.

Following up a course

A course is of value only if something happens as a result. This means that the follow-up to any course is a very important part of it. This is not possible for national or regional courses, but is for local courses.

Follow-up should be planned at the same time as the course and adequate time allowed for it. It is better to run fewer courses and to ensure their effectiveness by adequate follow-up than to run many which do not have effect in classrooms.

Following up a course may involve the following activities:

1 *Observing in classrooms and helping teachers to use what they have learned.* A course tutor involved in a course which is concerned with classroom practice should aim to see all the course members at work in the classroom or should be in touch with someone who will undertake this activity. Some teachers will need help and many will need encouragement to try out new ways of working or new material, especially where only one teacher from an institution attends a course.

2 *Working alongside a teacher to introduce new material or ways of working.* Advisory teachers are generally used to working with teachers and are likely to find this a very effective way of following up course activity. It may also be possible to develop a corps of teachers who are expert in the work of a particular course, who can be released from their own establishments for a limited time to undertake this kind of follow-up with colleagues.

3 *Discussing the effect of the course with the headteacher or head of department.* When a teacher returns from a course, it is important that headteachers and heads of department are supportive of the teacher's attempts to implement what has been learned. Asking them about the effects of a course on a teacher will encourage them to look for results, if they are not doing so already and it may be helpful to discuss ways in which they are planning to support the teacher and, in due course, enable other teachers to make use of what one teacher has learned.

Evaluation

Since the advent of central funding for in-service activity, there has been an increased emphasis on evaluation. Circular 6/86 (DES 1986b) which gave details of the training grant scheme for 1987–88, placed a responsibility on the LEA to assess how the training had contributed to more 'effective and efficient delivery of the education services' and to assess how the training had contributed to the local 'objectives and policies'. The circular, Grant for Education Support and Training (DES 1990b), went a step further and required LEAs to collect data for specified performance indicators for each funded area of activity. LEAs therefore now have to show that they are evaluating in-service work in some detail and advisers and inspectors must play a part in this. The advisory/inspection service may provide advice on how evaluation should be carried out. They may undertake some evaluation and may also be needed to interpret evaluation.

Evaluation should be planned as an integral part of any in-service activity at the same time as planning for the activity itself. This often makes it possible to use parts of the activity itself as part of the evaluation process. For example, in the kind of problem-solving interviews described above, a question can be included in the discussion as to whether the interviewer was of any help in solving the problem.

Basic issues

Oldroyd and Hall (1988) believe that the following issues should be considered in relation to evaluation:

- the purpose and possible consequences of the evaluation
- the audience for the evaluation report
- the key questions
- the methods of collecting evidence
- the sources of the information
- the time available and the deadline

A further point to consider is that of who should undertake the evaluation.

Questions about courses

The following questions are common to most course evaluations:

1 How far has the course achieved its stated aims?
2 Were the techniques chosen by the course tutors the most effective to achieve the course aims?
3 How far has the course met the needs and expectations of the course participants?
4 What evidence is there that the course has affected practice?
5 What has been the cost of the course per participant?
6 Has the course kept within the budget allocated?
7 Could the same results have been achieved more cheaply?

Methods of collecting evidence

Evaluation involves sampling the evidence available. The evidence chosen and the size of the sample will depend upon the purpose of the evaluation and the resources available for undertaking it.

There are three basic ways of collecting evidence.

1 *Documentation.* Each course has documentation on the intentions of the planners, the course attendance and the resources available. This information may well be on computer and easily gathered.
2 *Observation.* Information can also be obtained from observing the course in action and from visiting the classrooms of the course participants during or after the course itself.
3 *Talking to people.* Evidence can be obtained by questioning course participants and tutors. Some information may also be gained by asking questions of the headteachers of the establishments from which the participants have come and possibly asking questions of students in the classes of teachers who have attended a particular course.

The following techniques may be useful:

Questionnaires These can be structured so that they simply require ticks in boxes or grading of different aspects of the course, or they can be much more open, asking questions which require more than a one-word answer. A useful form of questionnaire which is somewhere between the two gives sentences for the course participant to complete, for example, 'The best part of this course was . . .'

In designing questionnaires for evaluation, it is important to consider how they will be analysed. Structured questionnaires should, if at all possible, be designed for computer analysis. Open questionnaires are more difficult to analyse but often give more real information.

There is much to be said for allowing time during the course for the completion of questionnaires. If people take them away to complete some will not be returned. It may also be a good idea to circulate course members with another or the same questionnaire some time after the course when they have had the chance to try out the ideas considered.

Studying course documents A course evaluator needs copies of all the documentation of the course. This gives an overall picture of what was planned and some information about how it worked out. It may also be possible to get participants to write a report on parts of the course which the evaluator can use. Information about the finances is particularly important in assessing value for money.

Discussion A discussion at the end of the course can be useful, but if it is in the presence of the course tutor some people will not wish to voice adverse criticisms. It is generally better for an evaluator to conduct such a discussion without course tutors present.

Discussion is more likely to be valuable if it is carefully structured. Variations on the nominal group techniques described earlier can be useful. Another possibility is to take points raised by participants in an open questionnaire and use these as a starting point for discussion.

Interviewing An evaluator can arrange to interview individuals and small groups about their reactions to the course. This involves some thought about sampling, since different members of the course will have different views. A structured interview can be used, with everyone asked the same questions or there can be a more open pattern of interviewing following up any point which seems to be of interest. Both approaches are useful and probably the best results are obtained with a mixture of the two.

Observations Where a course has an evaluator who is present throughout the course or for some parts of it, observation of what is happening will be of considerable value. The observer can see how different people are reacting to what is offered and can look critically at the teaching techniques employed and their effects. The use of time can be measured and assessed and note can be taken of the extent to which the course members are participants compared with the time they are recipients.

Observation can also take place in the classrooms of teachers who are attending a course, both before and afterwards. If any judgement is to be made about the effect of the course, the evaluator will need some knowledge of how a particular teacher worked previously.

Evidence from pupils Pupils are the people most likely to be aware of any changes in the way a teacher works as a result of attending a course. Finding out their views need not be threatening to the teacher if the questions asked of them are carefully chosen. Their work should also offer some evidence.

Value for money

Current thinking involves assessing courses in the light of their value for money. This means collecting information about all the expenses of the course: fees and expenses of contributors, teachers' travel, the cost of supply cover if needed, the cost of the time of those who have prepared and run the course, accommodation, subsistence and any other expense. These then need to be translated into cost per course member which allows comparison between different ways of providing in-service education and looking at whether the same learning could have been achieved more cheaply.

Supporting in-service work in schools

In addition to playing a part in managing the LEA's in-service programme, advisers are likely to be asked to advise staff on the programmes they arrange for themselves. Every establishment should be encouraged to appoint a particular member of staff at a senior level to be responsible for in-service work and to involve the rest of the staff in the processes of needs assessment and programme planning, usually working with a small steering committee. Establishments also need to have a staff development policy and programme and to consider the development of all members of staff and not only those involved in teaching.

The report of the School Management Task Force (DES 1990a) suggests that schools should do the following:

- Prepare and publish a school management development policy incorporated within the school development plan which recognises that staff development is a major area of personal accountability for the head.
- Establish appropriate management structures to reflect new tasks and responsibilities.
- Provide adequate supervision and support for staff in their daily tasks.
- Establish integrated procedures for the review and appraisal of individual, team and institutional performance.
- Support individual teachers in reviewing experience throughout their career.
- Promote strategies for succession planning and career development providing:
  - preparation for and induction to new posts
  - new task, job or project opportunities

A staff development policy might include statements about the following:

1 Overall philosophy and attitudes.
2 The people whom the policy concerns (staff entitlement).
3 The possible professional development activities.
4 Responsibility for professional development.
5 The way needs will be assessed.
6 The part played by appraisal.
7 Provision for induction and probation.
8 Procedures for making applications for courses and giving feedback.
9 The provision for teachers to consult about possible courses and the support which will be available when a teacher returns from a course.
10 The way in which provision for individuals is built up.

11 The way in which the teacher's development and progress will be recorded.

12 The way the establishment will monitor and evaluate its programme.

It is very easy to think of staff development simply in terms of in-service work. In practice the most effective development comes from the day-to-day work in schools and colleges and all establishments need to be encouraged to look at how this can be used to develop staff. There are also opportunities like visiting other establishment and seeing other teachers at work which have considerable potential for development. This point is strongly made in the Task Force report. It is also worked out in some detail in *Developing managers* (Berkshire Education Department 1990a). This lists possible ways in which teachers might develop on the job, close to the job and off the job.

School-based development usually works best when there is a designated mentor who has responsibility for supporting, encouraging, advising, listening and counselling. In a secondary school this might be the head of department, but it could also be a task undertaken by other middle management teachers. In a primary school it could be undertaken by the head, deputy or other senior staff. The following activities may be useful in developing the work of teachers:

1 Acting as a voluntary deputy to a senior member of staff.
2 Action research in the school or college.
3 Coaching by a senior member of the staff.
4 Coaching a more junior member of staff.
5 Experimental work with children or young people.
6 Giving a talk to a group.
7 Job enrichment.
8 Job rotation.
9 Keeping a diary of what happens in the classroom and reflecting on it or discussing it with a colleague.
10 Observation and discussion with other teachers.
11 Personal reading and study.
12 Preparing a report.
13 Receiving support and encouragement from senior colleagues.
14 Reflecting on one's own performance.
15 Shadowing a student or becoming a student for a day.
16 Shadowing a senior colleague.
17 Taking on responsibility and involvement in decision-making.
18 Taking part in problem-solving activity.
19 Teaching a variety of groups.
20 Triangulation (observation by teacher, colleague and students).
21 Visiting other establishments.
22 Viewing a video tape of classroom performance.
23 Working with other teachers.

These approaches are discussed in detail in Dean (1991a).

Schools will also need some help with actually planning courses and the steps given earlier in this chapter will apply at school level as well as more widely.

Teacher appraisal

The appraisal of teachers and headteachers is now a requirement, and although there is a good deal of scope for the individual establishment to work out how best to do it, it is likely that advisers and inspectors will be expected to play a part in various ways.

Most authorities are in the process of arranging for the training of staff for appraisal and advisers will very often be involved in this in some way, initially perhaps as course members or perhaps as contributors. It is certainly important that advisers and inspectors are aware of what is involved in the appraisal process, because it is to them that the head is likely to turn for advice on the implementation of a programme of appraisal in the individual establishment.

Much that advisers and inspectors normally do as part of their work has an element of appraisal within it. They have experience of observing in classrooms which will enable them to advise teachers on how to do this as part of the appraisal programme. The suggestions given in chapter 5 for classroom observation in the context of inspection apply equally to the teacher who is observing a colleague at work in the classroom. Advisers and inspectors offer feedback to teachers and headteachers on their findings and this demands much the same skills as the feedback which an appraiser may be offering to the person being appraised. Advisers and inspectors are therefore in a strong position to offer advice to schools on the skills involved in appraisal.

Most courses and most teachers stress the need to make appraisal a positive activity, contributing to the development of the person concerned. Advisers and inspectors will need to monitor this to see if appraisal is really seen in this light and is contributing to professional development. There may be particular appraisers within an establishment who are posing problems and the adviser/inspector may need to help the school or college to deal with this, perhaps by discussion with the people concerned and perhaps by arranging further in-service training where necessary.

Advisers and inspectors are also likely to be invited to deal with appeals which have gone beyond the scope of the establishment to sort out. There will be teachers who are dissatisfied with what has happened who have sought satisfaction within the school or college and not achieved it.

The most important task that will involve advisers and inspectors in some way is the appraisal of headteachers. This may not mean that an adviser or inspector is directly involved in the actual process of headteacher appraisal, but it will certainly mean discussing a head's performance with whoever is acting as appraiser, since the adviser/inspector is the external professional person most likely to know the establishment and what is happening within it.

It could be that a group of advisers or inspectors, judged to be credible to the heads concerned, act as a panel with direct responsibility for head-teacher appraisal, perhaps working in tandem with practising headteachers chosen for involvement with the scheme. If advisers are used in this way, they will need to be freed from a great deal of other work, since the appraisal of heads is likely to be a very time-consuming task. It will involve not only knowing the establishment and its staff and the work of the head, but collecting views from governors, staff and anyone knowing the institution well.

This task will be made more difficult by the fact that the governors now have power to determine a head's salary and the appraisal report has to be made available to the chairman of governors. This will make it more difficult to deal with appraisal solely as a developmental process, although it may be possible to separate the two functions of development and reward for good performance. It may also be that a governing body decides to go in for performance-related pay and this will have an effect on appraisal even if the two are kept separate. Generally speaking the experience of industry is that relating appraisal to pay is unsatisfactory.

Chapter 8

Relationships

Advisers and inspectors are expected to relate to a large number of people. The major relationships are with the advisory team, teachers and the administration, but most advisers and inspectors will also have some contact with HMIs and with colleagues in other authorities and may also have contact with education committee members and with school governors. The need for this wide range of contacts takes up a lot of advisory time, but it is difficult for advisers and inspectors to work effectively without being in touch with most of them from time to time.

Another problem about the relationships advisers and inspectors are expected to maintain is that they create a certain amount of confusion, both in their own minds and in those of the teachers. Advisers and inspectors are on the one hand representing the authority to the establishments and on the other representing the establishments to the authority. Teachers may very easily feel that the adviser or inspector is more on the side of the authority than on that of teachers and the administration may feel that the contrary is the case. Winkley (1985), suggests that some advisers solve this dilemma by coming down firmly on one side or the other. He suggests that advisers fall into four groups:

- Conservative – defenders of the teachers
- Conservative – defenders of the authority and its management system
- Radical – wanting change by imposition/development at authority level
- Radical – wanting change at a professional level by persuasion and support of teachers

It is not easy to stay in a neutral position.

The advisory/inspectorate team

The advisory/inspectorate team should be the group with which each adviser and inspector identifies most closely. This means that the team should meet on a regular basis as well as using informal contacts in the course of day-to-day work. One effect of the Education Reform Act (1988) has been to stress the need for a much greater emphasis on the team element in many authorities.

Where the team is small and centrally based it is likely that its members will come to know each other fairly quickly. Where the team is large and based in a number of different places, it may be necessary to work to bring the members of the team together. This can most easily be done by providing opportunities for in-service or to discuss plans and policies for the whole team to enable people to work with colleagues from different areas and with different skills and specialisms. This not only provides the opportunity to get to know the team as a whole, but also allows its members to know the skills and knowledge available to them among their colleagues.

The administration

There is a good deal of evidence to suggest that in the past the relationship between the advisory service and the administration has been an uneasy one, with neither group fully appreciating the pressures and constraints on the other. This was often because the boundary between the services tended to be blurred and the way they were expected to relate was not clearly stated, so that both groups acted with a measure of uncertainty in some situations. There is also the problem that people often come into the advisory service having been in a decision-making role and they find it difficult to accept that the service is advisory and that decisions, which will tend to be taken elsewhere, may very well not be those which advisers or inspectors would have wished.

There is some evidence from research of the slightly uneasy past relationship between advisers/inspectors and administrators. For example, Bolam *et al* (1978) found that many advisers felt that the administration did not understand what they did. They felt that communication with the administration was inadequate. For example, one stated that 'the advisory team is kept singularly ill-informed of administrative decisions'. Many wanted more and better contact. Winkley (1985) found that problems seemed most striking in authorities where advisers were least engaged in administration themselves or with decision-making at a high level.

Bolam's study also found that the patterns of contact with the CEO in particular were linked with the structure of the local education authority and the advisory service. Where the team was centrally based, the chief adviser was likely to have daily contact with the CEO and deputy but less frequent contact with heads and deputies. Where the team was based outside the administrative headquarters these contacts were reversed.

The Audit Commission (1989b) indicates that there are a number of areas in which officers and members will in future require advice from the adviser/inspectorate team. They list the following:

- the withdrawal of delegation from governing bodies
- major developments of premises and equipment through capital programmes
- initiation of procedures for closing, amalgamating or opening schools or colleges
- setting the budget
- proposals to the Secretary of State for modifying the formula
- provision of INSET where this is paid for by retained funds
- overall strategies for monitoring the National Curriculum and the prepar- ation of bids for curriculum development

This suggests that many of the areas in which it has been traditional to provide advice to the authority have now become areas where it will be directed to establishments and their governing bodies. Many local authorities are now defining the roles of each group more clearly, following the criticism in the Audit Commission report of the lack of management of advisory services and it seems likely that the relationship between administrators and advisers/inspectors will in the future be a much clearer one. In a number of cases the advisory services and the administration are working on combined tasks under the leadership of a chief adviser or assistant CEO who has joint responsibility for advisers/inspectors and some administrators. In other cases there is a definition both of the role of the advisory service and of its chief adviser, who is clearly seen as a member of the CEO's management group and is in a position to maintain communication between the centre and the advisory team. The chief adviser should also be part of the authority's decision-making process. Dean (1991b) maintains that there has been a considerable change in the level at which chief advisers operate, with 65 per cent now at second-tier level in the authority. This has implications for the status of the whole team.

The existence of a chief adviser would seem to have an effect upon the status of the team within the authority. If the chief adviser is a member of the management group, he or she is in a position to control the work coming to the advisory service to some extent and should be able to prevent the situation which has obtained in the past of administrators turning direct to individual advisers or inspectors and asking them to undertake new tasks without any clear knowledge of the extent of the work they are already doing. Pearce (1986) described this as a lethal combination for an inspectorate without positive management. He noted that 'its members share commitment which routinely becomes a low status reluctance to say 'No' to a demand, while the demands for their highly prized knowledge and skills are unfiltered by any firm priorities'. There is a need for an agreed pattern by which administrators pass requests to advisers and inspectors which allows priorities to be maintained and as far as possible avoids overload. This is not easy to achieve because an urgent need for the assistance of advisers/inspectors may come up at any time in response to a current problem. What must be accepted is that new work undertaken will be at the expense of existing work, not in addition to it.

It is important that advisers, inspectors and administrators should see themselves as working to the same end, that of supporting and improving what happens in classrooms. This will happen only if there is adequate communication between the groups and frequent discussion about aims and priorities. This is most likely to take place if the groups are in the habit of working together, each contributing its particular expertise.

Advisers and inspectors new to the service often find it difficult to know whom to ask about a particular issue. Very often they will be guided by more experienced colleagues who are able to answer their questions. Some questions need to be asked of administrators, however, and it is important that advisers and inspectors know the various responsibilities held by officers of the authority. New advisers and inspectors should be introduced to all the senior officers and to any at more junior levels with whom they are likely to need to work. This is as useful to the officers as it is to the advisers.

Advisory teachers

The management of the advisory teacher team is uncertain in many authorities.

Advisory teachers (Harland 1990) feel the need for a wider support from advisers and inspectors. Harland suggests that there is an element of threat on both sides between advisers/inspectors and advisory teachers, particularly as advisory teachers are likely to be taking over some of the work which was formerly the province of advisers. There is also mutual respect for each other's work.

Where the advisers and advisory teachers in a team do not meet as a total team from time to time, members of each group will be known to only a few of the other group. This is not helped by the fact that most advisory teachers are seconded to their posts. Yet both groups are serving the same establishments and need to know what the other is doing.

Members

The extent to which advisers and inspectors have contact with the education committee varies considerably from authority to another. Bolam et al (1978) study found that 52 per cent of advisers had some direct contact with the committee. Others had indirect contact via administrators and tended to be very critical of this.

Contact with members will vary according to the size of the authority and the size of the team. In a large authority with a chief adviser and several senior advisers, advisers in general are less likely to meet members, particularly if the team is area-based, than in a small authority centrally based.

There are a number of reasons why advisers and inspectors should occasionally be present at some committee meetings.

1 Members may want specialist advice from a particular member of the team in relation to a particular decision. This would seem to be better offered directly than through the agency of an administrator.
2 Advisers and inspectors are now the arm of the service through which, in the main, the authority meets its commitment to monitor the work of its establishments. Others may also be involved, but this is a major responsibility for the advisory/inspectorate service. Members will therefore want reports from this service from time to time.
3 Chief and other senior advisers/inspectors may be involved in the policy-making process either through involvement in the CEO's management group from which suggestions go to members or they may be directly involved with members in policy-making.
4 Advisers and inspectors should know something of the political climate in which they are working. This means that they need occasionally to see committees in action. If the team is a large one, the occasions when an adviser or inspector not in a senior post is asked to attend a committee will be very rare. It may be that each member of the advisory/inspectorate staff should attend a committee meeting as part of the induction process.

Other advisory services

Local authorities have a number of services which offer advice to teachers, although some of these are now becoming independent organisations whose services can be bought in. Advisers and inspectors will, from time to time, have contact with the school psychological service, the careers service, the youth service and the library service. Where these services are still part of the local authority there is a case for joint task groups and projects so that there is a real reason for them to meet. Working together is likely to lead to mutual trust and respect.

The school psychological service

In a number of authorities the school psychological service is responsible to the chief adviser/inspector and this makes the linking of the two services easier. Whether this is the case or not, the two services need to work closely together because they have many interests in common. Educational psychologists are not only interested in dealing with the problems of individual pupils but are concerned about what is happening to those pupils in schools and colleges and are anxious that there is the kind of climate and programme which is supportive to pupils who have learning and behavioural difficulties. They often have a very positive contribution to make to in-service programmes and in particular to work on managing children in school. Many educational psychologists are also interested in organisation development and could contribute to work on management.

The careers service

The careers service will have a particular interest in work which schools are doing on linking with industry as well as in their careers programme. Advisory and careers services need to talk together about their aims in these areas of work so that, where possible, their advice is complementary. This is more difficult where the careers service has become a separate organisation, to be bought in by the schools.

The youth service

The youth service is generally more concerned with out-of-school activities. The advisory team should know what it is aiming to do for young people and the way this relates to the personal and social education programmes being offered in schools.

Other local authority departments

Advisers and inspectors will, from time to time, have occasion to work with officers from other departments of the authority. The most common link in the past has been with the architects' department, where the adviser/ inspector was often advising on the requirements for new, reorganised or improved buildings. There may be fewer opportunities for this in the future because building will be the responsibility of governors. However, it is likely that governors will need the advice of advisers/inspectors and this will maintain the contact with the architects' department. There may also be a case for contact with private architects employed by some governing bodies.

It is tempting both for advisers/inspectors and for teachers to try to do the architect's work for him or her, particularly if the architect seems to lack knowledge of educational requirements. It is better, if possible, to give a brief which poses the problems and expects the architect to come up with solutions which adviser, architect and school can consider together. A good architect will have many ideas about ways of solving problems and these will add to the adviser's ideas and to those of the teachers involved so that the eventual building is as good as those concerned can make it.

HMI

Contacts with HMI can be extremely fruitful and are necessary, if only to avoid both groups spending time in the same establishments. This can be something of a problem, since the schools and colleges HMI plan to inspect are often chosen by computer without regard to those which the local team plans to inspect. It is therefore important to plan well ahead and discuss plans with local HMI as soon as possible, so that clashes can be avoided.

Probably the most profitable discussions with HMI are those where advisers, inspectors and HMI share their knowledge of particular establishments. HMI will be interested in all aspects of the work of the local advisory team and should be kept informed of plans and their outcomes and be given copies of papers produced. They may be able to contribute to the thinking of the local team in a number of ways, not least because they have contacts across the country and may be able to suggest places where similar ideas are being pursued.

There should also be a two-way arrangement for contributing to advisory training. Each group has something to offer the courses run by the other group.

Governors

Circular 7/88 (DES 1988a) includes the statement 'the LEA will sustain and support governing bodies with professional advice and guidance on the full range of issues affecting schools'. There is also a specific requirement on the LEA to give advice on appointments, and the governors have a duty to consider that advice.

It is likely that a good deal of the professional advice offered to governors will come from advisers and inspectors, sometimes indirectly through education officers and sometimes directly by their attendance at governors' meetings. In a number of authorities it is now becoming customary for advisers/inspectors to attend governors' meetings in order to offer professional advice. This is time-consuming but, since the governors' meeting is now very much the decision-making body, advisers may well find such attendance profitable.

Many of the same problems are present in governors' meetings as are present in education committee meetings. There may be political tensions. The way a suggestion is worded may be important and an adviser or inspector attending a governors' meeting to offer advice would do well to spend time listening and getting an idea of the frames of reference of different governors before making suggestions. They may have ideas of what constitutes good practice in education very different from those of an adviser/inspector or a headteacher.

Governors will certainly want to have reports from advisers and inspectors on the state of their school. This may not be easy to do if the school is not working well. The head may expect the adviser to support him or her, but there will be situations where this is not possible. The wisest course is probably to be honest at all times, but to temper honesty about problems with praise for what is good.

Public relations and the advisory team

There is now a situation in some authorities where advisory work is something which establishments may or may not purchase and this approach may spread. It is a situation which makes new demands on advisers, who will need to have a far greater regard for public relations and spend more time and money on it than was necessary in the past. If the local service is not attractive to schools and colleges they will seek their advice elsewhere and this could see the advisory role of the service disappearing.

Oxley (1987) stresses that public relations is an exploration of human relationships and defines it as 'the management of all the relationships that exist between a complexity called an organisation and all the other groups or individuals with which it interacts'. The main groups with which advisers are concerned are teachers, headteachers and governors. Advisers will be regarded in many different ways by schools and colleges according to their previous experience of the service and their beliefs, opinions, interests, values and prejudices. The task of a public relations project will be to raise the image of the service by helping establishments to understand what is on offer and how the service works. To do this effectively the service will need to find out what schools and colleges really want. This might be done with a mixture of questionnaires, meetings and individual discussions.

Compiling questionnaires which are likely to be returned with answers that can be analysed is quite a skilled task. The compiler must first remember that people will not bother with anything which makes too many demands. A short questionnaire in which the questions are straightforward, not requiring the writer to look up information or get it from elsewhere, is more likely to be completed than one which asks more complex questions or is several pages long. The way the questionnaire is set out is also important. It is more likely to be completed if it looks well-organised and well laid out. This also makes it easier to analyse the answers.

It is very easy in writing a questionnaire to ask questions which turn out to be ambiguous. It is therefore wise to pilot the survey with a small number of people before using it more widely. The letter that comes with a questionnaire needs to be carefully written, stressing the intention to offer a service which really meets the needs of the schools and colleges. It may also be helpful to meet sample groups of teachers, headteachers or governors and discuss their needs with them.

Once this kind of information has been collected, it should be possible to provide publicity material. This should be of high quality and professionally laid out. It may be necessary to produce different material for different stages of education, partly because their needs are different, but also because the language is different. It should set out clearly the different services offered and what they will cost.

Producing material for headteachers and teachers is very much easier than producing similar material for governors. Headteachers and teachers come from the same background as advisers. They have similar ways of talking about education, although values and interests may still differ widely and it is in the interests of the advisory service to be aware of this. Governors pose much more of a problem because of the wide range of people represented. Material produced for schools and colleges will not be appropriate for governors. The knowledge that can be taken for granted with professionals cannot be assumed and as with inspection reports language likely to be seen as jargon must be avoided.

The success of an advisory team in this new situation is likely to be judged to a large extent by the extent to which its services are used. It will be possible to increase the team if they are fully employed and decrease it if there is not enough work. It will probably be of interest to look for new fields of endeavour and it may be that teams will wish to circularise independent schools, grant-maintained schools and city technology colleges, all of whom have no formal source of educational advice.

One of the most difficult tasks when schools and colleges are asked to pay for advice is to work out costing. Unless it is subsidised it must be based on the salaries of advisers plus the overheads of accommodation, support and materials. This is likely to come as a shock to schools and colleges in the first instance, but advice given is likely to be taken very seriously.

If the team is to stay in business, it will be important that its members are competent. Training as people join the team will be essential and there will need to be constant updating of skills. There will also be the problem of deciding whether the choice of person to deal with any request is a matter for the team or for individual heads, teachers and governors. The reputation of some team members is likely to be better than that of others and this could make some people underemployed while others have more work than they can cope with. The solution lies in getting everyone's skills to a high level and keeping the decision within the team except where the request is specific.

An advisory team will also need to maintain good public relations with all the groups discussed above because they will often be in a position to recommend members of the team to schools and colleges.

Chapter 9

Making appointments

Although the process of appointing staff has now been passed to governors and headteachers, advisers and inspectors are still likely to play an important part, both in advising on the process of appointment and in taking part as a member of the interviewing panel. This chapter is mainly written as advice on appointing advisers, inspectors and advisory teachers, but the process described is much the same when appointing teachers and headteachers.

Appointing advisers, inspectors and advisory teachers is a very important part of the work of an LEA and it is an area where there has been little research. However, much of the work on the appointment of secondary school headteachers, described by Morgan *et al.* (1983) applies also to these appointments.

Advisers, inspectors and advisory teachers are appointed to undertake particular kinds of work. The first requirement is therefore to appoint someone whose previous experience and training make it likely that he or she will be able to do the job, although it must be recognised that both groups will usually require further training after appointment. The second requirement is that the person appointed has the kind of personality which makes it possible to carry out the tasks involved.

The first task is to attract applicants. This is a major problem in some areas where there is a limited field of applicants for advisory posts. Stillman and Grant (1989) suggest that it would be helpful in getting the best people to apply for advisory posts to:

– give those in schools and colleges a better understanding of the nature of the role
– reduce the gap between schools' perception of what advisers should be doing and the reality of the situation
– encourage the establishment of a pool of advisory experience

Much holds good about the appointment of advisers and inspectors for that of the latter advisory teachers. In the past they have often been appointed from within the LEA and their work has been known to those making the appointment. This has meant that the appointment procedure was a more limited one than might have been the case if the applicants were not known. In the future advisory teachers may take on much of the work that advisers and inspectors are now unable to do because of the demands that inspection is making on their time. It is therefore likely that more appointments will be open to national advertisement and the appointment procedure now needs to recognise that the work has become much more demanding.

It cannot be stressed too strongly that the appointment of advisers, inspectors and advisory teachers is a very important activity. It is therefore essential that enough time and care is taken over the appointment process. LEAs generally take less time over appointments than many industrial concerns and the pressures on those involved in the appointment should not get in the way of making a thorough assessment of those presenting themselves for selection.

Appointments are a two-way process. The applicants are also deciding whether the LEA in question is the place they would like to work. Ample information should be given both in advance and on the day when the appointment is being made, so that applicants are in a position to decide whether the post is for them. In particular the way in which candidates are welcomed and treated during the process of appointment will affect their view of the LEA. They also need to see the conditions under which they will be working. Many teachers in senior posts in schools or colleges are shocked by the poor accommodation offered to advisers, inspectors and advisory teachers and by the lack of adequate clerical help. They should be aware of these problems before and not after appointment.

The task of matching person to post involves collecting all the evidence available and weighing it against the demands of the job. Morgan *et al.* (1983) suggest that there are four questions to ask in planning selection:

— What is the job?
— What skills and knowledge are needed to perform the job?
— How will these be assessed?
— How will the final decision be reached?

Pre-appointment tasks

The job description

The starting point for making an appointment is the job description. It should define the responsibilities of the post and make it clear to whom the person appointed is responsible and where the boundaries of the job are. In the past the job descriptions of advisers and inspectors have been extremely wide and one effect of the 1988 Act and the reports of the Audit Commission (1989b) and NFER (Stillman and Grant 1989) is to define more clearly what they are expected to do.

Job descriptions for advisory teachers, where they exist, are usually less wide, but here too there is a need for a clear job description which guides appointment and action in post. The notes on the job descriptions given in chapter 2 will be relevant for making appointments.

The person specification

In addition to a job description it is helpful to have a person specification which defines the kind of person those making the appointment would like to see appointed. It should contain statements of what is required by way of:

1 Qualifications, knowledge, skills, abilities.
2 Experience.
3 Special aptitudes.
4 Particular interests

The job description should be made available to the candidates. The elements of the person description should be incorporated in the further particulars of the post.

The criteria for appointment

The task in making the appointment is to assess the potential of each candidate in relation to the various items of the job description and person specification. These provide the criteria by which judgements may be made.

Stillman and Grant (1989) discovered significant variation in the criteria adopted by chief advisers, by headteachers and by heads of department. Chief advisers looked for in their study of advisory services subject expertise and a flair for innovation, the right personality and broad experience in education, including senior management experience. Headteachers thought the subject specialism less important than a wide range of experience and the right personality. Heads of department thought that advisers should have a realistic and practical view of teachers' workloads, the right personality – approachable, enthusiastic, innovative and energetic – and have an extensive range of management skills.

The following criteria are suggested for an adviser/inspector's post:

1 Good teaching experience, some of it at a senior level.
2 Some experience of working with adults, such as in-service work, involvement in LEA working parties, acting as an advisory teacher or some similar activity.
3 Very good knowledge of current developments in education.
4 Very good knowledge, expertise and enthusiasm in the specialist field which the appointment is being made.
5 Skill as a problem solver.

6 Ability to look critically at work in the classroom.
7 Skill in presentation, both orally and in writing.
8 Ability to form relationships with adults.
9 Ability to cope with pressure and stress.

The criteria for advisory teachers will be similar. They too, need good teaching experience and some experience of working with adults. The remaining criteria also apply, although an authority would expect to appoint advisory teachers at an earlier stage of their career than advisers and inspectors and rather less might be expected under each heading.

The advertisement

The next task is to prepare the advertisement. This is likely to be constrained by the LEA's advertisement style as well as by cost, but it should contain if possible some brief statement about the philosophy of the LEA and brief details of the following.

1 Title of post.
2 Some details about the advisory service such as size, location, structure.
3 Person to whom the successful candidate will be responsible.
4 The responsibilities of the post.
5 Particular experience, knowledge and skills required.
6 Salary.
7 Starting date
8 Where to write or phone for further information.
9 Closing date for applications.

Further particulars

These should include the following details:

1 *Information about the LEA* This might include a statement of any overall aims or philosophy; an account of the education service, giving such details as the number of establishments and their organisation and any relevant details of the organisation of the education office.
2 *Information about the advisory service.* Information about where advisers and inspectors are based; the support available to them; the way the service is organised; the roles of the chief and senior advisers; the opportunities provided for professional development; the role of advisory teachers.
3 *Salary details.*
4 *Information about the particular post.* Details of the responsibilities which cover those given in the job description and the qualities given in the person specification. The criteria for the appointment should also be given in some form.

5 *Information about the arrangements for the appointment.* The dates on which appointment procedures will take place.

Application forms

Many LEAs use for advisory posts, forms which are appropriate for administrative appointments. Sometimes there is an authority form which is intended for all authority appointments. These forms are usually inappropriate for advisers and inspectors because they are often designed with quite junior posts in mind, asking for very elementary qualifications and not giving space for the kind of experience which is required for an advisory post. Candidates for advisory teacher posts are very often given forms designed for teachers. These are usually rather more appropriate than those designed for administrators but as advisory teacher posts become more important, these forms become less satisfactory.

If it is at all possible, a form should be devised especially for advisory posts. With desk-top publishing this need not be an expensive item and, if produced in-house, it can easily be changed if it is found not to meet the requirements of the appointment. If this is not acceptable, it may be possible to provide an insert which asks for more details about experience, in particular of previous work with teachers which was of an advisory nature. Such an insert may also make it clear what is required in a statement supporting the application.

The application form should contribute specific information to the file being compiled on each candidate. An application form should include space for the following information:

1 Name (including any previous names, which may be needed for salary purposes and for pension calculations).
2 Home address.
3 Home telephone number.
4 Work address and telephone number.
5 Present post, including the type of institution employed.
6 Education (location and dates):
   • secondary school
   • higher education institution(s)
7 Qualifications (name, where obtained and dates):
   • teaching qualification
   • degree(s) (subject and level of pass)
   • degree equivalent qualifications
   • other high level diplomas
8 Any full-time employment outside education: names of employers, dates, titles of posts.
9 Advisory experience: titles of posts, authorities, dates.

10 Teaching experience:
  • LEA or other employer
  • Type of institution
  • Age range
  • Single sex/mixed
  • Age groups taught
  • Full or part-time
  • Period of service

  Full information on teaching experience is important for the compilation of the short list. Where a briefer statement is allowed it is difficult to assess the actual nature of a candidate's experience. A person applying for a primary adviser's post, for example, who simply puts 'primary' on the application form may have no experience of the youngest children and may not be very knowledgeable about infant or first school work.

11 Health record. It is useful to ask about any absences of more than two weeks through illness in the past two years.

12 Statement in support of application. This is potentially the most useful part of the form, but will only be of use if all the applicants comment on points related to the criteria by which the appointment will be made. It is therefore important to ask for some specific information while leaving scope also for candidates to include other information which seems to them to be relevant. A standard question such as 'Please explain how you feel your previous experience qualifies you for this post' may be useful.

Some LEAs do not provide a form but ask applicants to provide information in their own style. This gives interesting information about the candidates' ability to set out information but has many disadvantages. It is extremely easy to disguise the nature of particular experiences and present them as contributing more than in fact they can possibly do. It is also very difficult to make comparison between candidates who provide very different amounts of information.

Long-listing

Once applications are received a long-list must be drawn up of those candidates for whom further information will be sought. This requires a system of assessing application forms against the criteria. A suggested assessment form for use at different stages of the appointment is shown in figure 10.

When a decision has been made about which candidates to long-list, confidential reports may be requested. Here again, it is wise to ask specific questions, but there may be authority limitations on what is possible. Where it is left to the referee to say what he or she wishes about a candidate it is easy to disguise weaknesses, whereas a question such as 'Would you appoint this candidate to a similar post in your authority?', pins the referee down and gives useful information. Some other questions which may be useful for advisory posts are:

1 Is this candidate knowledgeable about current developments in education?
2 Has this candidate a really good grasp of his/her specialist field?
3 Is this candidate able to look critically at work in the classroom?
4 Is this candidate good at solving practical problems?
5 Is this candidate able to present material competently?
6 Does this candidate form good relationships with other people?
7 Is this candidate able to cope with pressure and stress?
8 Has this candidate any particular weaknesses?

Headteachers and advisers/inspectors frequently have to write confidential reports on teachers. The following headings may be useful whether or not specific information is requested.

1 *A note of the context* in which the writer knows the candidate.
2 *An account of the candidate's recent work.* This should stress those aspects which are relevant to the post in question. It is important in the case of advisory posts to give information about any work with adults outside the school and any contributions to in-service education.
3 *An assessment of the candidate as a person.* This should give strengths and where appropriate refer to any weaknesses which are likely to persist in a new post. It is important to be honest but tactful about weaknesses. The whole system of confidential reports falls apart if people are dishonest. It is also helpful to know of people who do not do themselves justice in the interview situation.
4 *An overall assessment.* It is helpful if the overall assessment states whether the writer would whish to see the candidate in a similar post in his or her own LEA. If possible the report should conclude with a statement of the degree of support for the candidate using such sentences as 'I support this candidate strongly and without reservation' or 'I support this candidate without reservation' or 'I support this candidate with the reservations given above' or 'I cannot support this application'.

Although many reports may still be confidential there is a strong move to make all reports open. This is likely to make them less valuable, but even if they are confidential, candidates applying for posts should have a fair idea of what is being written about them. It is the responsibility of the writer of such a report to see that the person concerned is aware of any reservations he or she may have.

Assessment form for adviser appointment					
Name of candidate				Date	
Grade A - E under each teaching	Long list	Short list	Preliminary interview	Analogous tests	Final interview
Teaching experience					
Senior management experience					
Experience of working with adults					
Knowledge of current developments					
Specialist knowledge, expertise, enthusiasm					
Skill as a problem solver					
Ability to look critically at work in the classroom					
Skill in presentation orally and in writing					
Ability to form relationships with adults					
Ability to cope with pressure and stress					

Figure 10   Assessment form for appointing an adviser

Short-listing

Once the confidential reports have been received it becomes possible to make a short list. A good deal of information about the way the candidates match the criteria will be available from the application forms and from the confidential reports. Here again it is helpful in making a short list to use a form such as that in figure 10 which allows those short-listing to grade each candidate against each of the criteria. In a number of cases the grading will be the same as it was for the long-listing, but the confidential reports may shed light on each candidate's skills and abilities.

Once the short list has been drawn up, the chosen candidates can be invited for interview and selection. In sending out the invitations it is helpful to the candidates to give some account of the selection procedure to be adopted and the people who will be taking part.

The selection procedure

Presenting the authority to the candidates

We have already noted that the selection procedure should to some extent be a two-way exercise, giving the candidates a chance to sum up the LEA and the situation in which they will be working as well as giving the selection panels the opportunity to assess the candidates. If this is to be done adequately it will probably need about half a day. It is a good idea to arrange for the group of advisers/inspectors with whom the successful candidate will be working most closely to meet the candidates and brief them about the work and the LEA and give them a chance to ask questions. They also need to see where they will be working. The chief adviser/inspector will also wish to undertake some of the briefing and there should be some agreement about the points which the group of advisers and the chief adviser/inspector will cover. Advisory teachers also need to meet the people with whom they will be working and see where they will be based.

Topics which should be covered in this discussion include:

1 General information about the authority, including information about supporting services such as teachers' centres, the library service, the school psychological service.
2 The status of the advisory service within the education department.
3 The structure of the advisory service and the way it works out in practice, including the way advisers, inspectors and advisory teachers are managed.
4 The elements of advisory work which are laid down for advisers, inspectors and advisory teachers and what is left to their discretion.
5 The clerical and administrative support available.
6 The reports and records expected of them.

7 The training and support offered, and details of any appraisal system.
8 In-service arrangements generally within the authority.

Analogous tests

Interviewing is known to be comparatively unreliable as a selection procedure and there is much to be said for asking candidates to undertake tests which reflect skills which the tasks of an adviser require. The following might be possible methods of assessment. The first three would apply to advisory teachers as well as advisers and inspectors, the fourth is particular to advisers and inspectors and the last to inspectors only.

1 Candidates are invited to see a videotape of classroom practice and are questioned on what they observed.
2 Candidates are asked to interview a member of the advisory team who has a genuine problem in a school with which he or she would like help. The interview is observed for the skill with which the candidate achieves rapport with the interviewee, draws out information and leads the interviewee towards solutions.
3 Candidates are asked to make a ten-minute presentation on a given subject, e.g. the effect of recent developments in education. They are assessed on the skill with which they make the presentation and the quality of the content.
4 Candidates are given an in-tray exercise involving some of the problems which advisers and inspectors meet. They are then interviewed about how they would tackle some of the problems.
5 Candidates are given two sets of notes about an inspection and asked to combine them into a report which could be given to the school and to the governors. This is then assessed.

It is unlikely that there will be time for all of these types of assessment, but some of them would be valuable and would add considerably to the assessment which can be made during an interview. Here again, candidates can be graded on their performance.

Interviews

Before the interviews commence a decision needs to be made about whether to keep all the candidates until the end or to let them leave once they have been interviewed. With preliminary interviews they may need to stay if final interviews are to follow the same day or the next day. The advantage of keeping candidates to the end is that the successful candidate can be informed and the chief adviser can spend some time with him or her after the interview explaining more about the post. It is also possible when candidates wait to give them some individual feedback on how they did. On the other hand there is no reason why candidates should not be informed of the outcome by letter or telephone and unsuccessful candidates can be offered the opportunity to telephone to find out more about how they fared.

It was noted earlier that interviews are not wholly reliable as a way of selecting staff. They become more reliable as the time allocated to them increases. Two sets of interviews are likely to be more reliable than a single interview. It is also a waste of the candidates' time if they sit waiting to be interviewed, when this time might be used to find out more about them. The ideal would seem to be a double preliminary interview followed by a final interview of the candidates who have survived best in the earlier interviews and the tests. How possible this is will depend upon what the LEA's usual practice is and the readiness of those concerned to spend two days making an appointment.

The interviews should be devoted to finding how well the candidates match up to the criteria. Questions should be carefully prepared with these in mind. Questions about what a candidate has actually done often yield more reliable evidence than questions about what he or she would do in given circumstances, although there is also a place for this kind of question. In general it is better to ask each candidate roughly the same questions so that a comparison can be made, but they may be framed differently according to the experience of each person. For the posts of advisers and inspectors the final interview may involve LEA members and they should be given the criteria being used well in advance and asked to prepare questions with these in mind. Here again, it is helpful to use a grading system, matching criteria with interview performance.

At the end of the interviews all the evidence can be weighed up. The gradings given will obviously contribute to the decision, but the feelings of the interviewing panels will also be important and where two candidates fit the criteria equally well, the personalities of the people concerned will play a large part in the final selection.It can be useful in starting to discuss the candidates to ask everyone concerned to rank them in order of preference. This usually eliminates some candidates and concentrates attention on a smaller number who can be discussed in greater detail.

Providing feedback to unsuccessful candidates

It is helpful to those who were not appointed to give them some information about how they performed in interview. This should be as positive as possible, stressing their good points and giving them information about any areas in which they did not met the criteria and offering advice on presentation.

Evaluating appointments

The success of appointments is rarely evaluated in any formal way. It is, of course, impossible to know how the unsuccessful candidates might have performed relative to the person appointed. It is possible, however, to review the notes of an appointment some six months or a year afterwards and note the ways in which the person appointed differs in practice from the impression he or she made at interview and in any tests given. This review may cast doubts on some of the appointment procedure and lead to changes in the way future appointments are made.

Appointing headteachers and teachers

The appointment of headteachers and teachers is now in the hands of governors but the Education Reform Act specifies that the governors will be advised by the chief education officer. In a small authority the CEO may wish to do this him or herself for some posts but in other authorities advisers and inspectors will be the representative of the CEO concerned with many of the appointments. They can also be influential in talking to heads about ways of making appointments, particularly inexperienced heads.

Much that has been said about the appointment of advisers and inspectors applies also to the appointment of heads and teachers. Most establishments now have job descriptions for most members of staff, but it is not uncommon for there to be no job description for the headteacher. However, the responsibilities of the headteacher have been fairly fully defined in the 1988 edition of *School Teachers' Pay and Conditions*. There is also a full definition in Morgan *et al.* (1983).

The criteria for appointing headteachers might include the following:

1 Successful teaching experience, some of it at a senior level.
2 Successful management and leadership experience.
3 Good knowledge of current developments in education.
4 Skill as a problem-solver.
5 Good ability to form relationships with adults.
6 Ability to cope with pressure and stress.
7 The kind of presence and personality which supports leadership.

The criteria for appointing teachers will depend a good deal on the particular post, but in all cases except that of newly qualified teachers one criterion will be that of successful teaching experience. Another will be the ability to make relationships with children.

The advertisement for a headship or a teaching post will cover much the same ground as that for an adviser or inspector, although governors may have their own ideas about what should be included and in particular may want to add something about performance-related pay.

The further particulars for a headship might be expected to include the following:

1 *The establishment and its situation.* The history of the establishment, information about the site and buildings and any future plans; information about the catchment area and population trends; the age range of the pupils and the numbers on the roll and any community use of the buildings.
2 *Staffing.* The numbers of teachers currently in post and any vacancies; the teaching staff structure; non-teaching staff; arrangements for staff development.
3 *Governing body.* Composition; structure of meetings; sub-committees.
4 *Home/school relationships.* Existence of PTA or other organisation; parents' meetings; arrangements for giving parents information about their children's progress; involvement of parents in the school's work.
5 *Curriculum and organisation.* Pupil grouping for learning; provision for the most and least able.
6 *LEA support and inspection.* Arrangements for advisory support and inspection; other LEA provision such as library service, teachers' centres.
7 *Community links.*
8 *Salary details.*
9 *Details about the particular post.* Some indication should be given about what governors are looking for and the criteria by which the appointment will be made
10 *Information about arrangements for the appointment.* Details of the dates of interviews, the pattern the selection process is likely to follow and arrangements for seeing the school or college.

Further details for teaching posts might be based on this.

Most LEAs have forms specifically designed for headships and it is generally better to use these and also the appropriate forms provided for teachers. If they do not provide space for the information required it can be asked for separately. The information needed is very similar to that required for advisory posts except that advisory experience will not feature as a separate item. It is equally important where headteachers and teachers are concerned to ask specific questions, to be answered in the statement accompanying the application. These should be planned to abstract information about how well the candidate matches the criteria.

LEA forms often ask for information which seems irrelevant to teachers and laymen alike. For example, it seems somewhat unnecessary to include on headship forms information about GCE or its later equivalent. It is included on teacher application forms in order to check that candidates have passes in English and mathematics.

For all headteacher and teaching posts candidates need an opportunity to see the school or college and meet the staff. Candidates for headship also need time with the outgoing head, who can brief them about the establishment. It is helpful if an adviser is also present to put the authority's view and to tell candidates what the LEA has to offer. Candidates for teaching posts will similarly need time with relevant members of the staff.

Governors may want to meet headteacher candidates informally and it may be helpful for them to spend time talking with the chairman about the role of the governors and the way they are carrying out their responsibilities.

Headteacher candidates, like advisers, might be asked to undertake analogous tests. A range of suggestions about ways of doing this and possible tests are given in Morgan *et al.* (1984). This suggests among other things an in-tray exercise and an exercise involving chairing a small committee through a short problem-solving task. Candidates for teaching posts might be given a specific teaching task with a small group of pupils. Headship interview arrangements are a matter for the governors but they may be advised by the chief education officer's representative. The comments made above about interviewing for advisory posts apply equally to headteacher and teacher appointments.

Chapter 10

Training and the advisory service

It used to be assumed that anyone who was a good teacher could advise other teachers effectively. Stillman and Grant (1989) make the point strongly that this is not the case. Their study also gave some interesting information about the problems people find on coming into advisory work. It quotes these two comments by advisers:

> An adviser's job is a strange one and it should not be assumed that senior management work in schools or colleges prepares people in any significant way for a job with completely different demands:
>
> – a new work pattern, no set holidays, bells, periods etc.
> – a strange new work environment (office)
> – wider but less significant influence
> – jack of all trades, master of none
> – no significant feedback
> – no loyalty to an institution
> – involvement as a local authority officer, redeployment, unions etc.
> – sense of inadequacy to control education development, cf the head of a school can shape education for 1000 students – few advisers can shape education for an authority
> – increasing contact with political masters
> – continuing struggle to keep abreast of all educational developments from primary to tertiary – 'you can be asked to help anywhere and everywhere '

I have been in the post seven months. I don't really understand what is expected of me. It is totally different from what I expected. I have no way of judging whether I am having any effect, making progress etc. I feel overwhelmed by the number and range of different skills I am expected to employ without any training. Although I am not unhappy, I find it impossible to answer the two most common questions asked by teacher friends: 1) What do you do? 2) Are you enjoying the job?

Many of the problems listed here could have been avoided if the LEAs of these advisers had had an adequate system of induction and in-service training for their advisory staff. There is enough which is new in advisory work to challenge the most able without adding to this by failing to provide the necessary support in the early days. The same study listed other difficulties advisers encounter during their first and subsequent years of advising.

- balancing roles and establishing priorities – lack of guidance on what the role should be
- difficulties with schools/lack of experience with other sectors
- getting used to advisory work, its autonomy and the personal difficulties of being an adviser
- there being too much of the appropriate type of work to do/too much work
- lack of induction training
- lack of team ethos/lack of advisory service
- insufficient resources/not enough money to do the job/not enough time to do the job
- personal (time) management /learning to manage . . . work
- difficult and awkward communication with officers and members/red-tape/political interference
- too much administration and trivia to do
- learning new skills, committee work/negotiating skills, difficulties with providing and planning INSET
- coming to grips with changing and proliferating roles, greater LEA emphasis and involvement in initiatives
- coping with the diversity of tasks
- other difficulties

This list again demonstrates the need for training and suggests that, even with good training, adjusting to advisory work is not easy.

The study quoted above found that 82 per cent of advisers had had no induction. The National Association of Inspectors and Educational Advisers has for many years run an annual course in January for new advisers, but while this is a valuable contribution it does not replace the need for local induction and support in the first year of advisory work. Moreover, an adviser or inspector coming new to post in the early part of the year will be in post for almost a year before having the chance to undertake this course.

Advisory work is different from teaching and requires new skills which have to be acquired. Pearce (1986) suggests that LEAs should 'make plain that advisory work places a high premium on writing ability, time-management and the ability to cope with stress'. He also argues that advisers and inspectors need training in 'counselling skills, team-building skills, the dynamic of curriculum change, analysing organizational cultures, curriculum analysis and timetable construction, and awareness of their own impact on others'.

Stillman and Grant (1989) identified some of the problems in training advisers:

> training is perceived as taking advisers away from work. It is difficult to find time for it. It costs money and in the past it has not been given the priority it deserves. Effective adviser INSET requires management to have clear goals and an effective method for assessing group and individual needs. These are not always present. Advisory INSET is a relatively new art and little consensus exists about forms to meet specific needs.

Stillman and Grant (1989) gave chief advisers' views on the training that inspectors/advisers need. It included the following, given in the chief advisers' order of priority:

> acquisition of knowledge of phases and specialisms other than one's own, finance, education law, IT;
> management skills, leadership skills, the management of change and the management of time;
> general updating on curricular and other issues, central initiatives, DES reports, research etc.
> counselling, interpersonal, group and communication skills, stress management;
> appraisal techniques, school self-evaluation and review;
> inspection, evaluating, observing and supporting teachers, report writing;
> cross-curricular work, multicultural education, PSE, mainstream SEN, industry links, equal opportunities etc.

If little thought has in the past been given to INSET for advisers and inspectors, even less thought has been given to the needs of advisory teachers. It was assumed that, being good teachers, they would automatically be able to help other teachers and many did so very effectively. Advisory teachers were also often attached to particular advisers or inspectors and this gave them a kind of induction which was better than that experienced by many advisers. There was, nevertheless, a need for a proper in-service programme for this group as well as for advisers. Much the same is true of teachers' centre leaders except that they frequently do not have the benefit of the kind of support which an adviser or inspector may give to an advisory teacher.

The most notable contribution to adviser training is the Centre for Adviser and Inspector Development (CAID), which is based at Woolley Hall. This has offered a variety of valuable courses to advisers and inspectors at all stages and has made every effort to link these with each advisers local circumstances. However, it is still not a substitute for a coherent programme of professional development, based on identified needs, starting with induction and continuing throughout the adviser's or inspector's working life.

The changes that have come about in the advisory service as a result of the Education Reform Act are beginning to result in a much more coherent approach to training. Hereford and Worcester (1990), for example, make the following statement about training:

A programme for the development of inspectors ought to be no less thorough than that being recommended for teachers. Inspectors need equal but different opportunities to 'recharge their professional batteries' if the provision they are to make for teachers is to be of a consistently high quality.
   Possibilities which ought to be pursued include:

i)   Access to a wide range of short courses
ii) The adoption of a programme designed to grant each officer a sabbatical term at least once during his/her service
iii) The development of long term exchanges between authorities and/or short term visits to neighbouring authorities
iv) A system of exchanges between members of the inspectorate and serving teachers when a suitable professional context can be identified
v)   The creation of a number of research fellowships similar to those made increasingly available to teachers

Among the themes likely to merit inclusion in any programme of professional development for inspectors must be:

i)   An understanding of oneself in the role of inspector
ii) An examination of the main objectives of inspectorial work
iii) An examination and perhaps revision of the range of duties being undertaken
iv) An opportunity to review current theories of learning
v)   A consideration of aspects of curriculum theory, styles of teaching and learning and approaches to school organisation
vi) A review and refurbishment of the skills inherent in inspectorial work
vii) A study of team work and management theory and practice

Dean (1991) found that most authorities were taking the idea of training advisers very seriously. Ninety-two per cent had arrangements for induction and 63 per cent used the NAIEA induction course. Seventy-eight per cent had a compulsory in-house course and a further 28 per cent had a voluntary in-house course. Thirty-nine per cent arranged for advisers to attend a regional course, particularly in Wales, where this was well established. Sixty-seven per cent used the Centre for Adviser and Inspector Development (CAID) and 97 per cent provided for their officers to attend other courses. Sixty-five per cent provided for appraisal.

The highest percentages of types of course were for induction, inspection and updating, all above 80 per cent. There were also fairly high percentages of authorities providing training in interpersonal skills (60 per cent), supporting headteachers (62 per cent) and management (50 per cent). Rather less attention was given to in-service work (39 per cent), supporting teachers (48 per cent) and personal organisation (49 per cent).

Authorities were also asked about training for advisory teachers. Here 79 per cent were providing an induction programme and 65 per cent had a compulsory in-house programme. Eighty-six per cent provided an opportunity to attend other courses and 34 per cent provided appraisal.

Here the highest percentage of types of course were for induction (79 per cent), in-service education (61 per cent), supporting teachers (64 per cent) and up-dating (68 per cent). Interpersonal skills featured in 46 per cent of LEAs. There was considerably less attention to supporting heads (16 per cent) and somewhat less attention to personal organisation (37 per cent) and management (28 per cent).

The relative figures for advisers and advisory teachers suggest that many LEAs are now seeing advisory teachers as playing a larger part in in-service work and in supporting teachers, with advisers and inspectors playing a greater part in inspection and advice to heads.

The professional development policy

Every advisory team needs a policy for professional development. This may be part of a larger policy which is the concern of the whole education department or the whole service or it may be a policy devised simply for the advisory service. The policy might include statements about the following:

Overall philosophy The professional development policy of an advisory team needs to state the importance attached to the idea of professional development for advisers, inspectors and advisory teachers and to stress that every member needs to be concerned with keeping up to date and developing his or her skills.

The people whom the policy concerns Who is involved with the professional development programme will depend on the way the advisory service is organised. If the team is one where officers and advisers/inspectors work together then the policy and the programme need to concern both. If educational psychologists are part of the responsibility of the chief adviser, they need to be part of the professional development programme. Advisory teachers' should also be involved and possibly teachers centre wardens if the organisation makes this feasible.

The possible professional development activities Every team needs to have a regular programme of in-service activities and a number of other opportunities which occur from time to time. The policy also needs to make clear that advisers, inspectors and advisory teachers and any others covered by the policy will be given opportunities for development as part of their everyday work. The statement from Hereford and Worcester is a good example of this.

Responsibility for professional development Everyone needs to know where responsibility for professional development lies. It is likely that there will be one person with overall responsibility for in-service education and this responsibility may include the advisory service. If this is not the case, then one person, possibly the chief adviser in a small or medium-sized LEA or some other senior person in a large LEA, should be responsible overall for the development of advisers, inspectors and advisory teachers. People in line management roles also have a responsibility for the development of their colleagues.

The way needs will be assessed The advisory team, like other establishments, must take needs assessment seriously, starting when advisers are appointed and continuing as they become more experienced.

The part played by appraisal Many advisory teams are already undertaking appraisal and this will need to be spelled out in the policy statement.

Provision for induction The policy needs to state what the team expects to do for newly appointed members.

Provision for individuals There should be some statement of the way in which the team aims to provide for individual need and the kind of records of advisers, inspectors and advisory teachers which will be kept.

Organising for development

If advisers, inspectors and advisory teachers are to receive adequate training careful thought needs to be given to the way in which the work of the service is organised. Training needs to be integral to the work of the team, using opportunities arising in the course of daily work as well as making special provision. Advisers and inspectors, like teachers, learn from watching experienced colleagues at work and from feedback on their performance from experienced colleagues. The work of the team needs to be arranged so that opportunities for these activities are possible, particularly during the first year of service.

HMI has for many years used mentors whose task is to induct the new colleagues into the work. This is equally useful for advisory teams. An experienced adviser, working with someone new, can provide assistance in dealing with many of the problems listed above. He or she can help the new member sort out priorities, offer feedback on performance, make suggestions about ways of tackling problems and provide a listening ear when the new member wants to talk over his or her work.

Whether or not an advisory team uses a mentor system, there is a case for each adviser or inspector's line manager taking on responsibility for guidance. This arises naturally if there is an appraisal system. It is also part of the chief adviser's role to see that new members are being supported adequately and that they are learning the skills needed for their work.

In addition, an advisory team needs to have a programme of INSET in which the whole team or groups of people are expected to take part. Everyone will need opportunities to keep up to date with changes. Recently appointed advisers and inspectors and any others who feel they have a need require a programme designed for them. Advisers/inspectors also need the opportunity to attend courses outside the LEA in their specialisms and on other relevant topics. Small authorities may wish to join with others to provide development opportunities for their advisory team.

There should be an agreement that a certain proportion of the adviser/ inspector's time should be spent on personal INSET and some insistence that this is taken up. INSET for the adviser should not be regarded as dispensable when something urgent comes along. A number of days should be reserved for whole team INSET and a further proportion of time for work with small groups and individuals, and for individuals to attend courses outside the LEA or, where appropriate, those planned for teachers.

Needs assessment

Figure 11 is intended to offer both a means of assessing needs and the basis for a full programme of training. It covers all aspects of an adviser/inspector's work, but not all the skills and pieces of knowledge listed apply to all members of the team. Individuals can select what is relevant for them. It is suggested that it should be completed by all members of the team and worked through by new members with a senior member of the team. The team should then be asked to select a number of priority areas each year and this will then form the basis of the programme on offer.

This should give a number of topics common to the whole team, plus some identified by groups and others identified only by individuals. The whole team topics may then be the subject matter of the programme planned for everyone. Plans may also be made for groups. There should also be an individual plan for each person which is agreed with his or her line manager or with the chief adviser. Time for this should then be built into the programme for the adviser/inspector concerned.

Many of the sections in figure 11 will also apply to advisory teachers, although their precise application will depend on the particular role they have within a given authority. The proforma might be worked through with the adviser or person responsible for a particular advisory teacher. A good deal of the training of advisory teachers might take place alongside advisers and inspectors, since many of their needs are similar.

Induction

Some aspects and details of the proforma are particularly important at the early stages of advisory work and should form the induction programme offered to all new advisers and advisory teachers. There are also topics which should be part of the induction programme for advisers only.

It is suggested that the following topics should form part of the induction programme for advisers/inspectors and advisory teachers:

1 Local government.
2 The education service.
3 The advisory service.
4 Interviewing (for information and problem solving) and counselling.
5 Group leadership.
6 Talking to a group.

Advisory teachers will need early courses on:

7 Inspection and reporting.
8 Selection interviewing.

Advisory teachers will need an early course on in-service training. This will also be needed by advisers and inspectors but other topics may be more urgent.

The items in the first list might form the subject matter of a course run during the first week or so after new people take up their appointment. Where there is only one individual joining at a given time, the work on local government, the education and advisory services will still need to be introduced and time should be allowed with a senior adviser to provide this introduction. This early provision should include introductions to people within the education department with whom the new member may have some contact or who have important roles of which advisers, inspectors and advisory teachers should be aware. Some of them may take part in a course if it is possible to run one.

A course on the interpersonal skills needed in the job might involve more senior people as well as newly appointed advisers and advisory teachers until everyone in the team has been through the course. It might then be run in cooperation with other neighbouring authorities.

Other aspects of induction may be undertaken with a mentor or other

Aspects	Knowledge and skills 1	Good	Average	Weak

Essential legislation	Knows the main provisions of the:
	    Race Relations Act
	    Sex Discrimination Act
	    1981 Act (with reference to Warnock)
	    Education Reform Act
	    Teachers' pay and conditions documents			

Local government	Knows:
	    The organisation of local governmant
	    Its financial organisation
	    The structure of its committees
	    The structure of its departments			

The education service	Knows the structure and division of work within the education department
	
	Knows to whom to go for help with specific problems
	
	Understands the differences in role between administrators and advisers
	
	Knows within the LEA the organisation of:
	    Primary education
	    Secondary education
	    Special education
	    Nursery education
	    Further education
	    Adult education
	    Youth and community service			

Figure 11   The knowledge skills of the adviser

Aspects	Knowledge and skills 2	Good	Average	Weak

The education service (Cont.)	Knows the range of services available to support schools and colleges and the terms on which they are available
	    The school psychological service
	    The careers service
	    The youth and community service
	    The education welfare service
	
	Knows policies governing education			

Advisory work	Knows own team and the responsibilities of colleagues Is able to advise schools on the best person to help in a particular situation Knows advisory teachers whose work is relevant to the adviser's own			

Child development	Has knowledge of child development including:
	    Physical development
	    Intellectual development
	    Emotional development
	    Social development
	    Differences in development between boys and girls
	    Effects of environment			

(continued)

Aspects	Knowledge and skills 3	Good	Average	Weak
Child development (Cont.)	Is able to recognise aspects of development and maturity Is able to recognise the work which might be expected at different ages Is able to recognise match and mismatch of work to child's ability Is able to recognise problems and handicaps, for example poor sight and hearing			
Curriculum	Has knowledge of the framework of the National Curriculum and its assessment Has knowledge of the content of the core subjects Is able to advise schools and colleges on what they need to do			

Learning	Has knowledge of learning theories and teaching methods for:
	    Nursery/reception
	    Infant/first school
	    Junior/middle school
	    Lower secondary school
	    Upper secondary school
	    Sixth form
	    Special school
	    Adult education			

(continued)

Aspects	Knowledge and skills 4	Good	Average	Weak
Learning (Cont.)	Observes learning and assesses the appropriateness of the modes of learning and teaching methods for the particular situation Assesses development of learning behaviour and study skills at each stage of education			
Equal opportunities	Is able to assess how well a school is doing in providing for equal opportunities for children of different ethnic groups Is able to advise a school on how to provide equal opportunities for children of different ethnic groups Is able to assess how well a school is doing in providing equal opportunities for boys and girls Is able to advise a school on how to provide equal opportunities for boys and girls			
Organisation	Knows possible patterns of school organisation at each stage of education and the advantages and disadvantages of each Knows techniques for analysing school organisation Knows possible patterns of classroom organisation, including the organisation of the physical environment Is able to assess the appropriateness and effectiveness of a given organisation Knows how to arrive at the principles on which a timetable should be compiled Knows techniques for analysing a timetable and staff deployment			

(continued)

Aspects	Knowledge and skills 5	Good	Average	Weak
Management	Knows how to analyse the spending of a school and how to relate it to the school development plan			
	Understands the process of development planning			
	Understands the school budget preparation process			
	Is able to relate the school budget to development and maintenance functions			
	Knows how to determine success criteria and performance indicators			
	Knows the communication patterns needed in a primary school			
	Knows the communication patterns needed in a secondary school			
	Is able to evaluate the effectiveness of the administration of a school			
Pastoral care and discipline	Knows the possible patterns of pastoral care at each stage of education			
	Is able to evaluate the effectiveness of the organisation for pastoral care			
	Knows possible ways of establishing patterns of behaviour in schools			
	Is able to evaluate the effectiveness of a school's discipline and behaviour			
	Is able to evaluate a school's methods of dealing with discipline problems			
School self-evaluation	Knows how to establish a school self-evaluation system			
	Is able to assess the effectiveness of a school self-evaluation system			

(continued)

Aspects	Knowledge and skills 6	Good	Average	Weak
Assessment and evaluation	Has knowledge of current thinking about evaluation and of a range of techniques for carrying it out			
	Understands the main principles of assessment in the National Curriculum			
	Has knowledge of ways of recording pupil development and progress			
	Has knowledge of Standard Assessment Tasks (SATs)			
	Understands the relationship between teacher assessment and SATs			
	Is able to evaluate the effectiveness of a school's records of pupils			
	Is able to advise on the integration of assessment into the teaching and learning process			
	Is able to make judgements about a school's SATs results			
	Understands the moderation process for the assessment of the National Curriculum			
	Is able to make assessments and offer advice on provision for the most and least able			
	Is familiar with GCSE			
	Is able to assess the implications of a school's GCSE results and draw inferences from them			
	Is familiar with sixth-form examinations			
	Is able to assess the implications of a school's sixth-form examination results and draw inferences from them			

(continued)

Aspects	Knowledge and skills 7	Good	Average	Weak
In-service work within the school	Knows how to undertake a needs analysis			
	Is able to help a school to set up a staff development programme			
	Is able to help teachers undertake self-evaluation			
	Knows of informal ways in which teachers can develop their potential			
	Is able to help a school to use the everyday opportunities for staff development			
	Is able to help a school to plan and organise an in-service day			
	Knows techniques of appraisal interviewing			
	Is able to carry out appraisal interviews successfully			
	Is able to help a school to develop an appraisal programme			
	Is able to help a school to develop records for teachers			
Other in-service work	Has an overview of the in-service provision in the area			
	Knows of methods of planning and organising an in-service course in the particular LEA			
	Is able to use a range of training techniques			
	Is able to advise teachers on the in-service provision available in the area			
	Is able to select suitable forms of in-service provision for a given purpose			
	Is able to plan and run an in-service course			
	Knows methods of evaluating in-service provision			

(continued)

Aspects	Knowledge and skills 8	Good	Average	Weak
Career advice to teachers	Has knowledge of possible career patterns for teachers Is able to offer relevent career advice to teachers at different stages of education and at different stages of development Has knowledge of appropriate award-bearing courses for teachers in the area Is able to help teachers to choose suitable courses and to use what they are learning when it is appropriate			
Teachers who are failing	Knows LEA procedures for dealing with teachers who are failing Is able to support teachers who are failing Knows how to invoke and carry through the LEA procedures for teachers who are failing Is able to provide appropriate reports on the work of teachers who are failing			
Inspection and reporting	Knows what is involved in classroom observation Knows what is involved in looking at the management of a school Knows how to feedback observation to a teacher Knows how to feedback observation to a headteacher Knows what is required by way of reporting and the problems and dangers inherent in it Is able to give verbal reports Is able to provide written reports Is able to collate reports from colleagues			

(continued)

Aspects	Knowledge and skills 9	Good	Average	Weak
Making surveys	Knows how to make a study of an aspect of work in a number of establishments Is able to undertake large-scale evaluation Is able to use research and statistical techniques appropriately			
Advising on school building	Knows how school building is financed Understands plans of buildings Understands the process of designing a building and carring out the design Is able to provide briefs and suggestions within financial limits and within the constraints governing the architect Is able to offer suggestions about buildings at appropriate points in time Is aware of educational possibilities particularly where schools are being remodelled Is aware of what is available in furnishing and equipment for various aspects of work Is able to help teachers to choose wisely from what is available			

(continued)

Aspects	Knowledge and skills 10	Good	Average	Weak
Interpersonal skills	Understands what is involved in counselling			
	Is able to counsel			
	understands what is involved in negotiation			
	Is able to negotiate			
	Understands what is involved in consultancy			
	Is able to work as a consultant			
	Understands what is involved in working with governors			
	Is able to work with governors			
	Leads a group successfully in a formal meeting			
	Leads a group successfully in the performance of a task			
	Leads a group successfully in an exploratory discussion			

(continued)

Aspects	Knowledge and skills 11	Good	Average	Weak
Interpersonal skills (Cont.)	Knows and uses own strengths Is aware of own weaknesses and compensates for them Relates to other people Manages own work, including use of time Is able to prepare and give talks to groups of differing size and composition Interviews in situations requiring the obtaining of information Interviews in situations requiring problem-solving			
Making appointments	Is able to write a job description Is able to write a person specification Is able to write an advertisement for a teaching post Is able to write a confidential report on the work of a teacher Is able to identify criteria for selection for a given post Is able to make a short list, using application forms and confidential reports Is able to interview for a teaching post, looking for specific skills and abilities			

(continued)

experienced person. Stillman and Grant (1989) identified a number of types of induction experienced by advisers:

- accompanied visits, attachment to senior colleagues, observation of interviews etc.
- residential courses and workshops, NAIEA, CAID;
- locally-based tours, explanatory talks and observation, introductions to heads and department heads;
- locally-based induction courses e.g. talks on role etc.
- team meetings with other advisers, the previous incumbent, other new colleagues etc.
- informal discussion with colleagues;
- regular review meetings with the chief adviser and/or senior education officer

Newly appointed advisers, inspectors and advisory teachers need a good deal of information when they first join the service. It would be very easy to make an induction course a series of information-giving lectures. This is not only an unsatisfactory way of helping people to learn, but also a bad example of in-service work to offer to people with a major responsibility in this area. It is particularly difficult to take in and absorb information which will not be used frequently, for example, the organisation of the local authority. There will, of course, be a need for some information input in this area, but this is likely to be better absorbed if, for example, the group members are asked to work in pairs, preparing questions to ask various senior officers about the way the authority works, with the task of producing a paper at the end of it which they can use for reference.

Information about ways of working within the advisory team will gradually be absorbed with practice and the need here is for information on paper which can be referred to at appropriate times. Every advisory team needs a staff file or handbook which contains agreed policies, systems and routines. The file for one such advisory team contained the following:

1 Background information such as a list of names, addresses and telephone numbers of the advisory team, diagrams of the structure of the education department and the education committee, the aims of the education department and the advisory team, and a note about professional organisations for advisers.
2 Information on conditions of service such as travel and subsistence, leave arrangements, provision of materials and equipment for advisers, insurance, attendance at courses and conferences, professional development policy and appraisal, and arrangements for the induction of new members.
3 Details of the work of the service such as protocol in visiting establishments, inspection arrangements, details of teachers' pay and conditions of

service, notes on confidential report writing, on probation and on dealing with teachers who are failing and other disciplinary cases, policy on interviewing, regulations for educational visits, resources available to advisers and inspectors, and the various records they are required to keep.

4 Details of inspection policies, procedures for inspection, criteria for evaluation and monitoring, expectation regarding type and frequency of review and evaluation visits, reporting procedures, inspection schedules.

5 Details of the arrangements for in-service education.

6 Statements from each specialist and phase adviser on what to look for in his or her specialist area or phase.

This file of papers was issued to each new member joining the service before he or she took up the post and was discussed in a preliminary meeting with the chief adviser.

This kind of file can be built up gradually and the writing of appropriate papers for it offers a useful form of in-service training for those who undertake the task. In the file quoted, for example, a group of new advisers was given the task of writing a paper about the education department as part of their induction programme. It is also necessary to review the contents frequently to add, update or remove papers as patterns of working change. This too can be used as a staff development activity.

The part of the induction programme which requires practical activity is that concerned with the skills of interviewing and group leadership. These should be practised, as role play where necessary, with observers noting how individuals manage the situation and offering supportive comment on performance. Suggestions about this are given in chapter 3 and chapter 7.

This training should continue on the job, with the new adviser, inspector or advisory teacher observing more experienced people undertaking interviews, leading discussion and talking to groups and then undertaking these activities with a more experienced person observing and giving feedback on performance until everyone is satisfied with the new person's skill. This means that time must be allowed in the programme of the more experienced person to monitor the work of the newly appointed.

Provision for the experienced adviser

Experienced advisers need training opportunities to update their knowledge as changes occur. They also need occasional opportunities to review what they are doing and rethink aspects of their work. Advisory work does not provide many opportunities for taking time to think about the work and every team needs to ensure that such opportunities are made by reserving time for them.

CAID has been particularly valuable in this context and many experienced people have been able to spend a reasonable time thinking about their work and how to develop it. An opportunity of this kind should ideally be available to advisers and inspectors about every five years, so that no one has the chance to get stale. In practice this would require a much larger commitment nationally to in-service provision for experienced people.

Opportunities can be created within a team for thinking time. The most satisfactory arrangement is when a team can spend three or four days at a residential conference in a pleasant venue, out of reach of the office. This experience reinforces the sense of being a team and provides opportunities for talking about the work and thinking about ways forward. When a residential conference is not possible, then a period of several consecutive days of in-service work provides a possible alternative.

This kind of in-service opportunity, while requiring some stimulating input from outside speakers, should be mainly one for thinking and planning and talking together about the work of the advisory team. The discussion element needs very careful planning. It works best when the discussion centres on tasks to be carried out or papers to be written. For example, an initial conference of this kind might be concerned with the aims of the team, defining them if they have not already been defined and then using the suggestion for ideas collection in chapter 6 to suggest ways in which the aims might be achieved. A group might then work on one particular aim and endeavour to come up with a possible programme of activity which could be carried out.

Another part of the conference might include work on the professional development of the team. It might use the proforma in figure 11 to assess individual needs and then work in very small groups to select out of the needs identified by individuals a number which are common, perhaps using the nominal group technique described in chapter 7. The team might then go on to consider how such needs might be met and gradually evolve the framework of a programme.

Case studies of particular problems provide another useful activity. Individual members are each asked to bring a case study of a particular problem he or she is encountering and would like help with. They then work in groups of four or five, with a designated chairperson, taking each problem in turn and discussing it. A specific time should be allowed for each problem and it should be the chairperson's responsibility in each group to see that it is adhered to.

There will also be occasions when new skills or knowledge are required and a conference may be devoted to this. Where the acquisition of new knowledge is concerned it should be remembered that people need to become involved with it in order to make it their own. Lectures deliver knowledge quickly and efficiently but if it is to be retained more work on it is required. It is often useful to use the information circuit idea given in chapter 6, where experts in some particular area circulate a number of small groups, each of which has prepared questions to ask them. The groups are then asked to make a statement which covers the essential knowledge in the area under discussion which could be part of the staff file. Groups could also be asked to do this following a lecture, provided that everyone has been given advance notice that this will be required.

Skills must be learned through practice of various kinds. You cannot learn to play a violin from a lecture. However, there is usually a need for a summing-up talk, drawing together what should have been learned from the practical activities. All the various observer techniques suggested in chapter 6 apply here.

Sometimes work on a slightly unusual theme may stimulate thought and generate ideas. One team, for example, spent three days working on plans for the school of the future, resulting in a substantial statement about the way education might develop in the next century. This threw a certain amount of light on present practice.

Learning about other phases and specialisms

Most teams are now responsible for looking at all the educational establishments of their LEAs. This may pose problems if only a very small number of people are able to look at adult education and at primary and special education. In adult education in particular, there will be a need for specialist advice, and specialist advisers need to learn what is required. There will also be a rather different need for specialist advice at the primary stage and in special education as well as a need for more people who can view such schools as a whole. This requires specific training if the people concerned are to have credibility.

Informal opportunities for development

Much of the best learning in any job takes place in the process of actually doing the work. This can be purely incidental or it can be used deliberately as part of the overall professional development programme. This was discussed in relation to teachers in chapter 7.

The following may be valuable as learning opportunities for advisers:

Acting as a voluntary deputy Where a team has a number of people in senior posts it becomes possible to give others the opportunity for a given period to act as deputy to one of them. This needs to be seen as a professional development opportunity and should be for a fixed and limited period. The period needs to be long enough for the person concerned to learn the job, but not so long that the person concerned has difficulty in returning to his or her previous post or so long that it limits opportunities for others. A term might be a suitable length of time. This could be particularly valuable where a senior person has a heavy load and is a good trainer of others. The difficulty about it is that it takes a person away from the work he or she is doing and this has to be planned for.

Analysing one's diary Diary analysis is a very important way of learning about the work a person is doing and every team member should be encouraged to undertake it regularly. It is important to know how time is being used and the proportion being spent on the different aspects of the work. This should be part of the discussion with senior colleagues for both advisers and advisory teachers.

Being asked to investigate a problem or area of work Advisers, inspectors and advisory teachers learn by being asked to look at some new area which requires them to find out a good deal and put it together in some form of report or suggestion. For example, an adviser was asked to investigate the needs of gifted children and the way this question was being tackled in schools and in other LEAs. Another was asked to look at the possibility of a standard record for teachers and at what it might contain.

Being part of a problem-solving group The problem-solving group suggested above is a useful way of learning.

Being part of a task group Many of the problems and tasks faced by an advisory team are best tackled by appointing a working party to deal with them. Membership of such a group is normally likely to include those best equipped to deal with the particular problem. Such groups also offer learning opportunities, however, and it may be a good idea to involve one person who is there in a learning capacity. It may be appropriate to include advisory teachers in some such groups.

Discussing work with a more experienced colleague At every level it is helpful to discuss work. It should be a particular responsibility for those in line management roles to discuss work regularly with those for whom they are responsible.

The more senior people need the opportunity to discuss work with the chief adviser, who in turn needs an opportunity to discuss work with someone, possibly the CEO or deputy CEO. This is also one of the ways in which those in senior positions keep in touch with what is happening and get to know the problems of individual establishments. Advisory teachers also need this opportunity. It may be part of an appraisal scheme or simply a way of keeping in touch.

Shadowing or visiting with a colleague This has already been suggested as part of induction. It is also a valuable activity at any stage of an adviser's career, because it enables one adviser to see from another's point of view. As time passes it is extremely easy to become limited in what one observes and the opportunity to share observation helps to prevent this. It is also helpful to observe other people's methods of tackling problems and working with teachers and headteachers. This is useful training for advisory teachers as well as advisers and inspectors.

Visiting other LEAs   A visit to another LEA to see particular work and to discuss it with colleagues there is usually very useful, particularly when it is part of a study of some particular aspect of the adviser's work.

Working with teachers and children   Advisers are often tempted to exercise their skills as teachers, particularly at the stage when they are struggling to acquire the skills of advisory work. This can be a matter of self-indulgence. Advisers are not paid to be teachers and, since they should be trying to discover each teacher's style and advise in the light of it, showing someone how to do it may not be very useful: the adviser's approach may be at odds with the style of the particular teacher. On the other hand there may be occasions when an adviser is justified in doing investigatory work with children and teachers in order to develop curriculum and explore new ways of working.

In general, however, this is much more a task for advisory teachers than for advisers. It is normally part of their responsibility to teach and, while they too need to take care to recognise each teacher's style, there will be many occasions when they are working alongside a teacher, adapting to his or her situation and way of working.

Working with HMI   HM Inspectors have always been willing to discuss work with LEA advisers and to look at institutions with them. They are now also willing to undertake joint inspections. This has many benefits for advisers and inspectors at the present time, since it enables them to draw on the long experience of HMI in inspection.

Appraisal

As appraisal becomes part of the normal practice in instituions, advisory services will also need to have an appraisal system in place. Many have already done this.

Advisory work tends to be a lonely activity, even though it is work with people. The comments given earlier in this chapter show that many advisers and inspectors, particularly when they are new to the work, find it difficult to know how they are doing and to see any results for their work. It is only as he or she builds up experience in the job that an adviser or inspector can say, 'I helped that school to get started on that particular development' or 'I helped that headteacher through a difficult first year'. Initially advisers, inspectors and advisory teachers need as much feedback as colleagues can offer and appraisal offers one way of doing this.

A second aspect of advisory work is that it is very difficult for someone in a management role to know how colleagues are doing. Comments drift back from teachers and headteachers and from other members of the advisory service and one can learn about the work colleagues are attempting from talking to them. Appraisal offers a good opportunity to get to know how individuals are working and from this to see how well the service as a whole is working. It is also a good opportunity for feeding in ideas and offering direction so that the work of the advisory team is consistent.

While there should be many occasions when advisers, inspectors and advisory teachers discuss their work with senior colleagues, appraisal as such should probably take place once a year. More frequent appraisal is difficult to justify in terms of the time involved and less frequent appraisal would seem to be inadequate in view of the rapid changes taking place at the present time. However, there should be more frequent formal opportunities for newly appointed advisers to discuss their work.

Preparation for appraisal

Preparation is needed on the part of both the manager and the member of the advisory team. The manager needs to know something of how the adviser or inspector is doing and, while a senior or chief adviser learns a great deal from discussion with members of the team, it is only by visiting with someone that one can get an impression of how a particular person performs in institutions. Joint visiting therefore needs to be part of the senior adviser's role and it also provides a good development opportunity for the person with whom the visit is shared.

Points to look out for in observing an adviser or inspector at work might be as follows:

1 How well does the adviser/inspector relate to teachers and head-teachers?
2 Is the adviser/inspector a good listener? Is he or she skilled at questioning?
3 How acute is the adviser/inspector as an observer in the classroom and about the institution?
4 Has the adviser/inspector a variety of strategies for obtaining direct evidence?
5 How good is the adviser/inspector at problem solving? Are his or her techniques for dealing with problems in institutions sound ones? Does listening come first? Is the teacher concerned led towards his or her own solutions?
6 Is the way the adviser/inspector feeds in suggestions satisfactory?

7 How well does the adviser/inspector manage situations in which he or she has to be critical of a teacher or headteacher?

8 Does the adviser/inspector leave teachers feeling supported and helped and ready to use the suggestions given?

9 Are suggestions given on one occasion noted by the adviser/inspector and followed up on the next visit?

Similarly the adviser or inspector responsible for an advisory teacher will only be able to get a full idea of how the person works in schools or other establishments by visiting while the advisory teacher is at work there. Many of the above questions will apply also to the advisory teacher and the following might be added:

10 Does the advisory teacher take note of a teacher's style in planning work with him or her?

11 Is the teacher fully involved in the planning of joint work?

12 How convinced is the teacher about the joint working methods? Is the teacher likely to persist with the way the joint work has been organised?

The adviser or inspector concerned also needs to attend some of the in-service courses run by advisory teachers in order to see how well they are doing and to offer advice on developing the work further. Questions which might be asked about this are as follows:

1 How good is the planning of the course?

2 How well does the advisory teacher present material?

3 Is there an adequate level of member participation?

4 Does the course build on what the course members already know?

5 Is it at the right level for the majority of course members?

6 How satisfactory is the use of aids?

7 How good are handouts?

8 Is the course achieving its stated aims?

9 Are the techniques and strategies chosen the most effective ones for achieving the stated aims?

10 Is it likely that the course will affect practice?

11 Has the course kept within the budget?

Appraisal takes time, which must be allowed for in planning the work of the team. However, joint visits can be concerned with particular issues which need to be dealt with and which require visits anyway. An adviser or inspector responsible for in-service courses is also responsible for their evaluation and should be visiting them from time to time to see how they are going.

At the second round of appraisal, the senior person will also need to look at what was discussed and agreed on the previous occasion and to make notes about the points which need to be picked up both from observation and from previous notes.

The person being appraised needs to prepare his or her plans for the next period of time. These should fit in with the total plans for the service but each individual needs to have a personal plan. These plans should allow some time for fire-fighting but provide a definite programme of work to be done, which will be discussed and agreed. Part of the task of the appraiser is to see that the programme an individual is setting himself or herself is a reasonable one which can be achieved in the time available. It is a good idea to time cost what is planned so that its progress can be monitored.

It is also helpful if part of the appraisal process requires a diary analysis of the past year, looking at how time has been spent on the different aspects of the job. This can then be discussed and the balance of time considered. Advisers/inspectors and advisory teachers will need long notice of this so that they can analyse their diaries week by week during the year.

Another valuable piece of evidence, which should if possible be on a computer, is the pattern of visiting over the period reviewed. It is important that all establishments are properly served and it is the line manager's task to ensure that this is happening. If there is no computer record, then it is probably easiest to ask the adviser or inspector concerned to prepare a list of all the establishments visited during the period.

It is also helpful if there is either a form to be completed for appraisal or a list of points which will be discussed. The form might contain such questions as:

1 What do you feel you have achieved in the past year?
2 Which pieces of work gave you most satisfaction and which the least?
3 Can you account for this?
4 What are you planning for next year?
5 What are your goals for the next year?
6 What training needs do you feel you have?
7 Is there any way in which your senior colleagues could do more to help you?

The appraisal interview

It has been said many times that appraisal interviews for teachers must be positive and developmental. This also applies to appraisal interviews for advisers, inspectors and advisory teachers. The appraisal interview offers an opportunity to praise and encourage in a formal setting and to record success, but also to deal with aspects of a person's work which are less than satisfactory.

It is important that an appraisal interview is carried out in a comfortable place without interruptions. The person being interviewed must feel that he or she comes first in the attention of the interviewer for the period of the interview. This means that the interviewer must spend a good deal of the time listening intently and encouraging the interviewee to talk. Initially the appraiser should explain his or her plan for the interview, particularly the first time it is undertaken. The plan should be used flexibly, adapting it to include the ideas the interviewee wants to discuss and departing from it if this seems wise, but coming back to it so that all the ground is covered.

The appraiser has four tasks as the interview proceeds. He or she needs to listen, question, respond and summarise. The way these tasks are carried out contributes a great deal to the success or failure of the interview.

1 *Listening*. This must be active, concentrating on what is said and showing by body language that listening is taking place.
2 *Questioning*. This may be of various kinds. Sometimes questions will be closed when specific information is required. Quite a lot of questions will be open. Very often questioning will be probing: 'Why do you think that was?' 'What happened then?' 'Are you happy with that particular plan?' Questioning may establish facts, elicit feelings, check understanding, stimulate thought, clarify ideas.
3 *Responding*. The way the interviewer responds to the interviewee is very important and to some extent determines the willingness of the interviewee to speak frankly. Responses should generally be positive and encouraging and demonstrate that the interviewer has been listening carefully. Responses may be evaluative, giving a judgement on what has been said; interpretive, making inferences and checking them; supportive or probing, asking further questions and exploring the other person's ideas.
4 *Summarising*. At intervals during the discussion the interviewer needs to summarise what has been said and check that he or she has the correct picture. These summaries add up as the interview proceeds and lead to a final summary which is likely to contain the subject matter of any report.

There are also likely to be occasions during an interview when an interviewer is concerned to help the interviewee to solve a problem. It is helpful to work through the following stages:

- Define the problem
- Analyse it
- Generate solutions
- Select a solution

Goal setting

The process of appraisal involves setting goals or targets. These should be something over and above normal work, singled out for special attention. They should be clearly defined so that they can be seen to be achieved and they should have a definite time limit by which they are to be achieved. This means building in a checking arrangement. In the interview it is helpful not only to discuss the goals but also to discuss the strategies for achieving them.

Being direct

An appraiser may need, as part of the appraisal process, to tell someone that his or her work is not satisfactory in some way. Appraisal offers a good opportunity to tackle this in a positive context. The timing of discussion of this should be carefully chosen within the interview. It is wise to discuss more positive things first and gradually lead the other person towards the problem, if possible getting him or her to define it by leading questions. Whether or not the other person arrives at the problem of his or her own accord, the interviewer needs to state it clearly at some point so that there is no doubt in anyone's mind that the problem exists and needs to be tackled. If the other person does not accept that the problem exists, it may be helpful to suggest that if a problem seems to other people to exist, something should be done about it so that they do not get a false impression. As soon as possible, discussion should move on to what can be done about it, identifying steps which can actually be taken. This should then be built into a programme which is monitored. This could be part of the goal-setting process.

Concluding the appraisal interview

The appraisal should end with a summary and with a formal statement of encouragement and praise for good work.

The appraisal report

Appraisal should involve a report of some kind. This may be a form covering the various areas of discussion or it could be a letter from appraiser to appraisee listing what has been discussed and the conclusions reached. If a form is used, it will be necessary to decide how the views of both appraiser and appraisee are recorded. The form could be agreed by both, or there could be space for the appraisee to comment on the report made by the appraiser. Where a letter is used, the appraisee can respond to it if he or she disagrees with anything in it.

Following up appraisal

Following appraisal there needs to be a pattern of review to see how progress to towards goals is being maintained. This probably means having rather briefer discussion meetings during the period following the appraisal.

Performance-related pay

Some LEAs are now in the process of introducing performance-related pay. Evidence from industry suggests that the appraisal interview should not be linked with this more than can be helped. On the other hand, people will interpret what is said in the appraisal interview as indicating whether or not they may qualify for performance-related pay, and this poses a considerable problem for appraisers. The task demands honesty and encouragement but these are susceptible to misinterpretation. Each team needs to define the kind of performance which will qualify for additional pay and make it clear to everyone that these are the criteria which are being applied. Much will depend upon the percentage of employees who might be given extra pay. If this is small, it may be easier to manage than if it is large. It is easier to accept that a small number of people get something extra than to accept that a small number do not.

Chapter 11

The organisation of the advisory team

There have been considerable changes in the organisation of advisory teams as they attempt to meet the demands of the Education Reform Act. There is a good deal of evidence from the past about the need for change and for better management of advisory teams. Pearce (1986) comments, as we noted in chapter 8:

> the inspectorate without positive management is exposed to a lethal combination; its members share a low status reluctance to say 'no' to a demand, while the demands for their highly prized knowledge and skill are unfiltered by any firm priorities.
>
> The same low profile makes many advisers accept inappropriate working conditions without complaint. In the management of time they often prefer a muddle which leaves them some control to any more orderly priorities controlled by others or by the group. In consequence most of their clients regard advisory time as infinitely variable.

The Audit Commission (1989b) notes the need for active management of advice giving to ensure that advice is as soundly based and pertinent as possible.

The Education Reform Act has helped to clarify the role of the advisory/ inspectorate service in that it has laid clearly on LEAs the duty of monitoring the work of schools and colleges. While other officers may be involved in this process it is the advisory/inspectorate service which is likely to be expected to play the major part. There is also a substantial task, part of the traditional role of the advisory service, in helping schools to implement the provisions of the Act.

Advisory services may also be affected in the future by a change of climate. We are in an entrepreneurial period, when many services provided in the past as a matter of course are being put out to tender. Some advisory services are beginning to be affected by this trend and, with the development of grant-maintained schools and city technology colleges, are likely to be asked to sell their services. This may have to be provided for alongside a much more tightly programmed work plan.

The Audit Commission survey defines the task facing LEAs with regard to their advisory services. They suggest the following practical steps:

1 Define the role the service is expected to play.
2 Staff the service with an appropriate range of inspectors and advisers, appropriate both in terms of numbers and in terms of the balance of skills and experience within the team.
3 Establish management arrangements appropriate to the new functions and staffing.
4 Train staff for the new tasks and working procedures.

This chapter looks at staffing the advisory service, planning the programme, the organisation of the advisory team, policy-making, the management of the service, records, communication and the evaluation of the work of the service.

Staffing the advisory service

The aims of the advisory service were set out in chapter 2. The Society of Chief Inspectors and Advisers (SCIA 1989) listed a number of basic principles which need to be met. The local advisory team should guarantee expert coverage of:

1 The curriculum of the LEA, encompassing the National Curriculum.
2 All phases and aspects of education provided by the LEA – a principle which would require substantial staffing increases in currently under-provided areas, such as pre-school, primary, continuing and community education.
3 Each institution's character and operation so that it will be known in some depth by one adviser.
4 Other coordinating functions needed at LEA level, such as staff appraisal.

The same paper defines a number of structural principles, as follows:

a) The chief adviser/inspector should have direct line responsibility to the chief education officer. The chief adviser should be charged with the operational co-ordination and management of all the inspection, advice and training functions.
b) Senior advisers should be appointed to support the chief adviser in a senior management team. They would have individual responsibility for a phase, area or work team, or for whole-service functions such as for appraisal, INSET, professional development, assessment or continuity.
c) The team should have an explicit line-management structure, with the chief adviser as head of the team.

d) There should be a support and development team of field personnel
directly responsible to the advisory division with appropriate supervision, co-ordination and management.

Dean (1991) revealed that many teams have now reorganised and that most
of the structures adopted would seem to meet these principles.

Barnsley Education Department (1990) set out a number of similar
criteria. There should be:

1 A clearly articulated curriculum philosophy 'owned ' by all members of
the service.
2 Understanding of patterns/processes of staff curriculum review and
development.
3 Clear roles and manageable goals across the service.
4 Line management arrangements which promote effective
whole-service working and access to the advisory team, absence of
counter-productive hierarchical structures, sound overall leadership.
5 Flexibility of working arrangements in order to allow for cross-team,
cross-curriculum and cross-phase activities.
6 Suitable bases for service activities, appropriately resourced.
7 A geographical location of service which promotes collaboration
between teams.

Planning the programme

Meeting the aims of the service as set out in chapter 2 represents a very large
task for the advisory team, and the service that can be provided needs to be
defined and costed in terms of advisory time.

As a preliminary to planning, the chief and senior advisers and inspectors
need to consider the amount of time which can be devoted to each of the
aims. Hard information will be available for some aims through the analysis
of diaries. Some teams have taken a sample of two or three weeks at random
and asked each member to complete a pro-forma stating the amount of time
on each of these activities. The pro-forma needs also to list time taken by
administrative work, by meetings and by travel. It is also useful to ask
advisers and inspectors to estimate the time taken by unexpected items
which must be dealt with immediately. A further useful piece of information
is the time being spent on the support of teachers who are having difficulty.
This information gives a basis for planning, although some items, like advice
on licensed and articled teachers, will not be possible to assess from
experience. Time must also be allowed for the in-service needs of advisers,
inspectors and advisory teachers, for the management responsibilities of
senior members of the team and for necessary meetings.

Many teams have started by allocating a percentage of time to each item for advisers/inspectors and for advisory teachers, but this needs to be translated into whole days for detailed planning to be workable. The total suggested for inspection ranges between twenty and thirty days in the year. One team has planned in modules of two months at a time. This would seem to have some advantages in that it is difficult to see too far ahead in planning some aspects of the work, whereas other aspects such as inspection can be part of a long-term plan. A pro-forma for assessing the amount of time taken by inspection is given in chapter 5 and inspection may be a good starting point for planning time, since this is now a major task for all inspectors and advisers. The time taken for appointments can be assessed from a time analysis. Other items need to be allocated time using the diary analysis and general experience, and this allocation may need adjusting as the plan is put into practice.

The time available for working with institutions is 195 days, but in practice the beginnings and ends of terms will not be very profitable occasions for advisory work. Work in institutions might sensibly be planned within 185 days.

Once the time pattern has been established a consideration of the team's aims might well form the basis of an annual in-service day in which groups of advisers, inspectors and advisory teachers consider together the implications of each aim for the work which needs to be done in terms of the time available. Such an exercise should end with a statement of what is possible under each aim. This then forms the basis of the overall plan. The following may need to be considered under each aim.

Inspection and reporting

The team needs to consider which of the patterns of inspection given in chapter 5 it wishes to adopt, in terms of the time and number of inspectors available and the cycle of inspection required. The pro-forma (figure 6) and formula given in that chapter provide a means of assessing how much time is required for each type of inspection in a given LEA.

School support

Every school and institution will require some advisory time to support teachers in the classroom and the head and senior staff in their management responsibilities. This may be given by advisers who are also inspectors, by advisers whose main role this is or by advisory teachers. The analysis of in-service provision for advisers, inspectors and advisory teachers given in Dean (1991b) shows 62 per cent of LEAs providing in-service education for advisers and inspectors for supporting headteachers and 48 per cent for advising teachers. Comparable figures for advisory teachers show 15 per cent of LEAs giving them in-service education for advising headteachers and 64 per cent for supporting teachers. This would seem to suggest that many authorities see advisers and inspectors as playing the main role in advising heads and advisory teachers and as having an important part to play in advising teachers.

The adviser's role will include not only advising teachers and head-teachers in general, but also dealing with teachers and headteachers who are having difficulties. This may be very time-consuming. The best way of looking at this aspect of work may be to decide on an entitlement of days for each school or institution, leaving some time for dealing with emergencies and failing teachers.

LEAs have also had to decide what exactly supporting heads and teachers involves, and many have set about this by agreeing an entitlement of time for this work and a minimum pattern of visiting. It should certainly include helping schools to prepare their development plan and monitoring its progress. It will also involve monitoring the progress of the National Curriculum. As assessment develops it will involve discussing this with the head and staff, and in the secondary school it may involve looking at the timetable and at examination results. Schools and other institutions may also need support for change.

Advisory teachers will often help by working alongside teachers to implement new work.

In-service education

Advisers and inspectors are now likely to need to confine their involvement in in-service work to planning and evaluation, except possibly for aspects of management education, leaving the implementation partly to advisory teachers and partly to other providers. The work involved in this is therefore not very easy to cost, since in the past very little work has been done by advisers and inspectors as general evaluators of in-service work and many LEAs have developed new systems for dealing with the planning of the programme. It is probably a matter of working backwards by deciding how much time can be allowed for this aspect of the work and then considering what can be done in the time available.

Advisory teachers should be able to give information about the time they are currently spending on in-service work and from this estimate what time may be needed in the future. Planning should involve follow-up of teachers who attend courses.

Appointments

The Education Reform Act provides a right for the CEO or his or her representative to give advice to governors on the appointment of staff. The representatives expected to give this advice in many LEAs will be the advisers/inspectors. However, there will be a limited amount of time available for this and it may be necessary to limit those appointments which can be supported to more senior posts and those where there are difficulties.

Provision for licensed and articled teachers and probationers

Advisers and inspectors will be needed to interview possible candidates for these forms of training and to monitor what happens to them. It should be possible to break down the possible tasks involved and estimate how much time would be needed for a given number of such teachers.

Many authorities are handing over the support of newly qualified teachers to the schools. Where this is done, there will be a need to ensure that schools are aware of what needs to be done by way of support and to monitor that it is happening, perhaps as part of the inspection programme.

It may be easier in terms of planning to make all these teachers a major responsibility for one person, who could be either an advisory teacher or an adviser.

The total set of tasks then needs to be translated into a plan for each individual adviser, inspector and advisory teacher. Each will have so many days to allocate to each part of the work. Some days will be determined by team tasks. This will be true of the inspection element in the work and of the tasks involved in coordinating assessment.

Meetings will also be arranged for teams and groups. The remaining time must be allocated by the individual adviser or inspector according to the pattern agreed and there should be considerable encouragement to see that each visit to an institution has a definite programme known by the head in advance. It may be useful for each adviser or inspector to agree his or her programme with the appropriate middle or senior manager, returning for further discussion when there is a need for a change.

Planning for the senior members of the advisory service will need to include inspection, some specific support tasks and perhaps the appointment of headteachers and a contribution to their appraisal, but a major responsibility will be to support, monitor and coordinate the work of colleagues. This may include visiting with them from time to time, particularly where there are difficult problems. It also needs to include time not only for appraisal, but also for regular discussion of work with each individual and for training new members of the service. Discussions can well take place when schools and colleges are not in session.

Planning in many authorities also includes working parties to look at particular aspects of the work, either in institutions or in the advisory service itself, each functioning for a limited time. Advisers and inspectors involved in this activity will have less time for some other activities while they are members of the working party. It may be wise to plan the inspection programme, for example, on the basis that a small group of people will be omitted from it in any one year. This will allow time for working parties and for advisers and inspectors to attend long courses.

Where advisers or inspectors are responsible for a small group of advisory teachers, time must be allowed for working with them on planning and support. Some LEAs are now appointing people to management posts within the advisory teacher organisation so that much that now falls on specialist advisers and inspectors can be taken care of, leaving only the specialist role for the adviser.

The organisation of the advisory team

Stillman and Grant (1989) suggested that the significant elements in the organisation of advisory teams were:

- the amount of the chief adviser's time available to the service;
- the presence or otherwise of a middle tier of management;
- whether the chief adviser is a member of the CEO's senior management team.

Factors interacting with these points were:

- whether the team has an area organisation;
- the overall status of the service in the LEA;
- the integration of officer and adviser work;
- the size of the advisory team.

The Audit Commission (1990b) suggests that specialisms are needed as follows:

Management in primary, secondary and further education.
Teaching styles and methods for early, infant and junior years.
Work in the primary phase on number, language and science.
All subjects of the national curriculum.
Religious education.
Special needs.
Cross-curricular themes such as information technology and multicultural education.

Since the publication of the Education Reform Act most LEAs have made changes in the organisation of advisory work. A small study of changes in thirty LEAs (Dean 1990) showed 83 per cent had reorganised or were in the process of reorganising. Dean (1991b) suggested that there were very few LEAs which had not reorganised. Both the Audit Commission and Stillman and Grant were critical of the lack of management of advisory teams and Stillman and Grant suggested that LEAs did not take the management of this service seriously enough. Stillman and Grant give 29 per cent of LEAs without any middle management, 12 per cent without a chief adviser and a further 6 per cent for whom the chief adviser did the job on a part-time basis, with the rest of the time devoted to other responsibilities. All the LEAs in the later sample (Dean 1991b) now had a chief adviser. One had two people dividing the work between them and another had three. Although eight LEAs in the earlier study were expecting their chief adviser to do other things as well, this was part of a carefully structured organisation in which senior advisers did much of the day-to-day organising of the advisory team.

The studies showed that since the Education Reform Act virtually all LEAs had introduced a management structure with at least one tier of middle management. There was also some evidence of a move to bring the administration and advisory services closer together, with some twenty-seven LEAs making their chief adviser an assistant education officer and eleven making him or her deputy CEO. A number of teams included a mixture of officers and advisers/inspectors and several LEAs have developed inspection teams which contain both.

Stillman and Grant (1989) suggested that the specialist teams of the early 1970s were no longer appropriate for the present time. These teams were predominantly staffed with people of secondary school background and primary schools tended to get an inadequate share of help and advice. It is clear that current developments in schools and colleges require not only good specialist advice but also general advisers and inspectors who can advise across the whole curriculum and can also advise headteachers. A change in this direction is reflected in the present number of advisers and inspectors with general roles. Seventy-six per cent of LEAs in the sample (Dean 1991b) now have people working in the general role. In twenty-one cases these are specialists who also have a general role. Seventy-seven per cent of authorities have at least some advisers and inspectors with phase responsibility. Seventy-seven per cent of these are for primary education, 67 per cent for secondary and 61 per cent for post-16 education. Fifty-one per cent of LEAs have an area organisation.

All this suggests that there are many possible patterns of organisation of advisory teams. The possible alternatives can be classified in various ways.

Inspection and advice

It is first of all necessary to decide whether the same group of people will both inspect and advise. A small number of LEAs have separated these two functions and have inspectors whose task is to inspect and advisers and/or advisory teachers whose task is to support. The advantage of this is that each group is clear about its responsibilities and can concentrate on what is involved in carrying them out. Different skills are required in the two activities, and each group will have greater opportunities for practising and perfecting them.

The disadvantage of this system is that it is less easy in practice to separate the two roles and something may be lost in the communication of findings by inspectors to advisers. It is easier to help a school where details of its practice are known from observation. It is also a less satisfying job to be inspecting schools and colleges all the time. However, it seems likely that the patterns proposed for inspection will force a separation of the two functions.

Specialist and general roles

An advisory team needs to be in a position to give l ᴖ.h specialist and general advice. This can be achieved by separating the two roles or by expecting every specialist also to have a general role. The separation of roles allows greater concentration on each aspect, and advisers may find either role in itself very satisfying. Stillman and Grant (1989) report these comments by advisers on the disadvantages for the specialist:

– it frustrates internal and external promotion where general experience is required;
– it creates a door-to-door salesman impression of subject advisers in schools/institutions;
– it creates salary divisions and resentments within the team;
– it accords seniority to phase advisers;
– it depresses the salary for new subject advisers;
– it creates paperwork, preferential treatment and prevents team involve- ment in the scrutiny of the advice given by general advisers to senior administrative officers and to institutions.

One might also add that it is difficult for someone who spends all the time dealing with one subject to see it from the perspective of the needs of the whole establishment and this can create pressure on headteachers.

If specialists are also general advisers many problems are overcome. This form of organisation has the advantage that the total number of establishments can be divided among the total number of advisers so that everyone has a group of reasonable size. It prevents specialists from thinking that their specialism is the most important in the curriculum. It is very demanding but many people find it very satisfying.

The disadvantages are that there is always a tension between the two roles and some people place more emphasis on one than on the other so that either general or specialist work suffers. It also makes for considerable pressure on individuals. It is at its most difficult when a team first changes to this organisation, sometimes against the wishes of some of its members. It becomes easier to manage as time goes on, with advisers and inspectors being appointed who want to undertake both roles.

Phase, area or theme organisation

There is a limit to the number of people for whom one manager is directly responsible. In moving from a flat organisation in which there were either no senior posts apart from that of the chief adviser or even no senior posts at all, many LEAs have developed a middle management structure. This structure is sometimes based on phases of education, sometimes on themes such as evaluation or in-service training, and sometimes on areas. In larger teams there may be an element of all three.

In phase organisation the senior primary phase adviser may have a small team to work with while the secondary phase adviser usually has to co-ordinate the work of a number of specialists, with whom the primary phase adviser may also have involvement. The primary phase teams usually work well. The coordinating role of the secondary phase adviser is often more difficult. There is also the problem that the phases may become very separate and there is a need to ensure that good links are established.

Thematic organisation may or may not involve small teams. In one LEA, for example, there are two general adviser teams, working on an area basis, a subject adviser team, an in-service team and a senior adviser working with the general advisers who has responsibility for evaluation.

Area organisation provides for a small team of advisers to be responsible for all the establishments in a given area of the LEA. The members of each team may also have a specialist responsibility across the LEA. When the team is led by an area adviser or inspector, members of each team can be supported by someone close at hand who also knows the institutions for which the team is responsible. There is also the advantage that each person has a limited group of establishments to cover and continuity between primary, secondary and further education poses few problems because the general adviser or inspector may well have a family of institutions and teachers and the local team get to know each other well.

Warwickshire (1990) has teams, each of which works closely with an identified education officer, with the following major roles:

1 To act as a first point of contact for schools in their dealings with the LEA. This establishes a link between the individual school/college and the authority and a link between institutions, avoiding insularity and a perceived lack of benefit (from a school perspective) of the services available from the LEA.
2 To provide access to the range of services available from the LEA and acting . . . as the school/college's representative on occasion.
3 To provide professional support in the process of monitoring and evaluation as well as reporting upon local schools and colleges.
4 To support the management and development of the school by . . . active involvement in the preparation of a negotiated school development plan and its subsequent evaluation.

5 To act as a channel for the interpretation of the policies of the LEA in
   its strategic role

It is advantageous for the area team to contain both primary and secondary
specialists who can advise colleagues. In a larger LEA it may be possible to
have area advisers or inspectors leading teams and phase advisers coordinating across the authority.

Adviser/officer roles

There would appear to be three areas in which establishments need monitoring. First, finance needs checking to see that public money is properly
spent; secondly, the LEA needs to safeguard its assets and see that health and
safety regulations are implemented by the governing body; third, it must
oversee the quality of the education offered. The third issue is very much the
responsibility of the advisory/inspectorate service, but the first and second
require the expertise of other officers, although advisers and inspectors will
need to be knowledgeable in both areas. This means that the process of
inspection is unlikely to be carried out entirely by inspectors, and any
organisation needs to work out how officers and inspectors are to work
together to deal with all three aspects. Some LEAs, like Warwickshire, are
dealing with this by developing teams which include officers; in others
advisory/inspectorate teams coopt for any given inspection those who are
expert in the areas needed.

Policy-making

An advisory team needs to have policies for all areas of its work. Some of
these have already been dealt with earlier in this book. Each policy should
be a matter for discussion by the whole team and a statement then drafted
for eventual agreement. Discussion is important if everyone is to be fully
aware of what any particular policy states. All policies will need to be
included in the advisory staff file. As time passes, some policies will need to
be updated. Policies will need to be discussed with new members who were
not party to the original policy formulation.
    Policies would seem to be needed for the following areas of work:

Inspection Suggestions about an inspection policy were made in chapter
5 but it may now be that there will be little latitude for local policy on
inspection because the overall pattern will be decided centrally. On the
other hand there may still be a need to decide the cost of inspection and
what can be offered for a given sum. There may therefore be a need to
decide the preliminary visits that can be afforded, the time to be spent on
observation in the classroom and elsewhere and the way in which the report

is to be arrived at and presented. There will also be a need to consider how the inspection is to be followed up and by whom.

Visits Suggestions about a visits policy have already been set out in chapter 6.

Supporting schools and other establishments The policy needs to state what general advisers are expected to know about the establishments for which they are responsible and the way in which visits might be used. There is also a need for a separate policy statement about the way the services of advisory teachers should be used, who should be responsible for calling them into an establishment and the work they might be expected to do there.

Newly qualified teachers Now that probation is disappearing, the advisory team needs to give some thought to what should be done to support newly qualified teachers. There will, in the first instance, need to be consideration of what may be expected of the school in supporting these teachers and the complementary role of the advisory service. Some schools will undoubtedly need the additional help of inspectors and advisers who may well have to see that newly qualified teachers are given sufficient time to develop before judgements are made about their competence.

Failing teachers With local management of schools it is likely that there will be an increasing number of cases where governors wish to deal with teachers who, they believe, are not pulling their weight. There will probably be pressure to move as fast as possible towards disciplinary proceedings and dismissal and it will be important for advisers and inspectors to have a clear plan of action. This should define how a failing teacher should be dealt with, what opportunities should be offered for improvement, the role of the school in both supporting and reporting, and the way in which disciplinary proceedings should be carried out if there is no improvement. It is very important that an advisory/inspectorate team is clear about how this should be done, and how long should be allowed for improvement before a further step is taken, since dismissal could well result in a tribunal at which the adviser or inspector may have to give an account of what has been done by the LEA to help the teacher to improve.

Licensed and articled teachers It will be necessary to define such matters as the criteria by which such teachers are selected, the support institutions are expected to give and the way the work of such teachers is to be assessed and by whom.

In-service provision Advisers and inspectors will need to know the process by which planning takes place and their part in it, the role of advisory teachers and their part, what is involved in evaluation, how and by whom it should be carried out.

Communication Decisions need to be made about the methods of communication both within the team and with other related groups. Responsibilities for particular aspects will need to be allocated.

Professional development of advisers, inspectors and advisory teachers
All advisers, inspectors and advisory teachers should have a clear entitlement to in-service education and to opportunities to develop their work. They need to know how to apply for courses they wish to undertake and the criteria by which decisions will be made about applications. There should be information about induction and the responsibility for this and the responsi- bility of senior members of the team for the development of their colleagues. There should also be details of any appraisal scheme and what it involves.

There may, in addition, be papers needed on conditions of service, such as the way to apply for leave, what to do when sick leave is required, travel and subsistence allowances, ways of obtaining books and materials needed and so on. Some of these will be covered by LEA documents. Others will need to be provided for the advisory service alone.

It will also be necessary to provide policy statements on other aspects of work as the need arises.

The management of the service

All the earlier studies of the advisory service stress the need for better management. As advisory teams grow, the need for managers at middle level increases and these advisers/inspectors need to have delegated responsibility within an agreed pattern for the work of their teams. These senior staff also need to be trainers, developers and supporters of those for whom they are responsible.

The Audit Commission (1989b) made the point that it is vital to decide who, within the LEA, is entitled to call on the services of the advisory team. It is also necessary to build in some safeguards to prevent agreed priorities being set aside when emergencies occur.

The role of the chief adviser

There is a good deal of variation from one LEA to another in the role the chief adviser or inspector is expected to play. He or she is increasingly likely to be part of the CEO's management team and the Education Reform Act has led to increased status for the whole service in a number of LEAs. Some chief advisers have responsibility for some parts of the administration as well as for the advisory service; and in several LEAs the chief adviser is responsible for the school psychological service and, in some, for the careers service and youth service also. This provides a good opportunity for coordinating the work of all these services.

The Audit Commission (1989b) suggested that the following should be the tasks of the head of the service:

- ensure coherence in the work of the team and allocate specific curricular and geographical responsibilities;
- establish the process of decision-making and help the team determine goals, priorities and policies;
- monitor the implementation of agreed policies and evaluate the effectiveness of the work of the team;
- ensure that there are effective channels of communication both within the advisory team and with other groups.

We might also add to this a responsibility for the development and training of members of the team.

Richmond upon Thames (1989b) identify the qualities required for the incumbent of the post of chief inspector. Someone who:

- has the personal and professional qualities needed to lead on educational issues throughout the service;
- is able to motivate a well-established team of inspectors through a period of significant change;
- places value on the the development of constructive working relationships with schools and colleges.

The successful candidate will have:

- substantial and successful teaching experience;
- a track record of successful management in the education service;
- leadership skills with the ability to motivate and support colleagues in a fast-moving educational scene;
- detailed knowledge of current educational thinking;
- sensitivity, understanding and good humour in dealing with a wide range of people. both inside and outside the education service.

The only thing which appears to be missing from this otherwise excellent specification is experience of advisory work. It is difficult for someone coming into the leadership of an advisory team to support colleagues in work that he or she has not experienced.

The LEA's job description is as follows:

The chief inspector manages the staff and programmes of the inspectorate. He/she participates fully in educational policy and curriculum development in the education service and provides support to the director in the successful planning and implementation of the department's programmes and activities.

Main responsibilities:

- to lead a strong and well-motivated inspectorate and advisory service at a key phase in educational change and development;
- to develop and deliver the programme of inspection and advice proposed by the authority;
- to manage and coordinate the newly established pattern of inspectorial attachment to schools and colleges;
- further to develop systems of institutional evaluation and teacher appraisal;
- to ensure that the various activities supported by ESG, TVEI, GEST and the LEA complement each other in all aspects of the education service.

Job descriptions for chief advisers and inspectors are also likely to have reference to equal opportunities. Some might lay rather more stress on the task of supporting schools and other establishments.

The tasks of the chief adviser common to most LEAs are:

1 The overall direction of the work of the advisory team, including the determination of its goals and policies, priorities, organisation, deployment of its staff and planning of its work.
2 The organisation and implementation of a programme of monitoring and inspection.
3 The organisation of professional support for schools and other establishments.
4 The training and development of members of the advisory team.
5 The evaluation of the work of the advisory team.
6 The maintenance of channels of communication within the advisory team and with other groups.
7 The provision of advice to the chief education officer and elected members.

These can be looked at in greater detail.

1 *Overall direction.* The task of the chief adviser or inspector is to see that necessary action occurs, not necessarily to undertake it personally. Goal-setting, policy-making, setting priorities, organising the team and deploying staff all require considerable discussion with members of the team. The chief adviser is also responsible for team discipline.
2 *The programme of monitoring and inspection.* The task of the chief adviser or inspector or other nominated senior adviser is to see that the programme is developed, is clear to everyone involved and is fully implemented. Chief advisers will also need to see that the quality of reporting is adequate.

3 *The organisation of professional support.* The chief adviser needs to see that there is enough time allocated to this once the inspection and monitoring programme has been arranged. It is also important to see that time devoted to professional support is properly used.

4 *The training and development of members of the team.* The chief adviser needs to see that what is planned really happens and to monitor its effectiveness. He or she is also directly responsible for the development of senior members of the team, for their appraisal and for creating opportunities to discuss with them their work and ways in which they could develop further.

5 *The evaluation of the work of the advisory team.* This will include the definition of performance indicators and a variety of ways of assessing what is happening.

6 *The maintenance of channels of communication.* The advisory service needs to communicate with a large number of people and needs good systems for ensuring that information is properly distributed.

7 *The provision of advice to the CEO and elected members.* It is the responsibility of the chief adviser or inspector to see that advice is provided by the service for those who need it. This may be matter of collecting and coordinating advice or of putting those who want the advice in touch with the appropriate member of the team. This is not always an easy matter, since the need for detailed advice sometimes occurs unexpectedly and the information which allows it to be provided may not be available immediately. Part of the chief adviser's task is to anticipate the advice that may be called for and to see that it is available when needed. It is also necessary to leave sufficient space in the planning to collect advice needed urgently when it is not immediately to hand.

Other management roles

Other management roles are more difficult to define because they will vary considerably from one LEA to another. Some of the advisers and inspectors in middle management roles will have tasks similar to those of the chief adviser, in that they will be responsible for a small group of colleagues and will be expected to deploy them to the best advantage within the overall team plan, support and train them and help them to develop their work. These advisers/inspectors will be part of a two-way communication chain and it will be important that they discuss with their teams issues which they themselves have discussed with the chief adviser and feed back their views. They will also be providers of information and advice to the chief adviser and through him or her or directly to the CEO and his or her colleagues. Where the authority is organised on an area basis, area advisers will be an important source of information to area officers. Senior advisers, in whatever role, will also have a responsibility for evaluating aspects of the work of the team.

Where a senior adviser has a phase responsibility, he or she will be concerned with coordinating work in that phase and with helping to develop plans for inspection and support at that level.

Some authorities have appointed senior members of the advisory team with responsibility for evaluation. These advisers will clearly have an important role in helping to plan inspections and should have much to offer in helping the team to evaluate its own work. Another common senior appointment is for in-service work.

Records

It is essential that good records are kept of the work of each adviser, inspector and advisory teacher. This becomes easier if each member of the advisory team provides as part of the appraisal process a statement of what he or she has achieved each year but, even if there is no appraisal, this sort of statement should still be requested for the record. It then provides useful information when someone applies for a promoted post. It may also be useful in the context of performance-related pay.

The individual record file starts when someone is appointed. The application form and notes made at the interview provide a starting point, the latter providing material for evaluating at a later date the effectiveness of the appointment procedure. If the procedure has been effective, there will be few surprises when the person appointed takes up the post. If there are many surprises the procedure can be criticised as inadequate.

It may be helpful to use plastic envelopes within the file, to file different aspects of the adviser or inspector's work, since some material, such as the application form, will be permanent and other material, such as most correspondence, will be temporary. If a coloured sheet is put into each file each year at a given time, it is easy to discard outdated material.

The record then needs to contain the following in addition to annual updating notes on the work done in any particular year:

Information about professional development
When someone is appointed to the advisory team his or her professional development needs should be discussed, perhaps using a check list such as that given in figure 11, and a plan to meet them made. The needs thus identified should be recorded and the chief adviser, any middle manager and the adviser or inspector him or herself should have a note of what has been decided. There should then be a record of in-service opportunities undertaken. This is comparatively easy for some aspects of professional development if there is a form for applying for in-service courses which can be placed in the file. Other opportunities offered will need to be recorded individually.

A similar pattern should be followed for advisory teachers, with the adviser or inspector concerned or anyone else in a management role for this group undertaking a needs survey with the new team member.

Correspondence Correspondence with each individual will be part of the record unless there is good reason to file it elsewhere.

Appraisal notes In addition to the record of work done during the year, the adviser's personal record will contain other notes made during appraisal. There should be some agreement about how long such notes are to be kept, who has access to them and what happens when the adviser or inspector leaves the service.

Any service information Individuals may have particular aspects of the service which need recording. Long absence through sickness, for example, should be recorded in the file.

Equipment and materials on loan Many advisory teams have expensive equipment, like laptop computers, dictation machines and cameras and video-cameras. A record of these needs to be kept, preferably on a specially designed form signed by the adviser or inspector borrowing the equipment.

Any disciplinary procedures Where disciplinary procedures have been taken against an adviser or inspector, this must be part of the record. There will be local rules about how long such a record should be kept.

Notes of meetings A chief adviser, in particular, is likely to have many meetings with members of the team and any planned meetings should be recorded, sometimes by notes taken at the time and sometimes by a letter or memo to the person concerned giving a precis of the subject matter of the meeting. Some meetings with senior advisers in a management role should also be recorded in this way, particularly where they result in agreement about the plan of work of an adviser or inspector.

Communication

Stillman and Grant (1989), found that in general communication in the advisory service was not good. This is hardly surprising when the difficulties are considered. Advisers and inspectors need to communicate with a very large number of different individuals and groups and they may be based outside the central offices of the LEA. Even where they are based at the central office, they are by definition out of the office for a good deal of the time and likely to miss some of the communication which takes place over lunch and coffee with a group of people who normally work together. Communication within the advisory team was found to be often inadequate.

Three-quarters of all advisers said they rarely met about a quarter to half their colleagues outside formal meetings and working parties. Subject advisers, primary advisers and women appeared to get less communication than other advisers and to feel that they made less contribution to policy-making.

It may be helpful if communication responsibilities are clearly allocated and everyone is aware who is responsible for different aspects of communication. Communication also needs to be evaluated.

Channels of communication

Meetings The dispersed nature of the advisory team makes meetings a very important part of the communication system. The disadvantage is that they take time which might be spent in the field. In planning the year's work, the time taken by meetings needs to be estimated, probably from analysis of the previous year's diaries, and enough time, not only for meetings of the team but for the numerous other meetings in which advisers, inspectors and advisory teachers are involved, needs to be reserved. Considerable effort should be made, not only by the advisory team, but also by other people arranging meetings, to time them so that as many as possible fall outside or nearly outside school hours.

If the service is to function as a team, then it is essential that it meets regularly as a team, for communication sessions, forward planning and professional development. It probably needs to meet once a month or at least twice a term and to allow time for individual discussion between main sessions. Some of these meetings could normally be held at the beginning and end of terms, so that members are not out of the schools more than can be helped. It was suggested in chapter 10 that a residential conference once a year not only contributed to professional development but was also an exercise in team building. At least some of the meetings should include advisory teachers as well as advisers.

Much the same could be said of local or phase teams, which will need to meet regularly to plan and evaluate, and of the group of senior advisers and inspectors who will need to meet regularly with the chief adviser. All should have their own agenda and minutes which are circulated among members of the team. There may also be some other groups meeting regularly – for example, advisers or inspectors concerned with special needs meeting with psychologists. Advisory teachers will also need meetings to discuss their work with advisers or others who are responsible for the management of the advisory teacher team. It is essential that all such meetings are planned well in advance. It should be normal practice to plan a year ahead so that meeting dates can be reserved.

It is more difficult to plan for the many occasional meetings which crop up during the year. Meetings may be of working parties, with administrators, heads or teachers, or with advisers and inspectors and others from other

LEAs. Time for these meetings can be estimated only by assessing how much time overall was used in this way in the course of the previous year.

Everyone should be encouraged to look critically at the meetings he or she attends and be present only if there seems to be good reason for being there. Wherever possible advisers and inspectors should be prepared to represent each other at meetings and be responsible for reporting back, so that the presence of several members of the team at the same meeting is avoided. It should be part of a clear and well defined responsibility for those attending certain meetings to report back to others. For example, those attending the senior advisers' meeting who are leaders of smaller teams should report back to those teams and also be responsible for seeing that team opinions are reported to the senior advisers' group. It will also be important for the minutes of the senior advisers' group to be widely circulated within the team. There is a tendency for other members of the team to be suspicious of the senior advisers' meeting and it may occasionally be a good idea to open these meetings to anyone who wishes to observe what is happening.

It is not easy to ensure that meetings are effective. Stillman and Grant (1989) found only 53 per cent of advisers thought participation in team meetings was an effective form of communication. Meetings are most effective when the agenda is carefully compiled, bearing in mind the composition of the meeting, well prepared by the chairperson and firmly led, allowing for plenty of discussion but keeping to the agenda.

Individual discussions If those in senior posts in the advisory service are to keep in touch with the way that individuals are thinking and feeling, it is essential that they spend time talking with individual advisers, inspectors and advisory teachers. This may be partly a matter of using informal opportunities as they arise, but it is also important to see that there is discussion with everyone, so there is a need for some programmed discussion. A number of discussion meetings with the chief adviser may be a part of the team's pattern of induction for advisers in their first year of service. This enables the new adviser or inspector and chief adviser to get to know each other and gives the chief adviser first-hand information about how it feels to be a new member of the advisory team.

Much the same will be true for senior advisers and inspectors. Those who are team leaders will need to talk to members of their teams on a regular basis. Phase advisers may wish to talk to specialists about work at that phase. Advisers with a responsibility for coordinating in-service work will need to talk with each person to discuss plans for in-service work and the allocation of the money available.

This kind of individual discussion will go on all the time advisers and inspectors are together for any purpose, but there should also be planned meetings. Stillman and Grant (1989) found that 55 per cent of advisers thought individual meetings effective. Again it would seem likely that such meetings are most effective when the agenda is clear to both parties.

Written material   The scattered nature of advisory teams and the fact that advisers, inspectors and advisory teachers are not always available mean that written communication or communication by computer will play an important part in the communication system. The problem about written communication is that it can easily be ignored. Stillman and Grant found that only 52 per cent of advisers thought that written communication was effective. Short messages on no more than one side of an A4 sheet are more likely to be read than longer papers and good presentation will make information more easy to assimilate. Frequent headings help people to find their way around a document. A brief summary at the beginning may encourage people to read a longer document in full.

It is sometimes useful to have different-coloured paper for different kinds of communication, although this may also help people to ignore communications which they think may not interest them.

Communication by computer reaches its goal if it is brief and to the point and if the advisers concerned have good access to the computer and actually use it to receive messages.

Groups with which advisers and inspectors need to communicate

Advisers and inspectors need to communicate inter alia with other advisers, inspectors and advisory teachers, the CEO and administration, the education committee, heads and teachers, governors, teachers' centre wardens, teacher unions, HMI, course providers, professional and subject associations, regional bodies, examination boards, other LEAs and the press.

To some extent different advisers can specialise in the particular groups with whom they have contact, but this does not entirely overcome the problem. In the past advisory/inspectorate teams were probably too ready to allow themselves to be distracted from their main work by the need for other meetings, but it is now necessary to consider very carefully the need to be present at any meeting.

Advisers, inspectors and advisory teachers   Communication with other advisers, inspectors and advisory teachers is of considerable importance. This may seem obvious, but the evidence quoted earlier by Stillman and Grant (1989) suggests that there is a real need to ensure that communication within the team actually takes place. There is also a considerable need to ensure communication between advisers and advisory teachers. There is normally good communication between advisory teachers and the adviser or inspector who is responsible for them, but frequently other advisers are almost unaware of their existence. Visit records kept for advisers and inspectors should also be used in an adapted form by advisory teachers and advisers should be aware of the establishments in which advisory teachers are working. Ideally there should be a number of meetings when both groups work together. This will become more likely as advisory teachers take over some of the tasks which were previously carried out by advisers and inspectors.

CEO and administration Members of the advisory team should know the CEO and he or she should know them. This inevitably involves meetings, but it may be possible for the CEO to come to a specified advisers' meeting if this is arranged sufficiently far in advance. This should be an opportunity for the CEO to talk to the team about general policy and for the team to raise issues which concern them.

The administration and advisory services should work increasingly closely and there will be situations when work is shared on a different basis from formerly, with administrators playing a part in some aspects of inspection and advisers and inspectors contributing to policy-making. Different advisers and inspectors will have contacts with the administration according to their particular responsibilities.

Education committee members It would not be realistic for all advisers and inspectors to have contact with members of the education committee on a regular basis. The chief and possibly the senior members of the advisory/ inspectorate team should be well known to education committee members, and other advisers may have opportunities to meet them as members of governing bodies and in reporting on particular pieces of work. For example, in one LEA, it was the practice to produce one or two reports a year on a particular area of curriculum and for the adviser concerned to talk to the committee about this. It may also be a good idea to arrange for new members to attend a meeting, probably of the Schools' Committee or its equivalent, as part of the process of induction.

Headteachers and teachers It is self-evident that advisers and inspectors will need good communication with the heads of schools and other institutions and with teachers at all levels, but the problem is to keep in touch in some way with the whole teaching force and to get information about opinion. Much of this will be occur during regular visiting and supporting of establishments. Teacher unions and teachers' centre leaders will also provide information. In addition it may be helpful if the chief adviser meets groups of heads and teachers from time to time to hear their views. Specialist advisers can also meet heads of department on a regular basis.

HMI It is part of the responsibility of HMI to keep in touch with people in local authorities and in most areas HMI meet and often visit with advisers and inspectors in their particular specialism.

Course providers Most advisers and inspectors will need to be in touch with providers running courses in their particular area of work. If there is an adviser with overall responsibility for professional development, he or she will need liaise with the whole range of providers and with any regional provision.

Neighbouring LEAs It is helpful to know what other LEAs are doing, particularly where some shared provision is possible. Some provision for this will arise because of regional meetings and meetings of professional and subject associations.

Evaluation

The last major task for the chief adviser or inspector is that of evaluating the work of the team. Not much has yet been done by advisory teams to evaluate their own work, but many teams are gradually working out how this might be done.

Some information will come from comments by administrative colleagues, heads and teachers, who will make a point of telling the chief adviser when something is not working well and more rarely when something has gone very well indeed. More information is needed than this, however, and all members of the team need to be concerned with evaluating their work. Each of the aims of the advisory service needs to be evaluated. Over a period the programme of evaluation should cover the following:

1 The effectiveness of the inspection and monitoring programme.
2 The quality of reporting.
3 The provision of information and advice to the LEA.
4 The work of individual advisers, inspectors and advisory teachers in support of teachers and headteachers.
5 The contribution of advisers, inspectors and advisory teachers to the professional development of teachers.
6 The extent to which the National Curriculum and other local and national initiatives are being supported.
7 The work being done in curriculum development.
8 The quality of confidential reports.
9 The contribution of advisers and inspectors in interviewing and advising on appointments.

10 The contribution of the advisory/inspectorate service to appraisal.
11 The effectiveness of the in-service opportunities offered to advisers, inspectors and advisory teachers.
12 Communication.
13 The management of the service.

The following may be useful ways of assessing what is happening:

Documentation   The material an advisory service has on paper gives information about the topics which have been considered and the policies which have been worked out.

Visit records   If these are on computer, a good deal of statistical information can be gained from their study. They will make it clear how much time each adviser, inspector or advisory teacher has spent in institutions and how he or she has spent it. They will show how many establishments and teachers have been visited by each individual and whether there are any gaps in visiting which should be filled. A senior adviser in charge of an area or other team should study these records regularly to assess what is happening and records should also be studied as preparation for appraisal.

Diary analysis   The analysis of diaries as part of preparation for appraisal also gives an idea in statistical terms of how advisers are doing. It also provides an overall picture of how advisory time is spent.

Appraisal interviews   The chief and other advisers responsible for appraisal will learn much about how colleagues are working. Although the process is inevitably subjective, it not only tells the appraiser about the individual adviser's planning and achievement of goals, but also something about the way he or she approaches the work, the inferences which are being made about the work observed in school and how problems are being tackled.

Joint visiting   Visiting with another adviser or inspector in order to observe how he or she operates is a very valuable form of evaluation and has already been suggested as part of the appraisal process. One can see the sorts of relationships being formed and the way problems and difficulties are tackled and the regard in which the adviser is held by the institution.

Evaluation of advisers' and advisory teachers' in-service programme
There should be evaluation of what takes place by way of training of advisers and advisory teachers as part of the normal process of evaluating in-service work.

Questionnaires Questionnaires to a sample of administrators and heads and teachers provide a useful way of getting a wider view of how the service is being seen by others. Teachers and heads might be asked about the most recent visits by an adviser, inspector or advisory teacher and whether what came out of them was useful. They might also be asked about their views of the most valuable services the advisory team are offering them and any views they may have about other help they would like. Headteachers might be asked about the value of inspections and about the contribution of advisers and inspectors to appointments.

Administrators might be asked also about the services they have found valuable and any other help they would like from the advisory service. They might also be asked to comment on management and on communication

Questionnaires to advisers and advisory teachers may be helpful in assessing aspects like communication, management and the in-service provision offered to the service.

Meetings with heads, teachers and administrators, advisers, inspectors, advisory teachers Questionnaires might be followed up by meetings to discuss the views held by those on the receiving end of the advisory service. The main issues resulting from a questionnaire survey may be discussed with a sample group. Similarly, discussion with team members will offer useful information about their views of what is happening and such matters as communication and the management of the service.

Use of an external evaluator Advisory teams may occasionally have the opportunity to employ an external evaluator to assess how they are doing. Where this is done, it will be important to give the person concerned a clear brief, selecting from the many areas which could be evaluated those which are most difficult to assess from within. It will also be necessary to identify in advance the kind of report required. An evaluator may simply offer evidence for the team to discuss and leave them to draw their own conclusions, or draw conclusions from the evidence which can be discussed. This might be a task for an adviser or inspector undertaking a higher degree.

Performance indicators A number of teams are considering the performance indicators which might be useful in assessing their own work. The problem about this is that all the indicators which are easily measurable, such as the number of visits made, their duration and the number of teachers and headteachers seen, tell nothing about the quality of the work being undertaken, which is what really matters.

The following may be possible indicators in each of the areas listed above. It is not suggested that all these should be used at the same time. It may be that one or two areas are examined as part of overall evaluation each year.

1 *The effectiveness of the inspection and monitoring programme*
There is a written overall plan for the way in which monitoring and inspection are to be carried out.
The plan is generally carried out as written by most advisers and inspectors.
All members of the advisory/inspectorate service have received training in inspection and monitoring.
Changes have taken place in schools and colleges as a result of inspection.
Positive comments about inspection are made in questionnaires by head-teachers.

2 *The quality of reporting*
There is a written statement about the format and style in which reports should be written.
This is carefully followed so that reports rarely need rewriting.
All members of the service have received training in report writing.
Positive comments are made by headteachers in questionnaires about reports.

3 *The provision of advice to the LEA*
A number of reports have been made to the CEO and committee.
The administration turns to the advisory service for advice on many aspects of education.
Positive comments about the service are made in questionnaires from officers.

4 *The work of individual advisers and advisory teachers in supporting teachers and headteachers*
All establishments have been visited over an agreed period.
All headteachers have received visits and been offered appropriate advice over an agreed period.
An agreed number of teachers have been seen at work in the classroom over a given period.
All advisers have been trained to work with teachers and headteachers.
All advisers have been trained in working with the phases of education which now form part of their responsibility.
There is a written policy for dealing with failing teachers and headteachers.
Positive comments have been made in questionnaires to headteachers.
Positive comments have been made by senior advisers visiting with colleagues.

5 *The extent to which the National Curriculum and other local and national initiatives are being supported*
All teachers have had the opportunity of training in all the areas of work currently receiving attention.

Positive comments about this training have been made in questionnaires from courses and from headteachers.

6 *The contribution of advisers and advisory teachers to the professional development of teachers*

All advisers and advisory teachers have received training in provision for the professional development of teachers.

There is a well planned system for identifying training needs, planning, implementing, evaluating and following up in-service activities.

Each course offered has been carefully evaluated and criticisms noted.

There is a strong management education programme.

There are many positive comments from teachers attending courses.

There are many positive comments from headteachers whose teachers have attended courses.

Advisers are encouraging schools to use their everyday experience to help teachers to develop.

7 *The work being done in curriculum development*

There are working groups looking at aspects of curriculum.

Specialist advisers are encouraging teachers to develop a variety of ways of working.

There is work in hand to develop continuity between phases of education.

8 *The quality of confidential reports*

There are written instructions about how confidential reports should be written.

All advisers have received training in writing confidential reports.

Senior advisers assess this aspect of the work of their colleagues positively.

9 *The contribution of advisers in interviewing and advising on appointments*

There is a written statement of what is involved in making appointments.

All advisers and inspectors have received training in the process of making appointments, including interviewing.

Positive comments are made in questionnaires by headteachers about advisers' and inspectors' contribution to appointments.

10 *The contribution of the advisory/inspectorate service to appraisal*

There is a clear policy about the contribution of the advisory/ inspectorate service to appraisal.

All advisers and inspectors have been trained in appraisal techniques so that they can advise schools and other establishments.

Advisers and inspectors contribute to the appraisal of headteachers.

11 *The professional development opportunities offered to advisers, inspectors and advisory teachers*

There is a clear policy which supports the professional development of advisers and advisory teachers.

Training is provided in all aspects of the work.

A substantial number of external courses are attended by all advisers, inspectors and advisory teachers.

Positive comments are made in questionnaires about professional development by advisers, inspectors and advisory teachers.

Opportunities for professional development as part of the normal work of the service are used whenever possible.

Appraisal is provided for advisers, inspectors and advisory teachers.

Records are kept of each person's training needs and a personal development plan is made for each person.

A number of team members gain promotion.

12 *The effectiveness of communication*

There are systems for communication in all necessary areas of work.

There is a staff handbook or file giving members of the service all the necessary background information.

There are regular meetings of various groups.

Meetings are recorded and information about them circulated to all members.

Information about the work of the advisory team is regularly communicated to all establishments, the administration and other support services.

Positive comments about communication are made in questionnaires from the advisory team and from the groups with which the team communicates.

13 *The effectiveness of the management of the service*

The aims of the service are agreed and clearly stated and are used to plan the programme of work.

Appropriate and agreed policies exist in all the necessary areas.

Appropriate systems and routines have been agreed and are followed.

All members of the team have clear job descriptions which reflect what they actually do.

The overall programme of work has been arrived at through discussion with the team.

All members of the team have clear personal programmes of work which are known and agreed by the team management and these are followed in practice.

There is appropriate delegation of tasks.

Positive comments about the management of the team are made by administrators in questionnaires.

Positive comments about management are made by advisers in questionnaires.

Chapter 12

Personal organisation

There is a good deal of evidence to suggest that most advisers and inspectors work considerably longer hours than their contracts suggest and that they find organising their work something of a problem. For Williams (1981) the enduring impression resulting from his survey was 'of a cadre of inspectors in a stressful situation and experiencing increasing frustration over a self-perceived inability to achieve and maintain an appropriate balance between office and field work'. Pearce (1986), noted that a team of fifteen committed to an eleven-session week normally worked fifteen sessions and averaged 650 sessions a year against the 440 which were expected of them. Another survey found a team of forty-nine inspectors working an average week of fifty-six hours as against the thirty-seven and half stated in their contracts. It is probably also the case that most advisers and inspectors spend less time in classrooms than they would wish.

Advisory teachers may not have so many tasks, but they, like advisers, experience the pressure that results from successful work. Good work in one school not only results in further demands from that school, but other schools asking for similar help. Before long the adviser/inspector or advisory teacher has more work than it is possible to fit into the time available. In many LEAs the advisory teacher is protected to some extent by the responsible adviser or inspector who oversees the programme arranged and ensures that schools do not approach the advisory teacher direct to ask for help but apply to the adviser.

The use of time

Advisers, inspectors and advisory teachers need to be extremely self-disciplined if they are to work successfully. This demands first of all a proper attention to planning the time which is within their power to allocate. Some of the time of all advisers and inspectors will be dictated by others, often without much concern for the plans already made. The planning of other work, however, is in their own hands and it is the organisation of this time which is important.

It is helpful in planning the use of time to be aware of one's own best periods for different activities. Some people work best in the morning. Others work well later in the day. It is sometimes possible to organise work so that the most demanding tasks come at the best time, although for much advisory work the adviser/inspector has little choice about the timing. People also have preferences about the best way of setting about a large task such as writing a report. Some people work best when they have a long uninterrupted time to work at it. Others work better in a series of short and concentrated bouts. These choices may not be available on many occasions, but should be made when possible.

Good planning of time starts from having clear objectives. These should be discussed as part of the appraisal process and developed in the course of the year, so that there are long-range objectives which break down into short-range objectives for each week and day, normally stated as part of a 'to do' list, reviewed daily. This needs to be prioritised and plans made weekly and deadlines set where appropriate; and time needs to be allowed for this process. It then helps to highlight daily those items on the 'to do' list which have priority. Each week's work needs to be related to the long-term objectives so that what is urgent does not oust what is really important.

It is very easy in advisory work to spend too much time fire-fighting, although the current arrangements in most teams will make this much more difficult because time is being more closely planned. On the other hand, emergencies will arise and need to be dealt with. It is possible, if a diary is analysed, to assess how much time during the week is spent on important matters which are both unexpected and urgent. It is then possible to keep that free when making long-term plans, so that time can be rearranged when necessary to take account of matters that arise unexpectedly. If there are none, there will be some slack in the programme to allocate to tasks which need extra time.

It is always tempting to leave until last the tasks which are least attractive and possibly take a long time, with the result that they often get neglected. These should be scheduled first and tackled first if at all possible. All advisers and inspectors need to learn to use whatever time is available. Long tasks can often be broken down into a series of shorter tasks which can be fitted into shorter periods of time. It is all too easy to conclude that a quarter of an hour is too short to do anything useful, but short periods can be used profitably with appropriate planning.

The inability to say 'no' is a problem for many advisers/inspectors and advisory teachers. Planning will help to make this easier because more of the time is programmed, but the problem will still remain. Whether one accepts a task or not depends on one's objectives and priorities. It it does not fit into these then it should be refused. It helps in refusing if the reason for the refusal can be given and, if possible, other suggestions made.

Advisers, inspectors and advisory teachers need to look carefully at their attendance at meetings. It is first of all important to be sure that the meeting is really essential. It may then be possible to attend for that part of the meeting which is of particular concern. Advisers/inspectors and advisory teachers running meetings should plan them carefully so that they use time as effectively as possible. This means beginning on time, planning the agenda so that a given amount of time only is allocated to each item and ensuring that the group keeps to the point. It is also helpful to know how to draw a small meeting to a close. Most meetings can sensibly end with summing up. Gestures like closing a file or packing up papers then make it clear that it is time to finish. Meetings should also take place out of school time whenever possible.

Many of the reorganisation plans which have been made recently should help to overcome some of these problems, although the pressure and the need for self-discipline will still remain.

Managing paper

Advisers and inspectors are often daunted by the way the paper piles up on their desks every time they go out. It is important to be able to handle paper satisfactorily. It is useful to try to work on the principle of handling each item once only. It is very easy to spend a morning sorting out the paper on one's desk and to feel that this is achieving something. If each item is dealt with as it is picked up, as far as this is possible, much more genuine progress will be made. Of course, this is a counsel of perfection and in practice many of the items in the in-tray either need consultation with others not immediately available or cannot be dealt with without further information. However, many can be dealt with straight away and should be.

It is helpful is to keep a clear desk. Clutter makes work more difficult and it is useful to make a point of tidying one's desk each time one stops work. Work in progress should be filed away somewhere convenient and only in- and out-trays left on the desk top. Similarly it is helpful to make a point of taking everything out of one's briefcase once a week and making sure that what is being carried is only that which is needed.

Paper not only needs to be dealt with. It also needs to be available when it is needed. It can be helpful to spend time at the beginning of each week gathering together the papers which will be needed for each day's work. Coloured plastic folders can be used for each day and a note placed in each of files which will also be needed. This kind of preparation might be regarded as the task of a good secretary, but many advisers and inspectors have to work without support of this kind, and in any case gathering together the papers oneself provides an opportunity to prepare for the events in the coming week.

It is useful to have files for each month into which papers for coming events are placed, together with any pending material. These are reviewed at the end of each month and pending material moved on to the file for the following month. This is a particularly useful device for bringing forward notes of times to check that something is happening.

If paper is to be available when wanted a good filing system is needed. There should be some parts of the filing system common to the whole team, or a part-team where small teams are based away from the central office. School files are an obvious case for joint filing. In addition, most advisers, inspectors and advisory teachers will need their own files for the work which is particular to them. The filing system needs to be easily accessible to the adviser/inspector or advisory teacher concerned and to any clerical help available. This is more likely to be the case if the person concerned designs the system than if it is left to a secretary, although a secretary's knowledge of filing systems will be valuable to the adviser. An adviser/inspector or advisory teacher who marks up each item for filing is more likely to be able to find what he or she needs than someone who leaves it all to someone else – always assuming there is anyone else to leave it to! This also means that almost anyone can help with filing and a change of secretary is not a disaster. It also means that it is easy to return papers to the same file once they have been removed. A numerical/alphabetical system of marking takes less time than writing the name of the file on each piece of paper, although it may take time to get to know it.

It is very easy to leave filing to pile up. If papers are not filed daily, they are often not available when needed. A good deal of self-discipline is needed to file each day, whether it is done by a secretary or by the adviser/inspector or advisory teacher concerned.

Keeping notes

It is essential for an adviser or an advisory teacher to keep good notes of the work that has been done and the visits made. Every team should have some form of visit record, but advisers may wish to keep more comprehensive notes than this provides for.

It is a good idea to use a loose-leaf file for notes with a page for every institution. This can contain a standard sheet for each, giving statistical details like the number on roll, the group size, the staffing establishment and so on. It can also give a list of staff and details of the overall organisation and any special points to note. Notes of visits can then be added on a separate sheet and a copy of the visit record can also be included. These notes can then be transferred to school files as they become out-of-date.

It is important to remember that even an adviser's private notes can be called on by a tribunal if the occasion arises. There is virtually no document which is totally private and it is wise to make notes with this in mind. This is particularly the case when completing records which will go into school files.

Conclusion

Advisory work is to some extent an acquired taste. People coming into it for the first time often miss the close day-to-day contact with teachers and students. They find the lack of a clearly defined daily timetable difficult to come to terms with and it is difficult also to know how effectively one is working, since the results of advisory work take a long time to become evident.

On the other hand, the breadth of view which it affords can be rewarding. The opportunity to see large numbers of schools and teachers in action is not available to many people and it provides an opportunity to develop a broad philosophy of education. Teachers find satisfaction in watching children grow and develop. The comparable satisfaction for advisers and inspectors is that of seeing schools and teachers develop. It is very satisfying to see a school come into being from the drawing board stage and feel that one has had a hand in the development. It is also satisfying to see a teacher develop through the probationary year to the point where he or she is able to go on to more senior posts and again to feel that one has contributed to this development. Another satisfaction is to see a decision one has influenced take shape in the LEA's schools. Yet often only the adviser knows the part he or she played.

Recent developments have stressed the importance of inspection but inspection is of limited value if it is not coupled with a responsibility on the one hand for helping institutions and teachers, and consequently students, to achieve their full potential and on the other hand for helping to provide the thinking and information on which administrators, members and governors can build policy and make decisions.

It must be remembered that neither in the office nor in the institutions is the adviser's or inspector's role that of decision-maker, though there should be many occasions when he or she is influential in the decisions made. This can be difficult to accept for those coming into the work from decision-making roles. The task of the advisory service is to provide the information with which teachers, headteachers, governors, administrators and members can make wise decisions and in some cases to help them to weigh up the various possibilities open to them. Advisers and inspectors need to help others to think issues through rather than do their thinking for them.

The advisory service is also concerned with growth and innovation. Sometimes an adviser/inspector or an advisory teacher can help an instituion or a group of teachers to grow by the help he or she gives. Sometimes it is the adviser/inspector or advisory teacher who offers the help or encouragement which gives a teacher the confidence to move forward. Sometimes it will be an adviser/inspector or an advisory teacher who sows the seed from which new development grows and keeps it alive by his or her interest.

The pressures on the advisory service mean that it is essential to have a well articulated philosophy of education as well as wide knowledge of curriculum and method. This provides the criteria against which judgements can be made. Each team needs to have clear objectives and priorities so that the limited resource which the service represents can be used to the best advantage.

There is also a body of skills which is particular to advisory work. Perhaps the most important of these is the skill of observation. The good teacher learns to look for the clues which show the reactions of students. The good adviser or inspector needs to see the clues which show the interaction between teacher and students and between head and teachers. It is easy to make wrong judgements if the observation is inadequate.

An adviser or inspector needs to be able to evaluate what is seen, both in terms of his or her own philosophy and beliefs and in terms of what the teacher or the instituion is trying to do. It is often important to separate these two, since a judgement made in terms of a completely different philosophy will probably be unacceptable to the teachers concerned because it is not a fair assessment of their work.

An adviser/inspector or advisory teacher needs to be a good counsellor: sympathetic and understanding, yet firm when the need arises and able to persuade people to take wise courses of action. All advisers, inspectors and advisory teachers need to be enthusiasts and optimistic enough to go on being enthusiastic when progress is slow. They should be the source of inspiration for many teachers, finding good in unlikely places, stirring and stimulating and enlarging the experience of others.

References

Audit Commission (1989a) *Losing an empire, finding a role: the LEA of the future;* HMSO, London

Audit Commission (1989b) *Assuring quality in education: the role of LEA inspectors and advisers;* HMSO, London

Back K., Back K. (1982) *Assertiveness at work;* McGraw-Hill, Maidenhead

Barnsley Education Department (1990) 'Barnsley LEA advisory and evaluation service'; internal paper, Barnsley LEA

Berkshire Education Department (1990a) *Developing Managers;* Resources for Staff Development series, Berkshire LEA, Maidenhead

Berkshire Education Department (1990b) *Planning for Staff Development;* Resources for Staff Development series, Berkshire LEA, Maidenhead

Bolam, R., Smith, G., Canter, H. (1978) *LEA Advisers and the mechanisms of innovation;* National Foundation for Educational Research, Windsor

Coopers and Lybrand (1988) *Local management of schools;* HMSO, London

Crowther, R. (1988) 'An enhanced role'; *Education,* 16 September

Day, C. (1986) *Staff development in the secondary school: Management perspectives;* Croom Helm, Beckenham

Day, C., Whittaker, P., Wren, D. (1987) *Appraisal and professional development in the primary school;* Open University Press, Buckingham

de Boo, M. (1988) 'Supporting science: reflections of an advisory teacher' *Education 3–13,* October, pp. 12–16

Dean J. (1990) Survey of advisory teams (unpublished)

Dean J. (1991a) *Professional development in school;* Open University Press, Buckingham

Dean, J. (1991b) *The organisation of advisory/inspectorate teams;* Education Management Information Exchange (EMIE), National Foundation for Educational Research, Slough

DES (1982) *Mathematics counts* (the Cockcroft Report), HMSO, London

DES (1985) 'The role of local education advisory services'; unpublished

DES (1986a) *Local education authority training grants scheme; financial year 1987–88;* circular 6/86, Department of Education and Science, London

DES (1986b) *Better schools;* HMSO, London

DES (1988b) *Education Reform Act: the school curriculum;* draft circular, Department of Education and Science, London

DES (1988a) *Education Reform Act: local management of schools;* circular 7/88, Department of Education and Science, London

DES (1990a) *Developing school management: the way forward the report of the School Management Task Force,* HMSO, London

DES (1990b) *Grant for Education Support and Training*; draft circular, Department of Education and Science, London

Donaghue, C., Ball, C., Glaister, B., Hand, G. (eds) (1981) *In-service, the teacher and the school*; Kogan Page, London

Elliott-Kemp, J., West, B. (1987) *Sigma (Self-initiated Group-Managed Action)*; Pavic publications, Sheffield City Polytechnic

Elliott-Kemp, J., Williams, G. (1980) *The DION handbook (Diagnosing Individual and Organisational Needs)*; Pavic Publications, Sheffield City Polytechnic

Eraut, M. (1885) *Evaluation of management courses*; National Management Centre for School Management Training, Bristol

Fisher, Roger, Ury, William (1983) *Getting to yes*; Arrow Books, London

Francis, D., Woodcock, M. (1982) *Fifty activities for self-development*; Gower, Aldershot

Gray, H.L. (ed) (1988) *Management consultancy in schools*; Cassell, London

Hall, V., Oldroyd, D. (1988) *Managing Inset in local education authorities*; National Development Centre for School Management Training, Bristol

Hancock, D. (1988) 'Speech to NAIEA Executive', London, January 1988; unpublished

Handy, C. (1976) *Understanding organisations*; Penguin Books, Harmondsworth

Harland, J. (1990) *The work and impact of advisory teachers*; National Foundation for Educational Research, Slough

Havelock, R.G. (1975) 'The utilization of educational research and development'; in Harris, Lawn L. Prescott, W. (eds) *Curriculum innovation*; Croom Helm in association with the Open University Press, Beckenham and Buckingham

Hellawell, D.A. (1990) 'Headteacher appraisal: relationships with the LEA and its inspectorate'; in *Educational Management and Administration* Vol.18 pp. 3–15 No.1

Hereford and Worcester Education Department (1990) 'The education inspectorate'; internal paper, Hereford and Worcester LEA, Worcester

Hewton E. (1988) *School-focused staff development*; Falmer Press, Lewes

Jane, E., Varlaam, A. (1981) 'Support for support teams'; in *Insight* 5, 1 (1981–2); ILEA

Lavelle, Mike (1984) 'The role of consultancy in curriculum and organisation development innovation in education'; in *School Organisation* Vol. 4, No. 2, pp. 161–170

Lewin, K. (1951) *Field theory and social science*; Harper, London

Margerison C. (1978) *Influencing organisational change*; Institute of Personnel Management, London

Microelectronics Education Support Unit (1988) *Course materials*; Microelectronics Support Unit, Sheffield

Montgomery, D. (1984) *Evaluation and enhancement of teacher performance*; Learning Difficulties Project, Kingston Polytechnic, Kingston upon Thames

Morgan, C., Hall, V., Mackay, H. (1983) *The selection of secondary school headteachers*; Open University Press, Buckingham

Nebusnuick, D. (1989) *Monitoring and evaluation and the 1988 Education Reform Act*; Education Management Information Exchange (EMIE), National Foundation for Educational Research, Slough

Oldroyd, D., Hall, V. (1988) *Managing INSET in local education authorities*; National Management Centre for School Management Training, Bristol

Oxley, H. (1987) *The principles of public relations*; Kogan Page, London

Pearce, J. (1986) *Standards and the LEA*; NFER–Nelson, Windsor

Pedlar, M. (1983) *Action learning in practice*; Gower, Aldershot

Petrie, P. (1988) 'Primary advisory teachers: their value and their prospects'; *Education* 3–13, October Vol. 16, No. 3, pp. 3–5

Poster, C. D. (1991) *Teacher appraisal*; Routledge, London

Revans, R.W. (1980) *Action learning*; Blond and Briggs, London

Rhodes, G. (1981) *Inspectorates in British government: law enforcement and standards of efficiency*; Allen and Unwin, London

Richmond upon Thames Education Department (1989a) *Appointment of chief inspector*; Richmond LEA

Richmond upon Thames Education Department (1989b) *The inspectorate's contribution to evaluation in LB Richmond upon Thames*; Richmond LEA

Robson, M. (ed.) (1984) *Quality circles in action*; Gower, Aldershot

Rudduck, J. (1981) *Making the most of the short in-service course*; Schools Council Working Paper 71, Methuen Educational, London

Sayer, J. (1988) 'Identifying the issues'; in Gray, H. L., *Management consultancy in schools*; Cassell, London

Schmuck, R.A. (1973) 'Consultation in organisation development: report of a research programme at the University of Oregon, USA'; paper prepared for course E321, Open University

Schools Council (1983) *Guidelines for Review and Institutional Development (GRIDS)* Longman, London, for the Schools Council

SCIA (1989) *LEA advisory services and the Education Reform Act*; Society of Chief Inspectors and Advisers, London

SCIA (1990) *Evaluating the achievement of schools and colleges: performance indicators in perspective*; Society of Chief Inspectors and Advisers

Secretary of State (1990) *Letter to CEOs*; Department of Education and Science, London

Secretary of State (1988) Speech to Society of Education Officers, January, unpublished

Stephens, J. (1989) 'How does your garden grow?' June 9 *Education*

Stillman A., Grant, M. (1989) *The LEA adviser – a changing role*; NFER–Nelson, Windsor

Straker, N, (1988) 'Advisory teachers of mathematics: the ESG initiative'; *Education Policy*, Vol. 4, pp. 371–84

Suffolk Education Department (1985) *Those having torches*; Suffolk County Council, Ipswich

Suffolk Education Department (1987a) *Teacher appraisal: a practical guide*; Suffolk County Council, Ipswich

Suffolk Education Department (1987b) *In the light of torches*; Suffolk County Council, Ipswich

Trethowan D. (1987) *Appraisal and target setting*; Harper & Row, London

Turner, G. (1987) *Studies in school self-evaluation*; Falmer, Lewes

Warwickshire LEA (undated) 'A Warwickshire policy for inspection'; internal paper, Warwickshire LEA

Wheldall, Kevin, Merritt, Frank (1984) *Positive teaching: the behavioural approach*; Unwin Educational, London

Whitaker, Patrick (1990) *The development of advisory teachers*; Centre for Adviser and Inspector Development, Wakefield

Wilcox, Brian (1989) 'Inspection and its contribution to practical evaluation; *Educational Research*, Vol. 31, No. 3, November 1989, pp. 163–73

Williams, V. (1981) *Survey of advisory duties and responsibilities of LEA inspectors 1979–80*; University of Oxford Department of Educational Studies

Winkley, D. (1985) *Diplomats and detectives*; Robert Royce, London

Woodcock M. (1979) *Team development manual*; Gower, Aldershot

Index

For Product Safety Concerns and Information please contact our EU
representative GPSR@taylorandfrancis.com
Taylor & Francis Verlag GmbH, Kaufingerstraße 24, 80331 München, Germany

www.ingramcontent.com/pod-product-compliance
Ingram Content Group UK Ltd.
Pitfield, Milton Keynes, MK11 3LW, UK
UKHW010813080625
459435UK00006B/62